Gender as Love

Gender as Love

* * * * * *

A THEOLOGICAL ACCOUNT
OF HUMAN IDENTITY, EMBODIED DESIRE,
AND OUR SOCIAL WORLDS

* * * * * *

Fellipe do Vale

Baker Academic
a division of Baker Publishing Group
Grand Rapids, Michigan

© 2023 by Fellipe M. do Vale

Published by Baker Academic
a division of Baker Publishing Group
Grand Rapids, Michigan
www.bakeracademic.com

Printed in the United States of America

Library of Congress Cataloging-in-Publication Control Number: 2023016625
ISBN 978-1-5409-6697-1 (paperback)

Baker Publishing Group publications use paper produced from sustainable forestry practices and post-consumer waste whenever possible.

23   24   25   26   27   28   29   7   6   5   4   3   2   1

To William "Billy" Abraham,
friend, mentor, guide, and example

May eternal light shine upon him

CONTENTS

FOREWORD

I first met Fellipe do Vale when he was in the beginning stages of this work, and it's been my privilege to see the project realized in this deeply theological and elegant book. Fellipe do Vale is a careful thinker, a generous teacher, and—as this book will establish—an emerging ecclesial theologian whose voice we will want to listen to not only now but also in the years to come. Readers will see, in this book, his characteristic approach of carefulness, courage, and grace.

What of the topics of the book? What of gender and of love? The questions here keep me up at night. They stalk me by day. As a theologian who cares about gender—as a feminist, a parent, a friend, a spouse, and a member of the body of Christ—I worry about gender and love. I worry that we can't talk openly about these important matters. I worry that polarization keeps us from relationship and from healing. I worry that we're trying to approach all of this with the thinnest of resources and ignoring the thick love of God that would help us reach toward truth and goodness and beauty. As a theologian, I worry. As a woman in a world without gender justice, I worry. But as a woman, I am also tired, and I bear scars.

If there is one clear thing to be said about gender in this time and place, it is that gender is a source of pain. We see cultures and individuals struggling with the meaning, implications, and practical consequences of ideas about humans as gendered beings.

Some preach God's creational intention for the goodness of maleness and femaleness but fail to see that maleness and femaleness are enmeshed in sin and that those sinful constructs are hurting beloved children of God. Others preach the goodness of an endless diversity of gendered possibilities but can account neither for the real ways real bodies suffer in a specifically patriarchal world nor for the longstanding Christian claim that we must treasure bodies because we are pro-creation. Again, beloved children of God are left hurting.

Vitriol from both ends of both political and theological spectrums spews forth, in continued blindness to this hurt. And from both ends, drastic interventions are proposed that fail to take account of complexity, nuance, our real lack of knowledge, and the great human cost and hurt those interventions are likely to cause real human beings.

In this situation, we need courage to speak. And in this situation, we need to take care. Fellipe do Vale's book does so. As the author does in his person, so also in his work he offers care for hurting human beings and care for all that is at stake theologically, which always affects hurting human beings. In this situation, we need what the late John Webster called "theological theology." That is, we need to pay attention to God and to the things of God. And it is God who takes care of hurting human beings. Only God will help us here, but theology is part of the route by which we may know and navigate God's care.

This book is theological theology. It does not rely first on anecdotes or popular trends, on the things of this world. Instead, it treats carefully with who God is and with classic theological categories that help us to know the God who has acted in the Word, incarnate and written, that we might not languish in ignorance of the divine character and nature. As you will see as you read, theological theology must be concerned with justice if it is to be about the God we know in Jesus Christ. This means theological theology takes care.

In the face of hurt, Fellipe do Vale brings the balm that is the love of God. While the church is unlikely to come to perfect agreement about a theology of gender, we cannot avoid the conversation if we are to love the hurting people God so loves. I invite reader and church to consider Fellipe do Vale's proposals carefully and, with him, to seek theological solutions as we continue to struggle with what it means to love, as gendered creatures, in this broken world being redeemed by God. I know you'll be enriched by what you're about to read.

Beth Felker Jones, professor of theology,
Northern Seminary

ACKNOWLEDGMENTS

To write a book on gender is not an easy task, as the odds of saying something of benefit to a wide audience are often slim. This means that an author who attempts to do so requires wise and careful advisors, so that the resulting product would be, hopefully, a welcome contribution. I think I have benefited from such advisors. The book is dedicated to Billy Abraham, who was my doctoral supervisor and friend. He died shortly after its completion. If it were not for Billy, this project would not have been completed, and I would probably be in another field of work. Billy was a constant reminder of academic excellence and argumentative charity, while also serving as an exemplar for the expectation that theological work is nothing short of a divine calling.

Additional gratitude must be shown to D. Stephen Long, James K. H. Lee, and Beth Felker Jones, all of whom read and critiqued the entirety of this project as it was being produced. Beth also wrote the foreword, which is an honor, as she is a personal theological role model. I count each of these individuals as paradigms of the Christian theological vocation. Thanks must also be given to Kevin Vanhoozer, who saw the heart of this proposal almost immediately. Arabella Bryant, Bonnie Miller, and Makayla Payne gave remarkably helpful editorial feedback, indicating their possession of theological insight with a bright future. Madison Pierce promoted the project selflessly, and it would not have seen the light of day without her advocacy. Finally, I am grateful for the team at Baker Academic, especially Anna Gissing, who believed in the book and provided an enthusiastic and encouraging atmosphere.

My wife, Karla, has stuck with me through years of academic training and duress, and her enduring support and perceptive care were ingredient to the completion of this project. Karla and our children teach me daily why thinking about gender in a way that promotes flourishing, goodness, and love is an important task for our day. I can't imagine a life without them.

Kenosha, WI
Eleventh Sunday after Pentecost, 2022

PART 1

* * * * * * *

The Landscape
and Its Faults

* * * * * *

ONE

What Does It Mean to Give a Theological Account of Gender?

1.1 Introduction: Contemporary Theological Discussion about Gender

There is little doubt that in the contemporary theological landscape gender has emerged as a vibrant and diverse object of investigation. The contributions made by scholars from all of the established disciplines of theology have proliferated, so much so that Elisabeth Schüssler Fiorenza, one of the pioneers of the field, has testified, "I remember in the 1960s when I could read everything that appeared on feminism; in the '70s when I could still read everything in feminist studies in religion; in the '80s when I was still aware of everything published in feminist biblical studies; and in the '90s when I could still keep tabs on everything that appeared in feminist Christian Testament/Early Christian studies. Yet, today, I find it impossible to be aware of everything published in the field."[1] Perhaps due to this proliferation and diversification, there has arisen a great deal of uncertainty, obscurity, and intransigence with respect to theological analyses of gender. At the same time that theologians are focusing on the manifold ways in which gender implicates their discipline, it has come to light that there is no settled agreement on the object of their investigation nor on the best method for investigating it.

1. Elisabeth Schüssler Fiorenza, "Reaffirming Feminist/Womanist Biblical Scholarship," *Encounter* 67, no. 4 (2006): 362.

At the risk of generalizing, it seems to me that the current state of the discussion is plagued by two problematic yet broadly accepted bifurcations, and it is precisely their acceptance that has generated the intransigence of the field. The first bifurcation recognizes a distinction between gender as a *social construct* and gender as an *essence*. Much more will be said about each view as my argument proceeds, but their popular understanding seems to go something like this: On one side, some argue that gender is an essence, by which they mean that gender is entirely derivable from one's biological makeup.[2] Gender, on this view, can be read off of whatever biological components one considers to constitute gender identity, with the most frequent candidates being genes, gonads, hormones, other external genitalia, and average physical ability.[3] On the other side is the view that gender is a social construct. Social constructionists identify significant problems with the first option on account of the way it has made the traits that have been used to validate the oppression of women something "natural." Maintaining that gender is a social construct has the additional appeal of revealing these traits as produced by the assumptions, expectations, practices, and performances within a society that go on to establish what it is to be a "man" or a "woman." Thus, a distinction is made between "sex"—seen as the biological components that differentiate males from females from intersex/DSD[4] individuals—and "gender," which has more to do with the definitions of masculinity, femininity, or otherwise as they are socially expressed.

There is a well-worn debate between these two views, though it is fairly safe to say at this point that some version of the social constructionist view

2. Strictly speaking, such a commitment makes this view a *biological* essentialist view. It is not typically acknowledged that there are different types of essentialism about gender. It will be one of my burdens in this work to bring to light the greater diversity of options available for thinking about gender. Likewise, it would be a mistake to think that biological essentialism is the only or best way to take seriously the data of biology. Those inclined to do so need not take on all of the commitments of biological essentialism.

3. For a fairly recent example of this view, see Steven Pinker, *How the Mind Works* (1997; reissue ed., New York: Norton, 2009), chap. 7. Pinker's particular modification of this view involves his commitment to evolutionary psychology, which does much of the heavy lifting with respect to building a bridge between biological facts and social behavior.

4. I use the term "intersex/DSD" in order to reflect the diversity of the nomenclature. Some prefer "intersex," while others prefer "DSD" ("disorders of sexual development" or, sometimes, "diversity of sexual development"). More recently, "intersex and variations of sex characteristics" has also been used. Because there does not seem to me to be a settled preference, I will retain "intersex/DSD." This is a massively important topic in theologies of gender, and an adequate treatment of it requires patience and detail, something I hope to offer in chapter 6.

predominates among theologians, even if there is a sizable delegation of those who remain dissatisfied with it. Largely, and perhaps most vocally, these critics of the social construction of gender have come from certain branches of Roman Catholic theology.[5] But some feminist theorists have also resisted the social constructionist view because of its inability to provide the moral and political normativity necessary for social change, with some opting for alternative forms of essentialism[6] and others preferring to extend constructionist claims to sex *as well as* gender.[7] For the moment, it is enough to observe that the debate between those who think that gender is a social construct and those who think that it is an essence is far from settled, with many left wondering whether there is any clear answer to the question "What is gender?" Because it is concerned with the basic properties of gender—whether natural, biological, social, or otherwise—think of this first bifurcation as concerned with *ontological* matters.

A second bifurcation has made theological discussions of gender unduly complex, and it is more *methodological* in nature. As has been noted, though many theologians incorporate gender into their discussions, it is rather difficult to say with specificity just what makes their contributions *theological* in comparison with other academic disciplines. John Webster maintained that it has become "increasingly difficult for practitioners within the various disciplines of theology to state with any clarity what is specifically *theological*

5. See esp. Margaret H. McCarthy, "Gender Ideology and the Humanum," *Communio* 43, no. 2 (Summer 2016): 274–98; Abigail Favale, *The Genesis of Gender: A Christian Theory* (San Francisco: Ignatius, 2022). In point of fact, the official teachings of the Roman Catholic Church have consistently and explicitly rejected the social construction of gender. See Pope Paul VI, "Humanae Vitae" (encyclical letter, July 25, 1968); Pope John Paul II, "Mulieris Dignitatem" (apostolic letter, August 15, 1988); Joseph Cardinal Ratzinger, "Letter to the Bishops of the Catholic Church on the Collaboration of Men and Women in the Church and in the World" (May 31, 2004), 1.2; Pope Francis, "Laudato Si'" (encyclical letter, May 24, 2015), par. 155. Much of the influence lying behind these views comes from Pope John Paul II, *Man and Woman He Created Them: A Theology of the Body*, trans. Michael Waldstein (Boston: Pauline Books, 2006).

6. See here Anthony Appiah, "'But Would That Still Be Me?' Notes on Gender, 'Race,' Ethnicity, as Sources of 'Identity,'" *Journal of Philosophy* 87, no. 10 (October 1990): 493–99; and Mari Mikkola, "Elizabeth Spelman, Gender Realism, and Women," *Hypatia* 21, no. 4 (2006): 77–96.

7. Fiorenza opts for such a view, contending that the "attempt to separate biological sex from gender is . . . problematic since it does not sufficiently reflect that the cultural sex/gender system 'naturalizes' the category of 'sex' as biologically given rather than as discursively constructed. It does not take into account that primary and secondary physical sex differences are not 'biological facts' but are also discursively constructed" (Elisabeth Schüssler Fiorenza, *Jesus: Miriam's Child, Sophia's Prophet; Critical Issues in Feminist Christology*, 2nd ed. [New York: Bloomsbury T&T Clark, 2015], 42).

about their enquiries";[8] the very same can be said about those theologians who have turned their attention to gender. Typically, an unhelpful division has tended to occur between two different theological approaches. On one side of this divide are theologians who are eager to treat gender seriously and carefully, but their treatments too often look to anchor their views in some neighboring academic discipline, perceiving that discipline to provide whatever warrant is putatively missing from theological work. Theology is seen as ill-equipped to guide an inquiry into a topic such as gender, so it must be bolstered (or worse, supplanted) by some alternative theory or school of thought deemed to be more reliable. In the hands of such thinkers, the tools, topics, and sensibilities familiar to theology appear clumsy, antiquated, and artless, and if recourse is made to the recognizable traits of Christian theology, it is done with awkwardness. On the other side are theologians whose practice is immediately recognizable to those familiar with the long line of theological practice through the ages. Yet, though these theologians produce highly sophisticated and genuinely salutary work on the various loci of theology, there is a tendency on their part to confine themselves to texts and questions of their own traditions, and if gender is treated in their discussions at all, it is done with a sense of suspicion and reservation. This bifurcation, then, brings to light the question of which tools and methods are best suited to discuss gender, and here too there is more obscurity than clarity.

It is not difficult to find similar assessments of the state of affairs created by these two bifurcations. Thus Sarah Coakley: "It is rare indeed—although not completely unknown—for systematic theologians of any stature to take the category of gender as even a significant locus for discussion; and when they do, they tend to import a gender theory from the secular realm without a sufficiently critical *theological* assessment of it."[9] Resonances of Nicholas Wolterstorff's indictment of the modern state of academic theology can also easily be found in theologies of gender:

> It is my impression that a fair amount of what is not so good, and even whimsical, in theology is the completely predictable response by theologians to this indictment by our cultural elite. The theologian looks around for developments

---

8. John Webster, "Theological Theology," in *Confessing God: Essays in Christian Dogmatics II* (London: Bloomsbury, 2005), 22.

9. Sarah Coakley, *God, Sexuality, and the Self: An Essay "On the Trinity"* (Cambridge: Cambridge University Press, 2013), 34. See also Kathryn Greene-McCreight, "Feminist Theology and a Generous Orthodoxy," *Scottish Journal of Theology* 57, no. 1 (2004): 107.

in the contemporary academy that seem to be generally esteemed, and tries to sail a bit of theology under those colors. . . . So the theologian looks to see what language the world is currently speaking, and tries to speak in that language. Ironically, I think the result of most such attempts to be relevant is irrelevance. . . . There is an opposite response, equally predictable. Because the world is "going to hell in a handbasket," it is best to ignore it, construct one's own little theological ghetto, read a few safe old texts from one's own tradition with one's students, and when they give the appearance of having been well indoctrinated, send them forth to propound what they have been told while railing against liberalism, postmodernism, or whatever happens to be the current demon.[10]

Either lose one's theological nerve or become parochial in one's theological conversations: those are the two equally unsatisfactory options on offer according to Wolterstorff's read of the situation, a situation that seems to have trickled down to the churches when they are concerned only to battle "the current demon." Even if it is ultimately overstated, judgments like his and Coakley's do seem to carry some intuitive appeal. Their diagnosis focuses on the fact that theologians interested in gender are forced into one of two rigid methodological alternatives: either take gender seriously but forsake the recognizable virtues of theology, or be a serious theologian but only think of gender in a maladroit way.

I have been generic in the above comments, but I suspect that this characterization of theology's current state of affairs is at least broadly recognizable to the reader. What is difficult to deny, in the end, is that there are ontological and methodological dilemmas when theologians turn to gender. Recently, however, there has been a change of direction as some theologians have recognized these bifurcations and sought to overcome them by questioning their very validity. For these theologians, Eugene Rogers's statement is a summons: "If you are looking . . . for 'strategies' to move the churches on controverted topics in theology and sexuality, your search will misguide you, if you imagine 'strategies' and theology to be at odds. There is no 'strategy' apart from better theology. There is no better theology—and thus no strategy—apart from better exegesis, better Christology, better use of the liturgy, better recovery of patristic and medieval resources, and so on."[11] What Rogers is proposing

10. Nicholas Wolterstorff, "To Theologians: From One Who Cares about Theology but Is Not One of You," *Theological Education* 40, no. 2 (2005): 83.

11. Eugene F. Rogers Jr., "Doctrine and Sexuality," in *The Oxford Handbook of Theology, Sexuality, and Gender*, ed. Adrian Thatcher (New York: Oxford University Press, 2015), 53.

is that discussions about theology and gender have unnecessarily been forced into a dilemma in which theologians restrict themselves to the basic categories that make up the opposing sides of the bifurcations, and our persistence in doing so is precisely what has hindered the advancement of theological treatments of gender.

It is not surprising, then, to see feminist theologians challenging both bifurcations. Regarding the division between gender as an essence and gender as a social construct, Elaine Storkey pronounces that "the time has come for me to leave these categories behind. They have done a useful job, but they have their limitations. They are adequate for a rough sketch but far too vague and nebulous if we are trying to copy a masterpiece."[12] Turning to the methodological bifurcation, Beth Felker Jones looks to recover the viability of theology to engage questions of sex and gender in no uncertain terms. Responding to the claim that Christian theology is a "highly compatible bedfellow" with patriarchy, she is adamant that "they are the least compatible bedfellows of all. . . . My conviction is that theology as such *is* feminist. In other words, there is no right theology that is not feminist just because God intends good for all creation, including male and female."[13] For Jones, theologians who hold to the recognizable desiderata of Christian theology have no reason to think that their tools are ill-suited for studying gender. Rather, exactly the opposite is true: it is when theology *fails* to adhere to its own principles that the theologian does the greatest harm. It is by aspiring to do theology *coram Deo*, with all that it requires, that the theologian will be able to engage justly the most pressing issues facing the church. In this sense, theology is a bit like a Formula One car. Famously, these cars have tires with no tread. When driving such a car, the temptation is to slow down when approaching a curve, but doing so causes the tires to lose their grip, sending the car off the track. Instead, drivers know to accelerate when approaching the curves, allowing the vehicle to better grip the track. It is when theologians let their foot off the gas that theology goes awry; when they approach gender by accelerating their theological engines, they find that they have not spiraled away.

12. Elaine Storkey, *Origins of Difference: The Gender Debate Revisited* (Grand Rapids: Baker Academic, 2001), 126. See also Beth Felker Jones, *Marks of His Wounds: Gender Politics and Bodily Resurrection* (New York: Oxford University Press, 2007), 5: "My intent is to move beyond the standard debates about essentialism versus constructivism."
13. Jones, *Marks of His Wounds*, 6.

The present work takes up these challenges and provides an account of gender that moves beyond the overly simplistic division between social constructs and essences. It attempts to do so *theologically*—that is, it provides an account of gender using the recognizable tools and virtues of theology, such as scriptural exegesis and the critical retrieval of classical Christian figures, all while keeping an eye on the implications my argument will have on the health and well-being of the church. The remainder of *this* chapter, however, will make a case for the methodological plausibility of the project by offering a view of what it means to give a theological account of gender that does not sacrifice any of the defining traits of Christian theology. It will do so by drawing on the research program of John Webster entitled "theological theology," arguing for the conclusion that gender is best accounted for theologically when it is situated within the divine economy, a term understood as the full display of God's acts in history to create and redeem humanity. This is God's "plan [*oikonomian*] for the fullness of time, to gather up all things in him, things in heaven and things on earth" (Eph. 1:10). The economy is the sum total of divine action with respect to human redemption considered in and organized by its temporal unfolding. Its shorthand, I believe, is the term "gospel." The feminist theologian Catherine Mowry LaCugna provides a lucid summary of the economy in Scripture: "In general, then, 'economy' refers to the plan made known in the coming of Christ. Economy is the actualization in time and history of the eternal plan of redemption, the providential ordering of all things."[14] It is by understanding how gender is "gathered" into this economy, I posit, that we account for it theologically.

1.2 Theological Theology Unpacked

My aim in this section is to present and argue for one particular view about how best to engage a topic of investigation as a theologian. I present and apply John Webster's vision for theology for at least two reasons. First, few individuals invested as much time and experience into carefully considering the task of theology. Webster helped a whole generation of scholars to rediscover the riches and life-giving effects of theological work. He was confident in the intrinsic merits of Christian theology, but he was also keenly aware of the

---

14. Catherine Mowry LaCugna, *God for Us: The Trinity and Christian Life* (San Francisco: HarperSanFrancisco, 1993), 25.

important role theologians played in the intradisciplinary life of a university.[15] His work, therefore, represents a clear articulation of what makes theology the discipline that it is. More relevant to our topic, however, is the manner in which Webster attempted to avoid theology's perceived cultural marginality. When theologians begin to speak about issues concerning the complexities of human life, he noted, one readily finds that they "are largely ignored, and occasionally repudiated, outside the sphere of the Christian confession; where they still retain profile, it is often only in crude versions."[16] This is certainly true of gender, and for this reason, attempts to account for it that draw on theological premises are often avoided because they come across as ham-fisted or parochially confined to debates regarding the grammatical details of a few biblical proof texts. Webster's remedy was neither to appropriate external disciplines to supply theology with greater credibility nor to retreat further into a theologically embattled enclave. Instead, he maintained that the theologian speaks most helpfully to those who are of other fields and persuasions when she makes concrete theological claims with clarity and confidence. Only then will her claims be judged according to their merits, and only then will disagreements be had with understanding and light. This, I think, injects new life into the kinds of contributions theologians can make in discussions surrounding gender.

In the light of these convictions, Webster advanced an approach to Christian theology he called "theological theology." One useful way to grasp its unique contribution is to make an initial distinction between something's being *minimally* or *maximally* theological. An inquiry is *minimally theological* when it meets whatever basic conditions are necessary for counting as theology *as such*, whatever its quality. Sameer Yadav has recently called these "the norms that tell us what counts as engaging in the dogmatic task *simpliciter*—norms that someone has to satisfy in order to count as engaging the task of dogmatics at all, whether well or badly."[17] By contrast, something is *maximally theological* when it *also* meets those conditions needed for doing the theological task *well*. Norms that are maximally theological "tell us what

15. Webster had many essays on theology's place in the university. Most recently, see John Webster, "God, Theology, Universities," in *God without Measure: Working Papers in Christian Theology* (London: Bloomsbury T&T Clark, 2016), 2:157–72.

16. John Webster, "The Human Person," in *Cambridge Companion to Postmodern Theology*, ed. Kevin J. Vanhoozer (Cambridge: Cambridge University Press, 2003), 219.

17. Sameer Yadav, "Christian Doctrine as Ontological Commitment to a Narrative," in *The Task of Dogmatics: Explorations in Theological Method*, ed. Oliver D. Crisp and Fred Sanders (Grand Rapids: Zondervan, 2017), 74.

counts as engaging in the dogmatic task *properly*, in doing it well rather than badly."[18] In order to give a maximally theological account of something, that account will first need to be minimally theological, but not every minimally theological account will also be maximally theological, or even maximally theological in the same way. There are different judgments about the conditions for being minimally theological, but they typically involve statements about the subject matter of theology and the tools best used for investigating that subject matter. On Yadav's view, an inquiry is minimally theological when it is "engaged in the task of making explicit some sense in which Christians are ontologically committed to a narrative of creation and redemption. To formulate and commend Christian doctrine, I claim, is at a minimum, to formulate and commend ontological commitment to a narrative."[19] To commend ontological commitment, moreover, is to hold that there is "something (or some things) that makes that [narrative] true."[20] Christians will differ on what that something is; for instance, classically minded theologians will hold that there is an objective reality depicted by the narrative, while those persuaded of the view that theological statements express attitudes of dependence or existential commitments will hold that those attitudes or commitments are the truthmakers for the narrative. Moreover, proponents will differ on the specific contours of the narrative, particularly the details of creation and redemption. This is precisely what affords this view the ability to accommodate alternative proposals for theological inquiries of gender, even when it rejects them. The point, in the long run, is this: as long as *some account* is given of what makes one's rendering of the Christian narrative of creation and redemption true, then it is ontologically committed; and if it is ontologically committed, then it is minimally theological.

"Theological theology," however, is not a view specifying the requirements for minimally theological proposals. It is rather a view about what it means to perform the theological task *well*, or how to be *maximally* theological. This requires providing further specifications of the details of the Christian narrative of creation and redemption as well as an account of the particular truthmakers for that narrative.[21] For Webster, as we will see, this means viewing

18. Yadav, "Christian Doctrine as Ontological Commitment," 74.
19. Yadav, "Christian Doctrine as Ontological Commitment," 75–76.
20. Yadav, "Christian Doctrine as Ontological Commitment," 79.
21. Alternatively, one might discover what it means to do theology well by distinguishing it from doing theology *badly*. For one such attempt, see Leah E. Robinson, *Bad Theology: Oppression in the Name of God* (London: SCM, 2023).

the narrative as an *economy* and viewing its truthmakers as the *actions of the triune God, with a basis in God's immanent life*. Those two elements, I posit, make up theological theology as a maximally theological method.[22]

Webster begins with what he calls the "subjective cognitive principle of theology"—namely, "regenerate human intelligence."[23] As a genuine intellectual discipline, theology does not proceed from any special human faculties, faculties not already possessed and in use when one reasons about other topics and disciplines. It is at least an activity of the mind, requiring no other creaturely mental equipment than what human persons already have. Theology's employment of the mind differs, however, from other disciplines in at least two ways. First, "Christian theology is biblical reasoning. It is an activity of the created intellect, judged, reconciled, redeemed, and sanctified through the redemptive works of the Son and the Spirit."[24] That is, the work of theology requires a mind in which the healing and reparative work of God on one's epistemic faculties has begun. Those who stand in epistemic antagonism in relation to God cannot reasonably be said to come to know God and say true things about God, especially when "know" is not only taken to be knowledge *about* God but also knowledge of God by *acquaintance*. Because we have become "futile in [our] thinking" (Rom. 1:21), we need God to do the work of "scattering the darkness of sin, reconciling lost creatures, overcoming ignorance and establishing the knowledge and love of himself."[25] Here I take Webster to be practicing a form of virtue epistemology, according to which certain data are unknowable (or at least unknowable in the right kind of way) apart from certain moral states obtaining in the knower. Webster was well known for his insistence that the task of theology and the reading of Scripture (more on which below) require both the revelation of God *and* the right kind of reader. "Reading Scripture is thus a moral matter," he asserts.

22. I have attempted to articulate these principles with closer attention to divine action in Fellipe do Vale, "Divine Action Is Constitutive of Theology: William Abraham, John Webster, and Theological Theology," *Irish Theological Quarterly* 86, no. 4 (2021): 388–403.

23. John Webster, "What Makes Theology Theological?," in *God without Measure: Working Papers in Christian Theology* (New York: Bloomsbury, 2016), 1:217.

24. John Webster, "Biblical Reasoning," in *The Domain of the Word: Scripture and Theological Reason* (London: Bloomsbury, 2012), 115.

25. John Webster, "On the Clarity of Holy Scripture," in *Confessing God: Essays in Christian Dogmatics II* (London: Bloomsbury, 2005), 42. See also John Webster, *Holiness* (Grand Rapids: Eerdmans, 2003), 8: "Theology is an aspect of the sanctification of reason, that is, of the process in which reason is put to death and made alive by the terrifying and merciful presence of the holy God."

"It requires that we become certain kinds of readers, whose reading is taken up into the history of reconciliation."[26] The language of virtue is apposite here, but these virtues should not be mistaken for virtues acquirable through normal means. The virtues in question—like attentiveness, consistent prayer, fear of God, teachability, freedom from self-preoccupation, studiousness, and the like[27]—are direct products of the redeeming work of Christ applied by the Holy Spirit, and so they are gifts of grace. Thus, though no new faculties are employed in theological theology, those faculties require reparation by God before they can perform the theological task well.

The second way in which theology's employment of reason differs from that of other disciplines is that it has God as its object and inquires about all other topics in the light of God as their source and true end. For Webster, disciplines are not known or evaluated on the basis of some external or universal standard for what counts as rational or as knowledge; rather, they are known and evaluated on the basis of their objects and what it might take for those objects to be successfully known (criteria that will be discipline-specific).[28] For our purposes, note that the "principal object or matter of Christian theology is God."[29] But though that is a *necessary* condition for a maximally theological account, it is not a *sufficient* condition, for God is an object of investigation in other disciplines as well (say, psychology, philosophy, religious studies, and sometimes even nuclear physics!). What makes theology unique is that it speaks of God *in terms of divine action*: "The distinctiveness of Christian theology lies elsewhere"—namely, "in its invocation of *God as agent* in the intellectual practice of theology. In order to give account of its own operations, that is, Christian theology will talk of *God and God's actions*."[30] Or

26. John Webster, *Holy Scripture: A Dogmatic Sketch* (Cambridge: Cambridge University Press, 2003), 87.

27. This list is an ad hoc set of examples drawn from a variety of Webster's writings. For particular discussion, see Webster, *Holy Scripture*, 90; John Webster, *The Culture of Theology* (Grand Rapids: Baker Academic, 2019), 145–47; and John Webster, "Curiosity," in *The Domain of the Word: Scripture and Theological Reason* (London: Bloomsbury, 2012), 193–202. Note, however, that it is not meant to be definitive, for "any selection of virtues for the purposes of portraying theological existence is bound to be occasional—that is, an idealized picture which emphasizes certain features over others because in the present context they are considered to be of prime importance" (Webster, *Culture of Theology*, 145).

28. See Webster, "Theological Theology," 15. This has significant overtones in common with William Abraham's advocacy of epistemic particularism when it comes to divine revelation and theology in general. See William Abraham, *Crossing the Threshold of Divine Revelation* (Grand Rapids: Eerdmans, 2006), chaps. 2 and 3.

29. Webster, "What Makes Theology Theological?," 213.

30. Webster, "Theological Theology," 25 (emphasis added).

again: "A theological account of theology describes its nature and functions by invoking language about God, describing the human actions of creating and reading theology *in relation to divine agency*."[31] The unique object of theology, then, is not merely God. It is God considered through the array of actions performed in the history of redemption as well as the particular places all creatures have within that history.

If the object of theology is God and God's actions, then it is fruitful to inquire as to how this agent relates to the particular actions performed. Webster locates the source of these particular actions in God's *perfection* in the immanent Trinity and then maintains that God's acts are directly attributable to the character of that perfection. "Perfection" here does not describe any particular property had by God (like omniscience) but rather the quality of God's life considered within itself and not with regard to creatures. Thus Webster contends that "reflective participation in the economy of God's works prompts an intellectual . . . movement which considers God's works not only as they present themselves in their outer face or temporal structure and effect, but also in terms of the uncreated depth of God from which they flow. . . . What systematic theology may say of it is said because God's acts in time are transitive, directing theological reason to their agent and his mysterious, antecedent glory (1 Chron. 19:6f.)."[32] The task of the theologian is to see divine acts as derivative of the divine agent who performed them, specifically the kind of perfect life enjoyed by the triune persons and their relations. The basic point being made is trivially true: some of the characteristic actions I perform (say, writing a book) will indicate certain traits about me (say, my qualities as a writer). When this point is applied to God, however, we see that the actions appropriated to the divine persons reveal something about the particularities of those divine persons and the perfection they enjoy immanently. As the Son is sent into the world from the Father, for instance, we perceive between them the relation of eternal begetting (see, among many examples, John 3:34–35). Taken the other way around, we can say that divine action discloses God. God is necessarily trinitarian; thus, divine action must also be necessarily trinitarian in its disclosure. It thereby reveals to us the perfection of that necessary trinitarian life. In the end, this captures the

31. John Webster, "Reading Theology," *Toronto Journal of Theology* 13 (1997): 55 (emphasis added).

32. John Webster, "Principles of Systematic Theology," in *The Domain of the Word: Scripture and Theological Reason* (London: Bloomsbury, 2012), 143.

very old Christian confession that the trinitarian missions correspond to the trinitarian processions and that the actions of God are indivisible with respect to the three persons, all of whom share in the perfect life of God.

This brings us to the point at which Webster defines his particular construal of the narrative of creation and redemption to which Christians are ontologically committed. The theologian has as her object God as a divine agent who performs characteristic divine actions, and those actions have a certain overall *structure* or *order* to them, what Webster calls the "divine economy," in keeping with scriptural (see Eph. 1:10; 3:2) and patristic terminology. The economy is the "historical form of God's presence to and action upon creatures," so, as God acts, those actions comprise a structure or pattern given to it by the missions of the divine persons.[33] But just what is included in the economy? Webster uses very expansive terms to answer this question: "By 'the economy,' we refer to the comprehensive scope of God's dealing with creation and humanity—as creator, as savior, and as the one who will bring his purposes to perfection. The panorama of what the triune God does is the execution of God's being."[34] Or again, the economy "is a history of comprehensive scope, *gathering up all of God's acts toward the creature.*"[35] The economy, it appears, is the narrative of human history told from the perspective of what God has done to create, redeem, sustain, and perfect creatures. History is evaluable for Webster, and a correct evaluation of it must make reference to the acts of the Creator of all things and the appointed ends of those actions brought about through Jesus Christ. The divine economy, then, is the story of human history told with specific reference to what God has done and is doing to create, redeem, sustain, and perfect creatures. These acts are triune, for as the Father, Son, and Holy Spirit enjoy a perfect immanent life, the Father sends the Son and the Spirit to impart that life to creatures who, once lost in sin, now find their identities in this grand drama. A simpler way to make this point is to say that the divine economy is the great story of the gospel.[36]

Of course, all of these details are by no means *obvious* to the observer of the events of history, even to the Christian who stands as a beneficiary of such

33. Webster, "Biblical Reasoning," 117.
34. Webster, *Holiness*, 40.
35. John Webster, "The Holiness and Love of God," in *Confessing God: Essays in Christian Dogmatics II* (London: Bloomsbury, 2005), 125 (emphasis added).
36. On this, see John Webster, "What Is the Gospel?," in *Grace and Truth in the Secular Age*, ed. Timothy Bradshaw (Grand Rapids: Eerdmans, 1998), 109–18.

divine gifts. At this point one must return to Webster's virtue epistemology and note that viewing history as an economy is only possible when one approaches it with the requisite epistemic virtues. Yet one must also attend to divine revelation. Webster's theology of revelation is nuanced and demands a treatment of its own, but we can rest satisfied with connecting it to his broader theology of divine action. For Webster, in its most basic description, revelation *just is* divine action. "Revelation is nothing other than the history of God's covenant with humanity in its own intrinsic perspicuity. God's actions are such that they draw us into the knowledge of God. . . . Revelation is the eloquence of divine action."[37] This is not a far cry from our considerations thus far. If certain characteristic actions performed by an agent indicate something about that agent, it is conceivable to say that those actions are *revelatory* of that agent. Thus, God is revealed by the actions God performs. This is centralized, moreover, in Holy Scripture, for "the revelatory presence of God is *set forth in Holy Scripture*."[38] God has acted to inspire Scripture in an effort to perform revelatory communicative actions. What we have in Scripture, then, is the norming norm of theology, that which provides theology with its subject matter *precisely because it reveals God and the divine economy*. Holy Scripture is not a mere repository of facts but something that, when read with the right Spirit-produced virtues, enables the reader to encounter God. Thus, Scripture both discloses the divine economy and plays a pivotal role within it.

The task of the theologian is thereby transformed on account of the fact that it has a *shape* to which it is accountable. It is not merely the creative assembling of perspectives into interesting bricolage but something to which the theologian must first listen before she can speak. This means that one of the "main tasks of theology is to exemplify and promote close and delighted reading of Holy Scripture as the *viva vox Dei*, the voice of the risen Jesus to his community." Indeed, "the theologian's occupation is primarily exegetical," and "the necessary concern with other business is only derivative or by extension."[39] All the same, we must not mistake Webster for an advocate of

---

37. Webster, *Culture of Theology*, 121. See also Webster, *Holy Scripture*, 13: "Revelation . . . is a way of talking about those *acts* in which God makes himself present" (emphasis added). In that same paragraph, Webster cites Barth as saying that revelation is "divine presence."

38. Webster, *Holiness*, 17 (emphasis original). Divine revelation is not *identical* to Scripture for Webster, for God can be revealed to individuals, say, in a dream. But Scripture is the primary and most authoritative locus of divine revelation, the source to which theologians turn in order to go about their business. Scripture is the appointed means by which we learn about the economy.

39. Webster, *Culture of Theology*, 64–65.

a certain kind of wooden exegesis from which it is very difficult to extract theological claims, the kind of exegesis concerned exclusively or mainly with the historical features of the text being studied. Webster was a proponent of *theological* interpretation, though he was not given the time to specify his own brand of approach.[40] We may assume that it involves careful attention to the way figures of the Christian past exposited Scripture,[41] as well as attention to cultivating readerly virtues. Yet, I maintain that Webster's central devotion to theological interpretation is marked out by a commitment to seeing the way a particular claim is *situated* within the divine economy.[42] But what does it mean to situate something within the divine economy? Here we must move beyond Webster to develop in a little more detail the exegetical task of the theologian.

We might consider the relationship between Scripture and a particular theological claim as occupying one of three levels, each describing the relationship whereby Scripture *validates* the claim. At its most basic level, a claim may be a mere translation of Scripture; one may argue for the view that God is love simply by citing 1 John 4:8, a passage that effectively says, in the same words, the claim being argued. This level of relation is very rare, for theologians are often more interested in making claims of a more complex nature. At a second level, then, a claim may be *entailed* by Scripture. In other words, a claim is entailed by supporting premises if it follows *necessarily* from those premises. It may be argued that the existence of God is one such claim; though no single Scripture passage says, *verbatim*, "God exists," if what Scripture has to say about God is true, then it necessarily follows that God exists. At a third level, a particular claim may be neither a mere translation of a biblical passage nor a necessary entailment of scriptural teaching but may be *inductively* related to Scripture. The options available here are broader and are open to negotiation and debate, but examples include the way that a particular claim is *most fitting* with respect to the breadth of biblical teaching, or

40. For statements of theological interpretation indebted to and influenced by Webster, see Darren Sarisky, *Reading the Bible Theologically* (New York: Cambridge University Press, 2019); and Daniel J. Treier, *Introducing Theological Interpretation of Scripture: Recovering a Christian Practice* (Grand Rapids: Baker Academic, 2008).

41. On this, see John Webster, "Theologies of Retrieval," in *The Oxford Handbook of Systematic Theology*, ed. John Webster, Kathryn Tanner, and Iain Torrance (New York: Oxford University Press, 2007), 583–99.

42. This is clearest in his dogmatic discussion of Holy Scripture. When one considers the reader of Scripture, one must always keep in mind that she is "located within the economy of grace" (Webster, *Holy Scripture*, 123).

how it has the greatest explanatory scope, or that it does the most adequate job of accounting for the entirety of the canon, or that it is most sensitive to the narrative progression of Scripture. However one construes it, it is at this third level that it becomes difficult to obtain scriptural validation, but it is also where the canny theologian is able to display her craft. Here, ultimately, one is able to situate a claim within the divine economy. A claim is validated scripturally when it recognizes its place in the economy and displays sensitivity to the scope and canon of Scripture.[43]

All of this counts as exegesis, and though Webster did not present his preferred exegetical method in just this way, I suggest that it is a particularly helpful heuristic for understanding how a claim may be situated in the divine economy, particularly when the divine economy is disclosed in the canonical text of Scripture. "Situating" something there is a matter neither of translation nor of entailment; rather, it is a matter of taking the whole breadth of the economy and seeing the way it implicates the subject matter in question. This will differ, I believe, depending on what claim or claims the theologian is considering for validation. I am concerned with how views about human personhood, particularly human *genders*, are situated in the divine economy. This will require its own considerations about how best to be situated in the economy, considerations likely unique to theological anthropology. We will turn to that next, but allow me first to summarize. A minimally theological account requires, recall, (a) ontological commitment to a narrative and (b) some account of the truth of that to which one is ontologically committed. All theology, if it is to merit the title, must meet these criteria. Maximally theological accounts, however, make claims about what it means to do theology *well* or *properly* by specifying the nature of the narrative and its truthmakers. Webster's is one such account (though, of course, there are others). On his view, (a) the narrative in question is the divine economy, revealed through God's triune missions in their appropriated divine actions, by means of which God reconciles lost creatures back to their true Source and End in God; and (b) the truthmakers of that narrative are the divine actions themselves, such that a defeater to the possibility of divine action would constitute a defeater to theological theology itself. With that established, we have an answer to the question of what it is for something to be treated theologically.

43. I have attempted to elucidate this view in much more detail in Fellipe do Vale, "On Thomas Aquinas's Rejection of an 'Incarnation Anyway,'" *TheoLogica* 3, no. 1 (2019): 152–57.

1.3 Theologically Theological Anthropology and Theologies of Gender

The pieces are largely in place for understanding what it would take to address human persons and their genders theologically, namely, to *situate* them in the divine economy so that we can see how the litany of divine actions disclosed by the gospel gives them their distinctive character. In the writing that Webster devoted to theological anthropology, he advocated precisely for this:

> The task of Christian theological anthropology is to depict evangelical (that is, Gospel-constituted) humanism. It aims to display the vision of human identity and flourishing which is ingredient within the Gospel's announcement that, in the being, action, and speech of Jesus Christ, the crucified who is now alive and present in the Spirit's power, the good purposes of God the Father for his human creation are established and their completion is promised. Christian theological anthropology offers a portrayal of the nature and destiny of humankind by explicating the Gospel's disclosure of the works and ways of the triune God. . . . The context in which a theology oriented to the Christian confession pursues its interpretation of human nature and destiny is a consideration of the economy of grace. What it means to be human can only be grasped in its full scope and integrity on the basis of a depiction of the gracious work of God, Father, Son, and Spirit, in his saving self-communication with us.[44]

Notice the emphases of this exhortation. Theological anthropology, the theological discussion of human persons, is to have as its focus the ways in which the gospel casts light on what it means to be and to flourish as a human. This will make reference to the "works and ways" of the triune God—that is, to divine action. This is what it means for humanity to be situated in the "context" of the economy of grace. To think theologically about human personhood (and gender) is to see the ways in which they are implicated by the divine economy.

As an overall view of what must be done, these statements suffice. But one further refinement remains necessary. It follows from the above considerations, particularly about exegesis as "situating" a claim in the economy, that theological considerations of human nature and their particularities must be *narratively indexed*—that is, humans have the properties they have in virtue of occupying a certain stage of the economy. We should generally be cautious of statements regarding human nature *simpliciter*, for it may turn out that

---

44. Webster, "Human Person," 219, 224.

the properties predicated of human natures are in point of fact mistaken or isolable to only one moment of the divine economy. A typical example from Christian theology is original sin: I have not met a human being who is not also a sinner, but it would be a mistake to conclude from this that *human nature* is sinful. Sinfulness does not belong to the *definition* of what it means to be a human; instead, the state of sin is a *universal* property shared by all humanity (exempting Christ and the saints in glory) downstream of the fall. Instead of broad-sweeping anthropological claims, we should commit ourselves to two principles. First, human persons have the properties they have in virtue of occupying one particular place in the economy or another. Specifying the moments of the economy will in turn detail what is most salient about humans at each stage. Beth Felker Jones has recently articulated this insight well: "No statement . . . on the body can ever be taken at face value without first understanding the place of that statement in God's work of salvation. Are we speaking of the body of Adam, good but able to sin? Are we speaking of the fallen body, plagued by the mutability which will bring it death? Are we speaking of the risen body, blessedly unable to do other than reflect the glory of God?"[45] Second, it is only with the *entire economy* in view that we can say with clarity just what is *natural* to humanity and not merely what is presently universal. Sin once again serves as a fitting example: only by recognizing that creation was good and without sin and that one day there will exist humans in the new heaven and earth who know no sin can we say that it is perfectly possible to be human and yet without sin. Far too often, hasty appeals to creation or to the life of Christ are invoked as warrants for broad claims about gender without consideration for the bigger story of which these episodes are a part and without consideration for the difference between properties that are universal to a moment in the economy and properties that are natural to human beings. We will revisit this in chapter 6 with regard to appeals to creation, but for now we should note that what is required is attention to the full scope of the divine economy with respect to humanity, maintaining an eye on how God transforms human beings along the way to salvation. Taking these two principles together results in a view in which gender must be run through the full economy to achieve a proper theological understanding.

This is not to deny that there is such a thing as a human nature or that it should be important for theological reflection on gender, only that we should

45. Jones, *Marks of His Wounds*, 36.

have noticeably different motivations at play for appealing to it. Feminist theology has *rightly* been concerned to point out how invocations of "human nature" are weaponized to oppress women. Far too often, the conditions for being human are confused with traits taken to be characteristic of an ideal man, and when those conditions are made necessary for inclusion, social recognition, and opportunity, it is not difficult to see why many women have been treated as subhuman. This is abject and should be corrected. It does not mean, however, that talk of natures is rendered bankrupt. It does reveal the enduring corrigibility of our understandings of human nature as well as the sinful motivations that produced such pernicious understandings of humanity. A theological account of human nature must be derived from and held accountable to the divine economy, and it must be formulated with a constant awareness of the motivations surrounding the sinful grasp for power over others. It must be held accountable to God. If it can be demonstrated that a particular understanding of human nature is facilitating systemic trauma to significant swaths of its participants, then that construal must be abandoned, for it could not be from God, for God is not a God of evil.

Where does this leave us with our original question? How can one give a theological account not just of anything at all, not just of human persons, but of *gender*? It will be the task of the remainder of this project to give an adequate answer. I will offer a theological account of gender's basic properties, shaped and informed by the ways gender is modulated in the different moments of the divine economy. I realize, however, that this amount of methodological specificity might run the risk of making a theological account of gender far too parochial and intolerant of alternative approaches. In an effort to circumvent such an objection, allow me to recall the new generation of theologians who are articulating theological accounts of gender that move beyond the bifurcations I posited. These theologians, it seems to me, are doing something not dissimilar from theological theology, especially to the extent that they are aware of situating gender in the economy. We have already seen Catherine LaCugna's articulation of the economy in the context of trinitarian theology. Sarah Coakley goes further, positing that the way beyond the simple alternatives of secular gender theory and unreflective Christian positions lies with the "theological concepts of creation, fall, and redemption which place the performances of gender in a spectrum of existential possibilities *between* despair and hope." When one allows one's theological vision for gender to be impacted by these concepts, "the fallen, 'worldly' view of gender relations is open to the future, and to change; it is set in an unfolding, diachronic narrative both of individual spiritual maturation and of societal transformation."[46] By situating claims about gender within this unfolding narrative, claims Coakley, one is able to see beyond the simplistic articulations of gender provided by current theories to a more theologically helpful vista. Beth Felker Jones advocates for precisely the same move. She attempts to "place gender and sexuality in theological context by thinking about them in relationship to the big-picture biblical arch from creation to redemption. . . . We're not just left in the lurch, for God has chosen to reveal his goodness to us. . . . Thinking about sex [and] gender in light of creation, fall, and redemption points us toward a hopeful vision of our bodies as witnesses to the God who is love."[47] Finally, in her monograph on theologies of gender, Janice McRandal affirms that "Christian doctrine tells a particular story of God, a God who creates and redeems." This story, McRandal argues, "can inform a contemporary discourse about difference, and can reframe theoretical questions for a contemporary feminist theology. . . . Within a Christian systematic theology the subject always and only ever subsists insofar as it is located in the movement of the divine economy. The subject is sustained by, drawn into, and lovingly transgressed by the Triune life."[48] All three of these feminist theologians have sought the solution for the apparently rigid divisions surrounding gender in the "works and ways of the Triune God," for it is by seeing what God has done and the structure of such deeds that one is able to see gender more clearly.[49]

This is not to say that the adoption of this method will always yield the same conclusions about gender's ontology or about any other gendered issue.

46. Coakley, *God, Sexuality, and the Self*, 53–54.

47. Beth Felker Jones, "Embodied from Creation through Redemption: Placing Gender and Sexuality in Theological Context," in *Beauty, Order, and Mystery: A Christian Vision of Human Sexuality*, ed. Gerald L. Hiestand and Todd A. Wilson (Downers Grove, IL: IVP Academic, 2017), 21.

48. Janice McRandal, *Christian Doctrine and the Grammar of Difference: A Contribution to Feminist Systematic Theology* (Minneapolis: Fortress, 2015), 17, 175.

49. See also Jana Marguerite Bennett, "Telling the Old Story in Gendered Keys: The Theological Revivals of Katherine Sonderegger, Kathryn Tanner, and Sarah Coakley," *Anglican Theological Review* 101, no. 2 (2019): 277–88. Bennett's focus is on the theological revival represented by the figures in her title, theologians whom I self-consciously will follow in this work. Her analysis is that what unifies the efforts of these figures and has made them so appealing is the fact that "we live in a time and place where big stories of God, as depicted in these systematic theologies, are crucial. . . . Proper attention to gender concerns will require not piecemeal essays, but rather telling the whole wonderful story of salvation—the 'old, old story'—yet again, with new tones" (278).

I have significant reservations, for instance, about McRandal's proposal, particularly her dissolution of the concept of gender into that of "difference." "Difference," though popularly used in feminist theory and theology, is not itself sufficiently informative to be evaluated on its own terms. The *kind* of difference in question, it seems to me, is important, and some instances of difference will be good (such as the difference between creature and Creator) while others will be evil (such as the differences that motivate racist distinctions). It is not enough to inspect "difference" on its face, but the relata being differentiated must be evaluated case by case. The same goes for "binaries," a term McRandal takes to be roughly equivalent to "difference." Some of these will be helpful and true, while others will not. Her failure to recognize this reveals a significant weakness in her book, yet I find it to be an entirely commendable project in the *way* it attempts to consider difference and gender. The method is difficult to distinguish from what I employ in the remainder of this work, even if the conclusions will be very different.

My theological account of gender will unfold as follows: In chapter 2 I will offer an explication and analysis of the most prominent view regarding gender's basic properties—namely, the view that gender is a social construct. After highlighting representative figures who have argued for this position, I shall put forward two objections related to the context-boundedness of social constructs. Chapter 3 offers an alternative account of gender that I believe to be broad enough to cover most understandings of gender. This account will serve as a "lowest-common-denominator" definition that is able to be refined in ways suitable to those who adopt it. I will present it in the form of four theses:

1. Gender is an essence, though this is not reducible to or identical with biological determinism or biological essentialism.
2. The complexity of gender, the noetic effects of sin, and the current conditions of oppression complicate our epistemic access to gender's essence. All the same, we can be assured that issues surrounding gender will be rectified in the eschaton.
3. Any theory or theology of gender must be consistent with and supportive of the cultivation of justice.
4. Gender is concerned with selves or identity and with the way selves organize social goods pertaining to their sexed bodies.

The remainder of the chapter will be dedicated to providing theological warrants for each of these theses, giving special attention to some *exegetical* reasons for maintaining them.

The fourth thesis provides the basis from which chapter 4 proceeds. If gender is concerned with who we are and how we organize social goods pertaining to our sexed bodies, and if this happens in a way that is social (but not socially constructed) and natural (but not biologically essentialist), then some account of what it means to bear an identity that adequately takes into consideration these features is necessary. The basic Augustinian point I bring to view is this: since our identities are defined by our objects of love, our *gendered* identities are defined by our objects of *gendered* love. Chapter 5 then introduces the argumentative core of the project. In conversation with Sarah Coakley's view that gender is intimately related to desire, I argue that gender is love, for love is how we acquire our identities. In the sixth and seventh chapters I will situate this account of gender within the different moments of the divine economy—creation, fall, redemption, and consummation—with an eye to the moral and contextual implications it raises.

Before moving on, I should make one final note. I am concerned with a question I take to be upstream of many of the heated debates that surround gender. That question is, "What is gender?" This deceptively simple question lies at the root of all gender theory and theology, and it can be expanded into a further question: "Is there a connection between the possession of a certain kind of body and the cultural roles, assumptions, and traits we associate with gender, and if so, what is the nature of that connection?" That is the question of this book, and while an answer to that question will have implications for current discussions, such as those about trans* identities and the ordination of women, it seems to me that far too many authors desire answers to those questions before adequately answering the more fundamental question of what gender is in the first place. One should be absolutely clear about the implications of that conceptually upstream question in order to cast light without heat in subsequent discussions. Therefore, while I will periodically indicate how this proposal impacts contextual issues, I take it to be conceptually prior to those issues—and, in fact, to be compatible with a variety of positions regarding important questions about matters like trans* identities, gay identities, and so on.

Ultimately, far too much theology has ignored gender, and far too many thinkers concerned with gender have been inhospitable to theology. But this need not be the case. The gospel of the triune God is sufficient, I believe, to guide our thinking about the most vexing of issues, and the Christian theologian can be confident of this. She can, ultimately, apply Nicholas Wolterstorff's final commendations to her thoughts on gender:

> To my young grad students who aim to become theologians I say, with all the emphasis I can muster: *be theologians*. Do not be ersatz philosophers, do not be ersatz cultural theorists, do not be ersatz anything. Be genuine theologians. Be sure-footed in philosophy, sure-footed in cultural theory, and the like. And struggle to find a voice that can be heard, if not agreed with, not just by theologians but others as well. But then: be theologians. There will be cultural theorists around to tell us how things look from their perspective; there will be sociologists around to tell us how things look from their perspective. What we need to hear from you is how things look when seen in the light of the triune God—may his name be praised!—who creates and sustains us, who redeems us, and who will bring this frail and fallen, though yet glorious, humanity and cosmos to consummation.[50]

Let us turn to doing so now.

---

50. Wolterstorff, "To Theologians," 91–92 (emphasis original).

TWO

Understanding the Social Construction of Gender

My aim in this chapter will be to explore the claim that gender is a social construct. Among those who write about gender in the academy, this is the view that predominates, so it merits careful attention. I shall begin with some contextualizing comments about the intuitions, motivations, and arguments that underpin the wide acceptance the view has generated. From there, I shall turn to an exposition of what it means to say that gender is a social construct, beginning with a historical overview of significant figures who have contributed to the view's basic tenets and ending with contemporary philosophical and theological perspectives on how best to understand it. This exposition will be followed by a set of objections that I take to be sufficient to consider it an untenable view. I shall conclude by considering the promise of claiming that sex as well as gender is socially constructed. In the end, this too will be shown to be indefensible and theologically unviable. My conclusion will be that social construction should not be the view championed by theologians who want to account for gender, but neither are they forced into a simplistic biological essentialism as the only alternative.

2.1 Contextualizing the View

When my wife and I found out from our doctor that we were having a daughter, we kept the sex of our baby a secret shared only between the two of us. We enjoyed having something that only we knew about, and it allowed us to paint a more defined mental picture of our anticipated daughter. With such a decision, however, came a complication: How were our loved ones to purchase gifts for us when they did not know the sex of the child? Initially, we did not realize this would prove to be an obstacle. When we did, my wife and I attempted to work our way around it in various ways; we recommended gender-neutral colors and items, but even this did not quite work. Even the most banal of items, like baby socks, proved to be gendered in some respect—*these* were boy socks, and *these* were girl socks, though what made each gendered in this way was beyond us (they were both white, after all!). In the end, our friends and family were able to find gifts, but when our daughter was born, much of what she had to wear was not *obviously* gender specific. So when we went out, those who encountered us could not tell if she was a little boy or a little girl (Where is the pink? Where are the sports figures?). Most of the time, we were told that we had a lovely little boy.

This short anecdote is not particularly shocking or unique, but it helpfully illustrates something that many contemporary theologians and theorists consider to be sufficient to show that gender is a social construct. Whether my daughter was going to be perceived as a boy or a girl depended on our ability to find the right social cues for others to recognize. The question of what kind of body she had was something we found out from the doctor (though even that has been argued to constitute an important part of social construction), but the question of whether she was recognized as a boy or a girl was tied to her ability to fit within categories defined by certain social rules and not others. If she was going to be a girl, she needed to have pink clothing, for instance; our failure to clothe her accordingly only revealed and strengthened the social conditions required for one's gender. At least that is how the thinking typically goes.

These sorts of scenarios pump the intuitions of many who hold that gender is a social construct. The Icelandic philosopher Ásta formalizes the intuition in the following way: "If a property chiefly figures in explanations of social facts, and not natural facts, that suggests that the property is a social property, and not a natural property. . . . One should consider in what kinds of explanations the property occurs."[1] Being a girl, on the example above, is indicated by wearing certain types of clothes and not others. Wearing clothes

1. Ásta, *Categories We Live By: The Construction of Sex, Gender, Race, and Other Social Categories* (New York: Oxford University Press, 2018), 70–71. The assumed distinction between

that are of one type or another is, of course, a social fact. So, being a girl must be a social property. It is because of these considerations that the view that gender is a social construct is simply *intuitive* for many. It may be anchored to some other nonsocial property, like the sex recognized on an ultrasound, but it is no less social considered on its own. As a result, *whether* gender is socially constructed is a foregone conclusion in many circles. Kate Bornstein's popular work, among many others, testifies to this: "There's a . . . simple way to look at gender. Once upon a time, someone drew a line in the sands for a culture and proclaimed . . . 'On this side, you are a man; on the other side you are a woman.'"[2] That, anyway, gives one a clue about the predominance, indeed the canonical status, of the view. It appears that it is simply assumed that if gender is recognized as *social* in a basic sense, then it must be socially *constructed* more specifically.

If one looks more closely, one also finds that supporting these intuitions are a series of other motivations and arguments. Perhaps the most common motivation many have for affirming the social construction of gender is its ability to challenge oppressive social structures. When social constructionist claims operate in this way, they have been said to be partaking in a "debunking project." The basic process of such projects is this: Take a trait that most people consider to be natural, or otherwise stable and unchangeable. If it can be shown that this trait is in point of fact *not* natural or otherwise stable, then one can engage in subsequent attempts to modify it. Thus, Sally Haslanger states, "This project of challenging the purported truth conditions for the application of a concept I call a 'debunking' project. A debunking project typically attempts to show that a category or classification scheme that appears to rack a group of individuals defined by a set of physical or metaphysical conditions is better understood as capturing a group that occupies a certain (usually 'thick') social position."[3] Once the property is debunked, the category can be done away with, or heavily revised. This is desirable because many of these categories have been shown to be oppressive, and social construction can be a tool used for debunking oppressive construals of gender, particularly

---

"natural" and "social" will be an important one to keep in mind throughout this book, especially since it will be questioned in the following chapter.

2. Kate Bornstein, *Gender Outlaw* (New York: Routledge, 1994), 22.

3. Sally Haslanger, *Resisting Reality: Social Construction and Social Critique* (New York: Oxford University Press, 2012), 132. For Haslanger, a "thick" social position is a position one holds in society with the ability to empower or disempower the continued performance of the individual holding the position.

ones that serve to disfavor women. For this reason, the social construction of gender is seen to have *political* benefits, meaning that the view is seen to be a powerful instrument for challenging oppression. This is one of its most compelling elements.

These, strictly speaking, are not *arguments* for the view that gender is socially constructed but rather *motivations* that support a common intuition. That being said, arguments for the view do exist,[4] and the most important one is an argument from *exclusion*. When the category "woman," so the argument goes, is under consideration, it is far too often the case that what one has in mind is a particular *class* of women, usually mirroring that of the person making the argument. The danger is that if the operative concept for a particular gender is restricted only to a subsection of persons of that gender, those who stand outside of that subsection will be excluded as proper members of that gender. A famous example of this is found in early feminist theories, which were alleged to be restrictively white and suited for women of a certain economic standing. When thinking of women's rights, then, the danger arose that those rights would not extend to, say, economically poor black women. In the words of Elizabeth Spelman, who provided one of the most influential articulations of this argument, "The real problem has been how feminist theory has confused the condition of one group of women with the condition of all."[5] The argument from exclusion is likely the most common and persuasive one in the literature, and we shall have recourse to return to it later. The basic idea is that once one realizes that it is *social* factors that provide the criteria for exclusion, one begins to see the ways in which the conditions for being of a certain gender are themselves constituted socially.

There are, then, some diverse motivations and arguments for thinking that gender is a social construct, motivations that empower the intuitions many already hold about the matter. Yet, as I mentioned in the previous chapter, I do not think that gender is a social construct. Nor do I think that it is a biological essence. Such a simplistic bifurcation is problematic. Still, this does not prevent me from seeing the purchase, both argumentative and intuitive, of the considerations just mentioned. It is highly counterintuitive

4. For more arguments in favor of the view, see Charlotte Witt, "Anti-Essentialism in Feminist Theory," *Philosophical Topics* 23, no. 2 (Fall 1995): 321–44.

5. Elizabeth V. Spelman, *Inessential Woman: Problems of Exclusion in Feminist Thought* (Boston: Beacon, 1990), 4. Of course, it was the experience of exclusion that led to the rise of womanist theory and theology, with Alice Walker as one of the main figureheads of the movement. In theology, the work of Delores Williams stands out as placing great priority on this point.

to think that there is *nothing* social about gender,[6] and the argument from exclusion is particularly powerful and far-reaching. Debunking putatively natural categories is also massively important, though I think such debunking is best done on epistemic rather than metaphysical grounds. So, though I will argue against the view that gender is socially constructed by the end of this chapter, my argument should not be taken as an attempt to repudiate it altogether as wholly untenable. In fact, some of its features will be rehabilitated in the next chapter. What is required, then, is an inquiry into whether social construction is the theory that provides the most satisfying explanation for these intuitions, motivations, and arguments. This inquiry will require understanding the finer points of the view. What does it mean, therefore, to say that gender is socially constructed?

2.2 The Metaphysics of the Social Construction of Gender

A chapter like this must begin by clarifying that there is no *one* view about the social construction of gender. In reality, it is a family of views clustered around some primary principles and convictions. There are things common to all social construction theories, as I plan to show, but it would be culpably reductionistic to say that there is just one way to think about it. This should suggest that at the center of this cluster of views are varieties of social construction that make stronger claims than the ones at the edges and that just outside of the cluster are views that *resemble* the social construction of gender but are not themselves construction views. Recognizing this diversity is the first step, I believe, in breaking the bifurcated deadlock between construction and essence. However, in virtually *all* social construction views, social construction is taken to be the direct and incompatible opposite of what is biological, natural, or essential.[7] Sometimes this assumption is a result of operating on terms that are poorly defined and understood; whatever the reason, it remains broadly held and creates one of our major bifurcations. To anticipate an argument I will make more fully in the next chapter, the assumption rests on a fundamental mistake: the identification of what is *biological* with what is

6. Though that does not of itself yield the conclusion that gender is socially *constructed*, especially if it can be shown (as I plan to do in the following chapter) that there are more ways of bearing a social identity than through construction.

7. Recall Ásta's distinction between "natural" explanations and "social" explanations; the distinction in that context is clearly between biological and nonbiological properties.

essential. Charlotte Witt makes this point brilliantly: "Although it is strictly speaking false to equate essentialism and biologism, biological descriptions are *one* way of specifying the essence of women, a way that has predominated in patriarchal thought both in the past and today. . . . It is thus assumed that the thesis that gender is socially constructed, in itself, entails a rejection of essences."[8] To illustrate why biology should not be conflated with an essence, consider the example of the computer on which I type.[9] It is not a biological entity, on the common understanding of that term; indeed, it is a socially constructed artifact. But does it have an essence? On one common definition of an essence—namely, the properties required for a thing to be the *kind* of thing that it is—the answer is yes. For my computer to be a computer, it must have the property of being able to, for example, process software. It is *essential* to its being a computer that it is able to perform such a function. If it cannot do that because it is broken, then we tend to think that it *should* be able to, given the kind of thing that it is. If it cannot process software because it does not have the requisite parts (perhaps because it is one of those cakes that are indistinguishable from ordinary household items), then we would be justified in thinking that it is not a computer after all. This computer has an essence, part of which is its ability to process software. But it is not a biological entity, and so it would be mistaken to think that only biological entities have essences. Yet it has been the motivation of many social construction theories to deny the existence of essences on the basis of their social construction. That approach, however, is ill-fated, and realizing this begins to question the very foundation on which this debate was founded. In light of these observations, let us turn to the finer points of this family of views.

2.2.1 The Theoretical Underpinning of the Social Construction of Gender

Social constructionist accounts of gender, it must be remembered, are not homogeneous. Nevertheless, they share some elements in common, perhaps the chief of which is the *purpose* to which they are put—namely, the advancement of justice through the uncovering of oppressive traits that have been wrongly seen as "written in stone." This was true even among its first proponents. Standard summaries of the view that gender is socially constructed

8. Witt, "Anti-Essentialism in Feminist Theory," 325.
9. My computer example modifies Witt's example of a Coke machine in "Anti-Essentialism in Feminist Theory," 325–26.

place its origin somewhere within the 1960s and '70s, or roughly the "second wave" of feminism. While this was when it gained the recognition it now enjoys, the view is in fact a good deal older than that. Its earliest articulations can be found in figures like François Poulain de la Barre (1647–1723), Mary Wollstonecraft (1759–97),[10] and John Stuart Mill (1806–73), who employed it in service of their deep concern for equal social opportunity for women, in terms of access to education and suffrage. They each arrived at a social constructionist position from a common conviction—namely, that there are *epistemic difficulties* in discerning universal traits concerning what it means to be a woman or a man, difficulties that originate either from prejudice or from the unjust conditions that cloud our ability to observe natural traits. In their time, as in ours, the traits associated with womanhood were taken to be natural to women simply because, on the observation of some, *all* women possessed them.[11] Yet, these figures argued, *even if* these traits are universally true of all women (which is a tendentious claim at best), one cannot infer that they are therefore *natural* to all women; there is an important difference between what is universal and what is natural. Universal traits could have come about from other means, from *social* means.

Poulain's view of gender as socially constructed relied on humanity's propensity toward "bias" to show that we are often mistaken about what is natural.[12] The bias he identifies is a false inference drawn from what is presently not the case to what *could not be* the case. Poulain noticed that many

10. Space does not allow for a treatment of Wollstonecraft, especially her landmark "A Vindication of the Rights of Woman," in *A Vindication of the Rights of Woman and A Vindication of the Rights of Men*, ed. Janet Todd (New York: Oxford University Press, 2009), 63–284. In my view, Wollstonecraft is best seen as an early feminist humanist, advocating for the human rights of women in the midst of social conditions that failed to recognize them. For that reason, I do not think she advanced the social constructionist position in the same way as Poulain and Mill, for social relations played a largely negative and prohibitive role in her theory of gender.

11. See, e.g., Horace Bushnell's galling argument against women's suffrage in *Women's Suffrage: The Reform against Nature* (New York: Charles Scribner, 1869). Bushnell's basic position was that it was *unnatural* for women to vote, a claim that he assumed did not require biblical support. Thus, after his basic argument, he says, "The Scripture has nothing to say of this matter, which is at all variant from what we see with our eyes" (73–74). Why is it unnatural for women to vote, for Bushnell? Because he had never seen a woman vote, so it must be universally true that women do not vote. And if it is universally true, then it is *naturally* true. This latter inference is highly problematic, as both Poulain and Mill will show, but it is still present today amongst those who wish to defend views of gender on the basis of natural law.

12. It is an irony of history that one of the earliest articulations of the view that has come to be representative of feminist theory finds its origin in a Cartesian philosopher and Calvinist theologian, even if both of these elements might now be seen as inconsistent with feminist

argued as follows: because women do not currently perform some task, it must be the case that women *cannot* perform it. But this argument is hugely mistaken, according to Poulain:

> If we press people a little, we will find that their strongest reasons come down to saying that, as far as women are concerned, things have always been the way they are at present; that this is a sign that things should be as they are; and *if women had been capable of studying the sciences and holding offices, men would have admitted them alongside themselves*. . . . No one reports ever seeing women otherwise. It is known that they have always been like that, and there is no place on earth where women are not treated as they are here. . . . People find it very difficult to imagine that things could easily have been different, and it even seems as if we could never change the current situation no matter how hard we tried.[13]

Such reasons are obviously false, and uncovering them led Poulain to conclude that "the common view about women is a popular and ill-founded prejudice."[14] We simply cannot conclude that because something has always been the case, it *must* be the case, says Poulain. Instead, it is far more likely that there is a *social explanation* for the current arrangement of things, an explanation whose central element maintains that "since men exercise all this authority, everything must be arranged for their benefit."[15] These putatively observable traits of femininity, concludes Poulain, are not natural, for we cannot infer what is natural from what is merely universally instantiated. Rather, these traits can be explained by social factors, with the result that gender is a social, not a natural, property.[16]

John Stuart Mill can be read as extending a line of thought Poulain had begun, though his agnosticism about knowing the nature of gender came not from an examination of bias but from an analysis of the pervasive inequality that exists between men and women, something that is itself unnatural.

thought. For more on Poulain's life, see Siep Stuurman, *François Poulain de la Barre and the Invention of Modern Equality* (Cambridge, MA: Harvard University Press, 2004).

13. François Poulain de la Barre, "A Physical and Moral Discourse concerning the Equality of Both Sexes," in *The Equality of the Sexes: Three Feminist Texts of the Seventeenth Century*, trans. Desmond M. Clarke (New York: Oxford University Press, 2013), 125–26.

14. Poulain, "Physical and Moral Discourse," 146.

15. Poulain, "Physical and Moral Discourse," 149.

16. For further detail and corroboration of Poulain's affirmation of the social construction of gender, see Desmond M. Clarke, introduction to Poulain, *Equality of the Sexes*, 43.

Under such conditions, he maintains, it is impossible to know the "nature of women":

> I consider it presumption in any one to pretend to decide what women are or are not, can or cannot be, by natural constitution. They have always hitherto been kept, as far as regards spontaneous development, in so unnatural a state, that their nature cannot but have been greatly distorted and disguised; and no one can safely pronounce that if women's nature were left to choose its direction as freely as men's, and if no artificial bent were attempted to be given to it except that required by the conditions of human society, and given to both sexes alike, there would be any material difference, or perhaps any difference at all, in the character and capacities which would unfold themselves. I shall presently show, that even the least contestable of the differences which now exist, are such as *may very well have been produced merely by circumstances, without any difference of natural capacity.*[17]

For Mill, it is presumptuous to assume we can know anything about the nature of women or men because any reliable information we have will be distorted by the current conditions of inequality and suppression. Far more likely is an explanation that has recourse to social circumstances that preclude women from access to equitable treatment.

I mention these two early social constructionists because their work represents a more epistemically driven set of arguments for social construction. They are fairly metaphysically restrained: we cannot say with a great amount of certitude what gender is because various things complicate our access to it. In the early twentieth century, however, a shift occurs. Whereas early social construction theorists relied on epistemic restraint about natures to make their case, more recent figures have turned to increasingly substantial *metaphysical* claims, and this shift will be important for my later argument. While the conclusion is the same, contemporary thinkers are much more willing to reconsider the properties of sex and gender *themselves*. The social construction of gender, in its most popular articulation today (and unlike its first defenders), has taken a metaphysical turn.

17. John Stuart Mill, "The Subjection of Women," in *J. S. Mill: "On Liberty" and Other Writings*, ed. Stefan Collini, Cambridge Texts in the History of Political Thought (New York: Cambridge University Press, 1989), 173 (emphasis added). Mill's treatise is filled with statements like these. See also: "I deny that any one knows, or can know, the nature of the two sexes, as long as they have only been seen in their present relation to one another. . . . What is now called the nature of women is an eminently artificial thing—the result of forced repression in some directions, unnatural stimulation in others" (138).

The most pivotal figure in this regard is Simone de Beauvoir (1908–86), whom many credit as the first to make explicit the distinction between sex and gender.[18] Beauvoir noted that the question "What is a woman?" is not as simple as it may seem.[19] While it may *seem* like all it takes to be a woman is to have an adult female human body, it is nevertheless the case that many women are told they are insufficiently feminine. She notes how "in speaking of certain women, the experts proclaim, 'They are not women,' even though they have a uterus like the others. Everyone agrees there are females in the human species; today, as in the past, they make up about half of humanity; and yet we are told that 'femininity is in jeopardy'; we are urged, 'Be women, stay women, become women.' *So not every female human being is necessarily a woman.*"[20] Beauvoir's central insight is that it is problematic to maintain simultaneously that being a woman is a matter of possessing a certain biological make-up *and* that one can possess such biological traits and still fail to be a woman. It seems like there are two different things being described, one biological and one that has to do with the roles one plays in society, and these things have different sufficient conditions. As Georgia Warnke aptly states, "Femininity can be in danger . . . only if it is not an inevitable outgrowth of being born female—in other words, only if gender is not the same as sex."[21] The dénouement of this observation is that what it takes to be of a certain sex (biologically understood) is not the same as what it takes to be of a certain gender (culturally understood); hence, sex is not the same as gender. Once again, we have a claim that gender is socially constructed, but in this instance the argument is about the metaphysics involved, not the epistemic access we possess.

Since Beauvoir, the literature on social construction has proliferated, whether applied to gender or to other socially constructed artifacts like money,

18. Some Beauvoir interpreters will deny that she actually held to this distinction. See Nancy Bauer, *Simone de Beauvoir, Philosophy, and Feminism* (New York: Columbia University Press, 2001); and Toril Moi, *What Is a Woman? And Other Essays* (New York: Oxford University Press, 1999), part 1. They claim that only when she is read through Judith Butler is she seen to be a social constructionist, but if read in the context of her cultural and intellectual inheritance, she appears to hold no such view. For more on this context, see Kate Kirkpatrick, *Becoming Beauvoir: A Life* (New York: Bloomsbury, 2019). In what follows, I will stay with the "mainline" interpretation of Beauvoir, fully aware that it may be incorrect; even so, the incorrect interpretation has had a significant impact on the contemporary landscape, and for that reason it is worth recounting.

19. Simone de Beauvoir, *The Second Sex*, trans. Constance Borde and Sheila Malovany-Chevallier (New York: Vintage, 2011), 3.

20. Beauvoir, *Second Sex*, 3.

21. Georgia Warnke, *Debating Sex and Gender* (New York: Oxford University Press, 2010), 5.

race, war, and so on.[22] Feminist theorists have made a significant contribution to this endeavor, articulating views of both what gender *is* and what it *ought to be*. Linda Martín Alcoff is an influential feminist theorist who maintains that gender "is not a point to start from in the sense of being a given thing but is, instead, a posit or construct, formalizable in a nonarbitrary way through a matrix of habits, practices, and discourses" throughout an individual's history. Because of this, "gender is not natural, biological, universal, ahistorical, or essential," yet one can still "claim that gender is relevant because we are taking it as a position from which to act politically."[23] (Notice, once again, the disjunction between what is social and what is natural.) Alcoff's particular contribution, as the quote indicates, is the theory of "positionality": "The positional definition . . . makes [a woman's] identity relative to a constantly shifting context, to a situation that includes a network of elements involving others, the objective economic conditions, cultural and political institutions and ideologies, and so on."[24] In contrast to definitions that ignore other identity markers possessed by an individual, Alcoff's definition of gender sees it as the *intersection* of all the relevant social positions in which one stands. One is gendered within a variety of social spheres, and the conjunction of these spheres helps to variegate what it means to be man or a woman or otherwise. Sally Haslanger's illustration gets at Alcoff's notion of intersectionality quite well: "Imagine race, gender, and other social positions to be like gels on a stage light: the light shines blue and a red gel is added, and the light shines purple; if a yellow gel is added instead of the red, the light shines green. Similarly, gender is lived differently depending on the racial (and other) positions in which one is situated."[25] Though she retains the biological distinction between males and females as grounding for gender,[26] Alcoff sees gender as the intersecting sum of all or many of the identities held by persons of a certain sex.

22. For an early and very influential account, see John R. Searle, *The Construction of Social Reality* (New York: Free Press, 1995). For a helpful survey of the different ways something can be said to be "socially constructed," see Muhammad Ali Khalidi, "Three Kinds of Social Kinds," *Philosophy and Phenomenological Research* 90, no. 1 (2015): 96–112.

23. Linda Martín Alcoff, "Cultural Feminism versus Post-Structuralism: The Identity Crisis in Feminist Theory," *Signs* 13, no. 3 (1988): 431, 433. It should also be noted that the notion of an "identity politic" is key for Alcoff: "The idea here is that one's identity is taken (and defined) as a political point of departure, as a motivation for action, and as a delineation of one's politics" (431–32).

24. Alcoff, "Cultural Feminism versus Post-Structuralism," 433.

25. Haslanger, *Resisting Reality*, 9.

26. See Linda Martín Alcoff, *Visible Identities: Race, Gender, and the Self* (New York: Oxford University Press, 2006), 172: "*Women and men are differentiated by virtue of their different*

It is important, given the diversity of accounts on offer, now to explore in greater depth the views of two representative theorists, one from the philosophical guild and one from the theological. Doing so will present the social constructionist view of gender in its greatest sophistication.

2.2.2 Representative Voices: Haslanger and Tanner

Sally Haslanger, a philosopher at MIT, was one of the first in the analytic philosophical guild to give explicit attention to the social construction of gender. The overarching thesis that structures her book is this: "Construed simply, genders are those social positions, within a particular culture, constituted by how sexed beings are viewed and treated."[27] Ingredient to her view, then, are the concepts of a *social position*, how that position is *confined to a particular culture*, and how it is produced by the views and treatments the bearer of the social position *receives from others*. In order to establish this thesis, Haslanger must provide a broader view of social construction into which her specific views of gender are situated.

The most general instance of social construction she calls "generic social construction": "Something is a social construction in the generic sense just in case it is an intended or unintended product of a social practice."[28] There is a certain ambiguity in this statement. On which end of the social construction process is the social entity encountered? Are social entities doing the constructing, or are they the result of construction? In actuality, Haslanger's view likely includes both. Something may be a social construct if it was produced by social practices, even if it is not itself a social entity (dog breeds are one such social construct). Call this type of social construction *subjective social construction*, since the relevant social entities are doing the construction, not resulting from it. Alternatively, if the resultant product is a social construct, even if the forces that produced it are not themselves social entities, it is an instance of *objective social construction*. Examples here are legion, including librarians, wars, parties, money, and so forth. It will turn out that on Haslanger's view, gender is both subjectively constructed and objectively constructed.

Within generic social construction are three further subdivisions: things that are socially distinguished, things that are socially caused, and things

---

relationship of possibility to biological reproduction, with biological reproduction referring to conceiving, giving birth, and breast-feeding, involving one's own body."

27. Haslanger, *Resisting Reality*, 196.
28. Haslanger, *Resisting Reality*, 86.

that are socially constituted.[29] First, some social constructs are *socially distinguished*: "We distinguish things by classifying them, and classification is a human activity and can be done in better or worse ways. . . . In this task I am appropriately guided by some epistemic goals (it would be a problem if my conditions for sorting were inconsistent, or if I applied them haphazardly), and some practical goals."[30] This is a very simple type of social construction. Every few months or so, my family will take time to look through our closets and think carefully about which items we need and which items we can part ways with. Thus, two piles are created: the "keep" and the "don't keep." These are socially distinguished categories. Moreover, paradigmatic instances of each pile begin to form. A particularly old shirt with holes in the collar characterizes the prime features for a suitable member of the "don't keep" pile, while a shirt I know I have worn in the last week is a "keep." It often becomes the case, as Haslanger observes, that "our attributions have the power to both establish and reinforce groupings that may eventually come to 'fit' the classifications."[31] She considers the distinction between "jocks" and "nerds," observing that those classified as jocks feel pressure to conform to the paradigm of the category, and the same for the nerds. When this happens, a further development of social distinguishing occurs—namely, "pragmatic construction." "A classificatory apparatus (be it a full-blown classification scheme or just a conceptual distinction or descriptive term) is socially constructed just in case its use is determined, at least in part, by social factors."[32] All that this means, claims Haslanger, is that the distinctions are in place to suit our own ends and intentions (e.g., what must be donated or kept, who is a jock or a nerd) and that the members of each classification feel social pressure to conform to the paradigms of each category. Within pragmatic construction, lastly, there are strong and weak varieties. A weak pragmatic construction is one that is only partly determined by social factors (retaining some kind of objectivity), while a strong pragmatic construction is an "illusion projected onto the world," having no objective basis for the distinction at hand.[33]

A second category of generic construction consists of those artifacts that are *socially caused*. This occurs when "social factors play a causal role in

29. See Haslanger, *Resisting Reality*, 190.

30. Haslanger, *Resisting Reality*, 188. This is also what Haslanger calls a "discursive construction."

31. Haslanger, *Resisting Reality*, 123.

32. Haslanger, *Resisting Reality*, 90. It is a bit puzzling why she says the apparatus is socially rather than pragmatically constructed. I take her to be saying something semantically equivalent.

33. Haslanger, *Resisting Reality*, 91.

bringing [something] into existence or, to some substantial extent, in its being the way it is."[34] For something to be causally constructed, it must be produced by social factors; this is another way of designating what I have called subjective social construction. Consider the example, cited briefly above, of dog breeds.[35] There are different dog breeds because *humans* have bred different types of dogs through social processes. These social processes have caused the varieties of dog breeds, making it a case of causal construction.[36] For Haslanger, gender is causally constructed: social practices have created the expectations, roles, and so forth that inform what is typically understood to make up masculinity and femininity. Interestingly, she makes the further claim that when gender is causally constructed, it becomes a case of pragmatic construction. For instance, a "husband is a legally married man. Being a legally married man does not *cause* one to be a husband; it is just what being a husband consists in."[37] What she means is that when social forces cause gender categories, those social forces just *become* the categories. To borrow a term from John Searle, they become "constitutive rules"—rules that both cause and constitute what it means to belong to a category.[38] Becoming legally married is what caused me to become a husband, but it is now also what *it means* for me to be a husband. Similarly, the rule "a ball fully crossing a goal line is a goal" caused the existence of goals in the game of soccer, but it is more aptly said that it defines what a goal is.

Haslanger's third category of generic construction demarcates those things that are *socially constituted*, or are "defined in terms of social relations." She explains: "These are constituted by a relationship . . . that holds between the members of each category."[39] This differs importantly from social causation, particularly when applied to gender: "The point being made is that gender is not a classification scheme based simply on anatomical or biological differences, but should be understood as a system of social categories that can only be defined by reference to a network of social relations."[40] Whereas the claim

---

34. Haslanger, *Resisting Reality*, 87. For an application of this to gender, see Haslanger, *Resisting Reality*, 130.

35. This example is offered by Haslanger in *Resisting Reality*, 190.

36. Note that the existence of subjective social construction, or in Haslanger's terms, causal construction, means that the opposite of "natural" is not social construction. A pit bull is a "natural" entity, even if it was produced by social practices.

37. Haslanger, *Resisting Reality*, 131.

38. See Searle, *Construction of Social Reality*, 27.

39. Haslanger, *Resisting Reality*, 185.

40. Haslanger, *Resisting Reality*, 130.

that gender is causally constructed concerns what was involved in producing it from social practices, to say that gender is socially constituted points out that what defines the category is not what caused it but the relations that obtain within it. Consider this a shift analogous to the change from subjective construction (social practices produce gender) to objective construction (gender is to be considered a social artifact). Here, we might say that gender is a social construct not (or not only) because society has *caused* the expectations attached to different genders but because of the social relations required of each gender. Suppose that it is a masculine trait to have a beard. One may say that society caused this trait to be masculine, but one may also focus one's analysis on the way this trait is extended within a web of social relations—say, the items in stores for facial hair grooming and related advertisements and the role they place in social interactions. From this we can see that gender has a "basis in social relations."[41] From these social relations, one acquires a "social position," which is the sum of social relations in which one stands.[42]

Recall from what I called Haslanger's "thesis statement" that this is where she believes gender is located: "Genders are those social positions, within a particular culture, constituted by how sexed beings are viewed and treated." This definition draws upon all three types of social construction, and the process can be summarized as follows: Once a social distinction is made between how the sexes are understood and gender is socially caused (which creates a pragmatic construction), one's consequent social roles constitute certain relations, the relevant ones of which become one's social position. When that occurs, one is then subject to "gender norms," which are "clusters of characteristics and abilities that function as a standard by which individuals are judged to be 'good' instances of their gender; they are the 'virtues' appropriate to the gender."[43] Thus, the social positions that constitute particular gender kinds have paradigmatic instances, and these exemplify the traits and relations to which the members *ought* to aspire. (Think of celebrities and models, athletes and musicians; there is an impulse for us to want to be *like* those figures.) Importantly, social norms function as representatives of the socially constructed kind to which they belong, so if the ideal is problematic, so is the kind.[44]

41. Haslanger, *Resisting Reality*, 40.
42. See Haslanger, *Resisting Reality*, 40.
43. Haslanger, *Resisting Reality*, 42.
44. Haslanger, *Resisting Reality*, 46.

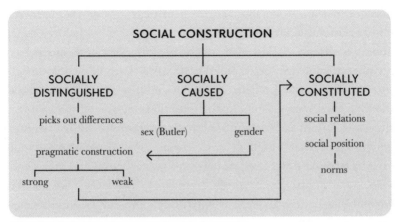

Fig. 2.1. Sally Haslanger's account of social construction.

Figure 2.1 provides an overview of this complex proposal. According to Haslanger, gender is socially constructed in each of the three ways depicted. Sexes are socially distinguished (those with one kind of reproductive role are on one side, and those with the other kind of reproductive role are on the other side), and these distinctions mark out the paradigmatic instances of each group according to some social purpose, making gender pragmatically constructed.[45] Gender is also socially caused, because it was society that created the norms, expectations, roles, and so on that define what it means to be of a certain gender. Finally, and perhaps most importantly, given how this fact informs our social positions, gender is socially constituted. It is the nexus of social relations that constitute a social position in which certain gender norms are present.[46]

Haslanger's philosophical understanding of the social construction of gender is helpfully positioned alongside Kathryn Tanner's views. Tanner, throughout her work, attempts to conceptualize the ways in which theology is embroiled in culture and how the traits of culture implicate the nature and tasks of theology. For Tanner, the social construction of gender is not particularly unique; all of reality is socially constructed, including the theology produced by theologians. Because of this, however, gender can be theologically

45. For her, the pragmatic construction is of the weak variety, since it will still have a basis in some nonsocial entity—namely, biological sex.
46. Haslanger has given a more specific, though much more controversial, account of gender in "Gender and Race: (What) Are They? (What) Do We Want Them to Be?," in *Resisting Reality: Social Construction and Social Critique* (New York: Oxford University Press, 2012), 221–47.

analyzed, with the particular goal of such an analysis being the charting of a new social vision for women and men.

Tanner is sharply critical of those theologians commonly labeled as social trinitarians for their attempts to craft a social vision modeled after the relations of the Trinity. Leveling a series of counterexamples and complexifications to their views, Tanner concludes that one should not look to the trinitarian relations for social principles, something of which theologians of gender are regularly guilty.[47] By extension, one should also not look to the Trinity to understand the ontology of human persons and their genders. Instead, for such answers we ought to look to *Christology*.[48] When we do so we find that human nature has a "lack of given definition, malleability through outside influences, unbounded character, and general openness to radical transformation."[49] She begins by affirming that the only being rightly said to be in the image of God is the Son, who in virtue of the divine nature has *in se* everything necessary for perfectly imaging divinity.[50] Though it is only the Son who is the image of God, we can nevertheless say that by the Son's direct involvement in creation (depicted in places like Prov. 8:27–31 and Col. 1:16–18), human creatures can approximate and participate in the image by means of their union with Christ established in the Spirit. In fact, this is what humans were created to be: "They are created to have within themselves something they are not."[51] In other words, to be human is to be created with a particular openness to relationship with the Son and to be transformed thereby. To be made in God's image, therefore, is to be made with a certain natural configuration suitable for union with the Son. If to be made in God's image is what it means to be human, then to be human is to be made for union with Christ.

---

47. "Clearly, then, trinitarianism can be every bit as socially and politically dangerous as monotheism. Everything depends on how that trinitarianism (or monotheism) is understood and applied" (Kathryn Tanner, *Christ the Key*, Current Issues in Theology [Cambridge: Cambridge University Press, 2010], 216). For a recent example of this strategy to understand gender, see Adrian Thatcher, *Gender and Christian Ethics* (New York: Cambridge University Press, 2021). It should be noted that appeals to the Trinity in an effort to make theological sense of gender are not characteristically "liberal" or "conservative"—they are readily found in theologies of both dispositions, in equally problematic measures.

48. See Tanner, *Christ the Key*, 236–37.

49. Tanner, *Christ the Key*, 1.

50. "A perfect image of God can only be a divine image. . . . Creatures by definition do not share the divine nature; and consequently human beings simply cannot be images of God in this way" (Tanner, *Christ the Key*, 6).

51. Tanner, *Christ the Key*, 22.

From this, Tanner derives a series of conclusions about human nature: "If human beings were created to enjoy Word and Spirit for their own, it no longer makes sense to give isolated attention to human nature in and of itself as if that nature were properly itself in some self-contained fashion."[52] Such a statement requires some disambiguation, particularly if we are going to be precise in what we mean by the word "nature." I take Tanner to mean that it is imprecise to think of human nature as a list of *intrinsic properties*, where an intrinsic property is one possessed by an individual apart from any relationships into which that individual enters (primarily relationships with other persons, human or divine). If a human nature lists the properties necessary and jointly sufficient for being human, then Tanner is arguing that it is mistaken to think these are exhausted by intrinsic properties. Rather, included within the properties constitutive of human natures are *extrinsic properties*, properties one has by virtue of one's relationships with other persons. Human nature, since it is defined by its capacity for union with Christ, includes within it an extrinsic property. From this it follows that we are not fully human apart from the relationship we have with Christ. Thus, Tanner contends, "Human nature must be characterized by an expansive openness that allows for the presence of God within it. It must be the sort of nature that has or makes room for the divine within its basic operations."[53] In short, human nature is defined not only in relation to itself but in relation to another—namely, Christ.[54]

Having established these conclusions about the image of God and human nature, Tanner extrapolates a broader account of human ontology. Though there are some natural faculties and capacities necessary for being human, she points out that there are no prescribed ways those faculties ought to be exercised: "Most of the innate and therefore fixed traits and dispositions of human nature underdetermine the character of actual human behaviors. These capacities, needs, and inclinations that make up human nature are designed to be culturally and environmentally sensitive in operation so as to take on a specific form only as shaped by environmental inputs."[55] It might be natural

52. Tanner, *Christ the Key*, 28.
53. Tanner, *Christ the Key*, 37.
54. For a much stronger argument for this kind of position, see Christa L. McKirland, *God's Provision, Humanity's Need* (Grand Rapids: Baker Academic, 2022). McKirland develops a theological account of "fundamental need" that gives greater metaphysical precision to Tanner's view, though it would not yield the same amount of plasticity with respect to human nature that Tanner desires.
55. Tanner, *Christ the Key*, 42–43.

to have hands, but there is no one use of my hands that is prescribed by their nature, claims Tanner. This means that there is a *cultural underdeterminacy* involved in human nature at the outset. Just as there is an extrinsic property that defines the image of God, it is also the case that there are extrinsic dimensions to all of the other properties constitutive of being human. She concludes, "One might say these self-formative capacities are determined by human nature, but the peculiar nature of humans as rational agents is just to have no particular nature to be true to."[56] One cannot account for what it means to be human, maintains Tanner, apart from the particular cultural and relational exercises of our natural capacities. This she calls human nature's *plasticity*, and it turns out that it is not just the particular exercises of our natural capacities that are labile, but also those natural capacities *themselves*, including our bodies: "It is . . . important to see the way that plastic or non-natured *bodies* are the ultimate issue even for these early church theologians. At the end of the day it is our bodies that are to be remade into Christ's body. . . . Humans demonstrate that, appearances to the contrary . . . , the material world itself is plastic—by extension just as plastic to divine influence, one might hope, as human lives."[57] There are extrinsic determinations even for physical bodies, leading us to believe that through the social exercise of faculties, particularly when they are exercised in relation to Christ, every aspect of human nature is labile. Tanner's conceptual moves thus proceed from the image of God being primarily true of the Son, to that image indicating that human nature contains some extrinsic properties, to claiming that natural capacities are themselves plastic, both in their exercise and in their basic features.

At this juncture, Tanner's argument proceeds far too rapidly. It is plausible to claim that human nature contains some extrinsic properties, even that our natural faculties require social manifestation, but this indicates nothing about the plasticity of the *faculties* themselves. There is still an identifiable shape to the human nature in question, with necessary and sufficient properties (even if they are extrinsic). The move from the social indeterminacy of natural faculties to the plasticity of the faculties themselves is unwarranted, particularly since the diverse ways that I can exercise my hands does nothing to indicate that their fundamental structure is plastic. It seems to me that there are deeper theological claims at play, ones drawn from particular readings of certain patristic authors. Since there are other authors who make these moves

56. Tanner, *Christ the Key*, 48.
57. Tanner, *Christ the Key*, 50, 52.

more explicitly, like Judith Butler and Sarah Coakley, we must await a deeper analysis of their validity. At present, it suffices to say that there is something missing from Tanner's presentation.

Having claimed that human nature, both in its capacities and in its exercises, is plastic on account of its dependence for definition on social relations, Tanner sees herself free to treat gender theologically. This is due to her account of the nature and tasks of theology, which presume the view that all things are socially constructed and fluid. In her book *Theories of Culture: A New Agenda for Theology*, Tanner enumerates the basic traits of a modern view of culture and shows how postmodern critiques require a reconfiguration of such traits, even if they are not done away with altogether. The sixth trait she lists is that "*culture is understood to constitute or construct human nature. Culture does not function to regulate or repress it. Indeed, there is nothing to human life with any definite form or shape of its own that might exist outside of culture so as to be regulated or repressed.*"[58] Notice that this claim is identical to the conclusion at which she arrived in *Christ the Key*—except that in *Christ the Key* she provided a theological rationale for her conclusion, whereas in this earlier work she is assuming the conclusion in an effort to set forth a theological method. Tanner maintains that the theological enterprise is objectively socially constructed; that is, the works that theologians produce are themselves social constructs: "The most basic contribution that an anthropological understanding of culture—postmodern or not—makes to theology is to suggest that theology be viewed as a part of culture, as a form of cultural activity. . . . Theology is something that human beings produce. Like all human activities, it is historically and socially conditioned; it cannot be understood in isolation from the rest of human sociocultural practices."[59] Human nature is a social construct, as are the efforts of theologians to understand it. This means that a correspondence or fittingness obtains between the ontology of human nature and the ontology of theology; both are constructed by social practices.

58. Kathryn Tanner, *Theories of Culture: A New Agenda for Theology*, Guides to Theological Inquiry (Minneapolis: Fortress, 1997), 27. Though Tanner is not an advocate for what she labels the modern view of culture, she does not criticize *this particular* tenet of it. In fact, she admits that the postmodern view does not differ massively in substance with the modern, only in the particulars: "After all these criticisms, what remains of the modern understanding of culture? Very few of the aspects of that understanding have actually been discarded. Most are retained with more or less their modern senses; they have just been decentered or reinscribed within a more primary attention to historical processes" (56). For this reason, I attribute this feature of culture to Tanner's own view.

59. Tanner, *Theories of Culture*, 63.

This is good news for the theological anthropologist, according to Tanner. It means that the theologian is free to turn her attention to anything within creation, considering their relationship to God.[60] The theologian who does this is "not like a self-determined creator of cultural artifacts—say, a writer of a novel or a composer of a symphony. He or she is, instead, like an active reader or an orchestra conductor metaphorizing the artistic creation of others, diverting it from its intended course, transposing it into a new register or key."[61] This means that the theologian has a freedom and a duty to inspect social realities, given that theology is itself entangled within the web of socially constructed artifacts occupying our social world. This does not mean that theology must meld its character with that of the other social sciences, but it can take their findings and "at least undergo a transposition into a religious key."[62] In short, the ontologies of theological work and human nature match up. Since both are socially constructed, the former is free to investigate the latter without ignoring its basic features. Theology is a social enterprise interested in social artifacts.

All that has been said up to this point is important for Tanner's own understanding of the social construction of gender. She has already said enough to commit herself to the view, for if every aspect of human nature is socially constructed (both because of her Christology and because of her broad understanding of culture), then it follows *a fortiori* that gender is socially constructed. And since the theologian is free to investigate socially constructed realities, then the feminist theologian can also study gender and must do so in a particular way. Applying her insights from cultural studies to theology, Tanner argues that feminist theologians ought to study gender with a view to finding out "the way oppression is built into the normal processes of everyday life by way of stereotypes and unquestioned norms, assumptions, and symbols," particularly "assumptions about men and women, and about ethnic and racial minorities, standards of proper behavior, dress, and beauty . . . [and also] the conduct of family life and its impact on economic opportunity for women."[63]

60. This is Tanner's main argument in "The Difference Theological Anthropology Makes," *Theology Today* 50, no. 4 (January 1, 1994): 567–79.
61. Tanner, "Difference Theological Anthropology Makes," 568. I take it that by the time she wrote *Theories of Culture* (published in 1997), Tanner would actually have denied the first part of this quote. Works of theology are *both* cultural artifacts *and* reflections upon other cultural artifacts.
62. Tanner, "Difference Theological Anthropology Makes," 578.
63. Kathryn Tanner, "Social Theory concerning the 'New Social Movements' and the Practice of Feminist Theology," in *Horizons in Feminist Theology: Identity, Tradition, and Norms*, ed.

Feminist theologians will do this particularly through the reconfiguration of Christian symbols, doctrines, and figures: "Alternative meanings and alliances of the same elements are also often circulating, with the potential, therefore, to dislodge the currently pervasive ones. Any secured meaning or articulation is only relatively secure, since it is the product of ongoing struggle with contending forces."[64] That is, theology's socially constructed makeup allows the feminist theologian, himself studying a socially constructed entity like gender, to reevaluate and reconstruct those features within theology that are typically taken to be problematic on feminist grounds.

It is worthwhile to note that Tanner has attempted something like this herself. In an article on whether it is right to retain Anglican liturgical references to God the Father and Son, Tanner retrieves the views of ancient Christian figures like Gregory of Nyssa in an effort to show that such labels were meant to exclude any creaturely or corporeal elements from their connotations. This allows for other names, especially biblical ones (like "Word" or "Wisdom" for the second person) to counterbalance any potentially sexist understandings and uses.[65] Or again, in a recent contribution to the *Oxford Handbook of Feminist Theology*, Tanner attempts to understand the impact of globalization on the lives of religious immigrant women, particularly the ways they are released from traditional gender expectations when arriving in a new culture.[66] Both examples serve as suitable instances of the confidence she believes the theologian can have in investigating cultural realities by means of her own cultural efforts. All of it depends, in sum, on gender's social construction, itself an extension of her convictions about the plasticity of human nature.

This concludes my exposition of the key features of the social construction of gender. I have attempted to expatiate the views of key representatives of the position in both philosophy and theology, demonstrating how they differ from and share similarities with the theorists who have come before them. Though the view that gender is a social construct is one with considerable

---

Rebecca S. Chopp and Sheila Greeve Davaney (Minneapolis: Fortress, 1997), 182–83. Notice that all of the objects of investigation constitute an inquiry into social structures, corresponding fittingly to a theological method that itself contributes to the social world.

64. Tanner, "Social Theory," 185–86.

65. See Kathryn Tanner, "Gender," in *The Oxford Handbook of Anglican Studies*, ed. Mark Chapman, Sathianathan Clarke, and Martyn Percy (Oxford: Oxford University Press, 2015), 400–412, esp. 402–3 and 410.

66. See Kathryn Tanner, "Globalization, Women's Transnational Migration, and Religious De-traditioning," in *The Oxford Handbook of Feminist Theology*, ed. Sheila Briggs and Mary McClintock Fulkerson (Oxford: Oxford University Press, 2011), 544–59, esp. 549.

breadth and variegation, its central commitments are sufficiently clear. With these in mind, let us now turn to their critique.

2.3 Objections to the Social Construction of Gender

At the outset of this chapter, I noted that one of the leading arguments put forward in favor of the view that gender is a social construct is an argument from exclusion. Conceptions of gender, it maintains, are often presented in ways that exclude significant portions of people who are themselves of that gender. It is alleged, moreover, that this happens when a failure of sensitivity to social factors (like the relevance of race and economics) occurs. Thus, early feminist theories were seen to exclude black women, Latin American women, Asian women, and so on. This was an early motivation for claiming that gender is a social construct, for doing so provides one with the theoretical framework to *include* these various social dimensions as well as to account for why they were excluded in the first place. My argument in this section, however, is that the view that gender is socially constructed is still susceptible to this very argument, even if its susceptibility takes on a slightly different form. I will claim that a social constructionist view commits one to the conclusion that there is no single social kind, "women" (and *mutatis mutandis* for any other gender); rather, there are numerically distinct social kinds corresponding to genders of different times and places.[67] What must be realized, however, is that this has devastating metaphysical and moral consequences. It results in an incoherence in gender theory and renders particular genders *morally unevaluable*, something I take to be necessary for advocating for justice in matters relating to gender.

The objection I have just articulated is recognized by most of the feminist theorists who write on the topic, and in this sense I do not think I am introducing a new feature to the discussion at this point.[68] Elizabeth Spelman, one of the architects of the exclusion argument, says as much: "For it may seem as

67. I should note that this does *not* mean that social constructs are not real. In fact, I am making the opposite claim: they are *too* real, yielding too many entities in the real world. There are as many genders as contexts that construct them, but I am focusing on the issue of *continuity*, not *reality*.

68. In fact, the problems I am outlining are summarized in much greater specificity in Theodore Bach, "Gender Is a Natural Kind with a Historical Essence," *Ethics* 122, no. 2 (January 2012): 234–35. What he calls the "Representation Problem" roughly corresponds to my second objection; what he calls the "Commonality Problem" correspond to my first objection.

if it is *impossible*, given the heterogeneity of women and women's situations, to make any well-founded yet nontrivial statements about all women. If that is *impossible*, however, its *impossibility* does not follow simply from the fact that such statements cannot be based on the situation of white middle-class women."[69] Spelman is willing to concede that the diversity of women in different times and places makes it "impossible" to say anything about women *simpliciter*, so long as what we mean by "differences" is not "differences *from* white middle-class women." In other words, the differences cannot be measured by an ethnocentric standard, but they exist nevertheless. Her solution is to appreciate the differences and to learn from other women about their experiences, particularly with regard to their racial and economic standing.[70] This, she assumes, can foster greater understanding among women despite cultural differences. Or again, Ásta's recent account of the metaphysics of social construction recognizes that "gender is radically context dependent." Certainly this is true with respect to different historical periods and geographical locations, but it is also the case that, for her, even "the same geographical location and time period can allow for radically different contexts, so that a person may count as of a certain gender in some context and not others."[71] What I will say, then, is not something new or unrecognized by feminist theorists; rather, I want to draw out the metaphysical and moral implications for this concession that often go unrealized or underappreciated.

The theory of the social construction of gender, at its most basic level, attempts to account for the basic features of the social kinds or categories we call "men" and "women" (and for any other gender category).[72] A kind specifies the properties necessary and sufficient for membership within it, and in the case of socially constructed kinds, the necessary properties are themselves social properties. As the thinkers we have considered so far have conceded, this means that social kinds are *context specific*, and contexts differ among times and places (indeed, even *within* times and places). Recall, for instance,

69. Spelman, *Inessential Woman*, 183 (emphasis added).

70. Spelman, *Inessential Woman*, 113. Of course, the very notion of "other women" is one of those claims Spelman thinks is impossible to ascertain or say anything about. It is difficult for a view like Spelman's to avoid the charge of self-referential incoherence, itself assuming the very thing it has said is impossible.

71. Ásta, *Categories We Live By*, 73, 74. Ásta goes on to say that "one can be a woman in one context and not in another, because the standards of relevance to the paradigm case vary with context" (87). This is so even though she has recourse to a Wittgensteinian account of "family resemblances."

72. For an explicit statement of this desideratum, see Ásta, *Categories We Live By*, 1n1.

that Haslanger's definition of gender restricts it to "a particular culture."[73]
Even Tanner, who is comparatively less interested in the metaphysics at play,
recognizes that cultures have to appreciate the amount of variegation that
occurs in time and place.[74] The most forthright admission of this is found in
Ásta's citation above, where I might be a man in my current context but it is
entirely possible for me to hop on a plane (or into a time machine) and find
myself landing in a context where I am no longer a man. This produces the
result that gender kinds like "man" and "woman" are context-dependent, such
that what it means to be a man in one time and place is not the same as in
another time and place. Consider just one example: in 1918, it was exhorted
by a clothing catalog that young boys wear pink to indicate their gender and
that young girls wear blue.[75] Red was accepted as the most masculine color
(because it represented aggressiveness), and pink was more proximate to red
than to blue, and therefore more fitting for little boys. Today, to indicate that
one is a boy or a girl, one must do precisely the opposite. This may seem like
a trivial fact, but remember that these are *necessary conditions* for membership in a social kind on the view that gender is a social construct. But it is
metaphysically impossible, even if it is only socially incongruous, for a social
kind to have inconsistent, even *contradictory*, necessary conditions. To be a
boy one must both wear pink and not wear pink; this tension must divide
one social kind into two.[76] I do not mean to deny the existence of inconsistent
standards for gender in the world. There are inconsistent conditions placed
upon women on a regular basis, and this is a deeply unjust state of affairs.
But such a recognition only heightens the metaphysical problem—namely,
that what we create is not one historically continuous social kind but two,
"boy$_{1918}$" and "boy$_{2023}$," and they are numerically distinct. If a boy in 1918
were to hop into a time machine and travel to 2023, he must abandon his
prior expectation to wear pink if he is to meet the expectations of boyhood

---

73. Haslanger, *Resisting Reality*, 196.

74. See Tanner, *Theories of Culture*, 26, 43.

75. For an interesting account of this, see Susan Stamberg, "Girls Are Taught to 'Think
Pink,' but That Wasn't Always So," National Public Radio, April 1, 2014, http://www.npr.org
/2014/04/01/297159948/girls-are-taught-to-think-pink-but-that-wasnt-always-so.

76. This remains true even if a gender term is a family resemblance term or cluster concept,
as suggested by Cressida Heyes in *Line Drawings: Defining Women through Feminist Practice*
(Ithaca, NY: Cornell University Press, 2000); and Natalie Stoljar in "Essence, Identity and the
Concept of Woman," *Philosophical Topics* 23, no. 2 (1995): 261–93. Neither a cluster nor a
family resemblance, it seems to me, can consistently tolerate outright contradiction and remain
operable in defining the term in question, not to mention the difficulty one would face in identifying "paradigm cases" for the resemblance to hold.

in 2023. In doing so, according to the social constructionist framework, he would become a *different gender*, not the same gender with different conditions. As a result, there are no "boys" *as such*, only "boys" with temporal and cultural modifiers and restrictors.

I take this result to be deeply counterintuitive. It seems to me that though I am relevantly different from my grandfather, who lived in Brazil in the twentieth century, I am also the same kind of thing as him: a man. He may have observed standards of masculinity to which I do not hold, but on the face of it, I do not think that he is something different than me. We might also consider the way that we point to exemplary women throughout history. It ought to be possible to point to paradigmatic and exemplary women of the past and raise them as examples for other women to follow. I hope to show my daughter, for instance, that she should aspire to be like the highly admirable women of history, women such as Harriet Tubman and Sojourner Truth, even if she is from a different time and culture than theirs. Additionally, Christianity benefits from the examples of biblical women, as we consider how their faithfulness can sustain our own.[77] Though this is not an argument but an intuition, it seems to me that it is not a problematic intuition to hold. In fact, it is a good and empowering thing to be able to do this in a world that consistently fails to display and highlight the achievements and faithfulness of admirable women. Finally, it is an intuition that seems to be scripturally assumed, minimally when Peter commends the example of Sarah in 1 Peter 3:1–6 to an audience living in a vastly different culture. The problem is that if the social construction of gender is true, this intuition must be rejected along with the actions we perform on its basis, for they are actually misguided. The social kinds occupied by Harriet Tubman, biblical women, and my daughter are all numerically distinct. They do not actually share in common the fact that they are women; strictly speaking, they are different genders confined to their own respective times and places. If there is any commonality between them, it cannot be because they are all women in an unequivocal sense.

The issue goes deeper than intuition. There are *theoretical* inconsistencies at play too. In feminist theology, for instance, it is often assumed that

---

77. For theological defenses of this, see Elaine Storkey, *Women in a Patriarchal World: Twenty-five Empowering Stories from the Bible* (Downers Grove, IL: InterVarsity, 2020); and Richard Bauckham, *Gospel Women: Studies of the Named Women in the Gospels* (Grand Rapids: Eerdmans, 2002).

the concepts "men" and "women" are in good working order for theological analysis. As will be discussed in further detail in the next chapter, most feminists are not *gender skeptics*, those who hold that gender terms have no stable meaning. Yet, the metaphysical incoherence brought about by the differences of time and place—the differences that make what it is to be a woman or man in different cultures so very different—lead into a gender-skeptical position nevertheless.[78] If it is impossible to state generally stable conditions for being a man or a woman, then those terms cannot be employed in theological argumentation. But this is precisely what feminist theology seeks to do. Consider a statement from the influential feminist theologian Rosemary Radford Ruether: "The critical principle of feminist theology is the affirmation of and promotion of the full humanity of *women*. Whatever denies, diminishes, or distorts the full humanity of *women* is, therefore, to be appraised as not redemptive. Theologically speaking, this means that whatever diminishes or denies the full humanity of women must be presumed not to reflect the divine or authentic nature of things, or to be the message or work of an authentic redeemer or a community of redemption."[79] This is a powerful statement that crucially depends on the stability of gender concepts. Yet, to a social constructionist, we might inquire: To whom does the referent "women" actually refer? If the necessary conditions were specified, one would find that they would be context specific, thereby excluding other women who exist outside of that context. If the social construction of gender is true, and if different conditions define different kinds, then there is not *one* referent picked out by "women," but at every point it must be made clear *which* women in *which* contexts. Is every diminishment or denial of women's humanity the same, and does that matter? Surely these denials will differ from culture to culture and in terms of degree, so much so that a woman experiencing one kind of oppression in one culture might not find solidarity with another experiencing something much different in another culture. Suppose, further, that enough progress is made that *some* women

78. For an argument that a true appreciation of the differences in gender terms between cultures leads one to think that gender terms apply only very restrictively, see Uma Narayan, "Essence of Culture and a Sense of History: A Feminist Critique of Cultural Essentialism," *Hypatia* 13, no. 2 (1998): 86–106. The upshot of Narayan's argument—that gender terms cannot sustain cultural generalization—strikes me as landing in close proximity to gender skepticism.

79. Rosemary Radford Ruether, "Feminist Interpretation: A Method of Correlation," in *Feminist Interpretation of the Bible*, ed. Letty M. Russell (Philadelphia: Westminster, 1985), 115 (emphasis added).

are treated as fully human; would they cease to be women? Ruether does not go into detail about the particular necessary conditions for participating in the social kind "women," though she does still employ the term in her theology. My point, however, is that if one employs a social construction-ist strategy for specifying these conditions, the contradictions and incoher-ence regarding what it means to be a man or woman in different cultures result in an inability to fix the referent of the term "woman" or to know the conditions for membership in that kind. If the category of "woman" is lost, however, then feminism would suffer, for unless there is "some sense in which 'woman' is the name of a social collective, there is nothing specific to feminist politics."[80] In short, if feminist theory and theology is intended to advocate for the liberation of *women*, then some stability is necessary in terms of what that category includes along with conditions for its persistence across changes of context, a clarity that cannot be provided by the view that gender is a social construct.[81]

Recall that my claim is *not* that feminist theologians are unaware of the cultural differences that obtain between women of different times and cultures. It is rather that the *implications* of the metaphysical position being advocated, the social construction of gender, are not fully perceived. As a result, "most feminist theologies nevertheless implicitly tend to operate with some analo-gous form of essentialism or totalizing thought, even if it is refined in terms of social construction. . . . Claiming that 'women's experience' is an identifiable, discrete category rests on the assumption of a totalizing anthropology of the feminine, even granted that we allow for the shaping of race and class."[82] The point being made is that the social construction of gender makes generalizing about a gender not only difficult but *impossible*. This is the result of views like that of Elizabeth Spelman and Ásta: statements about women *as such* are impossible, for that label may or may not apply in different contexts. But if feminist theology is anything at all, it is an attempt to talk about women *as such*. It promotes the liberation *of women*; it considers *women* in relation

80. Iris Marion Young, *Intersecting Voices* (Princeton: Princeton University Press, 1997), 13.

81. The objection applies equally to more generic statements about feminist theory. For instance, bell hooks defines feminism as the movement that seeks to end sexist oppression against *women*. See bell hooks, *Feminist Theory: From Margin to Center*, 2nd ed. (New York: Routledge, 2015), 26.

82. Kathryn Greene-McCreight, *Feminist Reconstructions of Christian Doctrine: Narrative Analysis and Appraisal* (New York: Oxford University Press, 2000), 61. Greene-McCreight is drawing attention to the ways in which feminist theology has recourse to women's *experience* in particular, something that only goes on to compound the issue at stake.

to God. This may be parsed out in ontological terms (Is there a kind with specifiable conditions such that there is something women share *qua* women?) or in semantic terms (To what do we refer, and how do we refer to it, when we refer to women?), but in either case, the problems persist with the category of "women," and with any other gender. Losing that category—or better, allowing that category to fission into variegated social kinds confined to particular times and places—is fatal for the practice of feminist theology and for feminist theory more broadly, especially if these hope to result in some kind of social or political change in the world.

The notion of political change brings me to my second criticism of the social construction of gender—namely, that it renders particular genders morally unevaluable. Serene Jones has alluded to this worry: "If no single description of women's lives is correct and all are equally valid, what standards are available for assessing harm or the nature of justice and injustice in women's lives? Don't we need normative standards for assessing what is good and bad?"[83] Following from these concerns, my contention here is that the metaphysics of social construction actually precludes any satisfactory answer to Jones's question and makes it impossible to name "women" as a social collective, thereby sacrificing its ethical purchase. If the necessary conditions governing the social kinds of gender are bound by context, then so are the moral norms that attend specific genders. Moral claims, therefore, cannot be made with respect to women and men, claims of the sort, "It is a woman's right to do x" or "It is morally wrong for a man *qua* man to do y." Rather, the best we can do, morally speaking, is to provide guidelines external to gendered concepts; the normative claims attached to masculinity and femininity are restricted to their own contexts, with the result that there can be neither good or bad *men* nor *women's* rights, for those normative evaluations are produced by the social constructs constitutive of their gender.[84]

83. Serene Jones, *Feminist Theory and Christian Theology: Cartographies of Grace*, Guides to Theological Inquiry (Minneapolis: Fortress, 2000), 41–42.

84. To anticipate this approach, one may witness the excellent work of Mari Mikkola, who maintains that the injustices about which feminists speak are wrong and harmful not because of anything within the definition of *women* but because of the conditions of what it means to be *human*: "These harms wrong women qua human (and not qua gendered) beings" (Mari Mikkola, *The Wrong of Injustice: Dehumanization and Its Role in Feminist Philosophy* [New York: Oxford University Press, 2016], 11). Though suggestive, I worry that there are some rights and obligations that are specific to one gender and not any others, such as reproductive rights had by women and not men. Due to counterexamples such as these, I do not think the general approach works.

The most obvious illustration of this objection is the ongoing controversy over female genital mutilation.[85] But for our purposes, perhaps a less controversial issue will prove more fruitful. Consider the example of Pitcairn Island.[86] Pitcairn is an island in the Pacific Ocean, halfway between Australia and South America. It was populated in 1790 by British mutineers who saw its locale as both uniquely attractive and isolated. Since then, a romantic culture has enshrined Pitcairn, with books, Hollywood movies, and ceremonies depicting it as a haven of adventure and natural beauty. Throughout its history, its population has hovered at about fifty people, many of whom have ties back to the original mutineers. The shroud of paradisal attraction, however, was lifted in 1999 when several Pitcairn girls confided to a British police officer on the island that they had been raped and sexually assaulted by many of the Pitcairn men.[87] This precipitated an investigation and trial beginning in 2004 and concluding in 2007. The results of the police investigation culminated with ninety-six charges being brought against thirteen Pitcairn men, and when the men who had died by the time of the trials are taken into account, nearly every adult male on Pitcairn faced allegations of crimes that likely date all the way back to the mutiny. When evidence that was dismissed in court is also included, what was uncovered was a vile and vituperative series of sexual assaults, all contained within one tiny island community.

On Pitcairn, there was a carefully cultivated culture of masculinity, a key aspect of which was an entitlement of adult men to "break in" young, virgin girls, always under the age of sixteen, sometimes as young as six.[88] These

---

85. For a discussion of this, see Martha C. Nussbaum, *Sex and Social Justice* (New York: Oxford University Press, 2000), chap. 4. Much of the controversy began around Alice Walker's book, *Warrior Marks: Female Genital Mutilation and the Sexual Blinding of Women* (San Diego: Amistad, 1996). (See also the film by the same title.) For a survey of the tensions involved, particularly those pertaining to the anti-colonialist argument against rejections of "Irua" (or Female Genital Mutilation), see Hope Lewis, "Between *Irua* and 'Female Genital Mutilation': Feminist Human Rights Discourse and the Cultural Divide," *Harvard Human Rights Journal* 8 (Spring 1995): 1–55.

86. Though the example of Pitcairn is quite specific, it should not be taken as irrelevant. The description that follows is not dissimilar to the cultures of toxic masculinity found in other island cultures. See Manuel Rauchholz, "Family and Gender Violence in Chuuk, Micronesia," in *Sex and Gender in the Pacific: Contemporary Perspectives on Sexuality, Gender and Health*, ed. Angela Kelly-Hanku, Peter Aggleton, and Anne Malcolm, Sexuality, Culture and Health (New York: Routledge, 2023), 181–91.

87. I have drawn the details of this section from Kathy Marks, *Lost Paradise* (New York: Free Press, 2009). Marks was one of the few journalists allowed onto Pitcairn to cover the trials and assiduously recorded all of the cultural details surrounding the occurrences.

88. For this language, see Marks, *Lost Paradise*, 192, 195. Shockingly, the most powerful men of the island got to "pick" the "most desirable" girls, while the weakest men got to pick

men would rape and assault these young girls, causing them lasting physical and psychological harm, in full knowledge of the other islanders. Interviews conducted by the police revealed that the islanders, including the adult women (many of whom were mothers of the assaulted girls), saw these horrendous acts as "part of life," "typical of the Pitcairn men," and held that if the men were prosecuted, it would "emasculate the community."[89] As one female Pitcairner stated, "You can't blame men for being men."[90] What it means to be a man on Pitcairn, evidently, includes the right persistently to sexually assault young girls.

Equally shocking are the results of the trials held by British and New Zealand courts. They were distressingly lenient on crimes that would have been punished more severely had they occurred elsewhere, simply because the judges wanted "to impose sentences which are appropriate for the island."[91] One of the men who was convicted of five rapes was given three years in a lenient and unhampered prison on Pitcairn (when the typical jail time then was about three to five times as long), only nine months of which he actually served before being sent home. The time he spent in prison was not drastically different than his day-to-day life prior to it due to the freedoms he enjoyed in custody. In comparison with a conviction in, say, England, the Pitcairners received little more than a slap on the wrist, leading many to conclude that their crimes were not taken seriously. More accurate, however, would be to say that they were judged *as Pitcairn men*, with moral norms restricted to the island's culture. The judges in charge of the trial attributed the comparatively short prison times to the vital role the men played in the upkeep of the island and, most importantly, to factors unique to Pitcairn, like its cultural and legal isolation. Throughout the trial, moreover, many in the media loudly defended the Pitcairners, claiming that the charges were based on racism and colonialism—that is, an imposition of standards from one culture to another. This led Marks to wonder: Were the crimes "somehow less serious because they were committed on a remote island with a small population? Was [the judge] saying that the Pitcairners deserved such extraordinary leniency because . . . well, because they were Pitcairners? . . . Did they not convey the message that the Pitcairners were special, and could, to a large extent,

whomever was left, such that the power structure of the masculine culture corresponded to the order in which girls were assaulted. See Marks, *Lost Paradise*, 275.

89. Marks, *Lost Paradise*, 43, 303, and 176, respectively.

90. Marks, *Lost Paradise*, 150.

91. Marks, *Lost Paradise*, 143.

get away with behavior that would be severely punished elsewhere?"[92] She concludes: "Their crimes—raping and molesting children—would normally have had the public baying for their blood. Instead, the islanders were seen as victims of a miscarriage of justice, perpetrated by their overzealous British rulers."[93] What seems to have happened, then, was that a unique set of rules and standards were applied to the men of Pitcairn on account of the fact that they were *Pitcairn men*, which is to say, the cultural specificity of their masculinity was seen to require an entirely different set of moral standards, one having to do with the expectations of masculinity ingredient to the island's operation.

Setting aside the legal complications surrounding the colonialist rule of a distant island, think of the Pitcairn trials instead as an instance of moral reasoning and moral judgment. The salient question was, ultimately, whether persons of a different culture could condemn practices that were seen as *constitutive* of Pitcairn masculinity. The awkwardness and leniency used to apply the sentences serves as a revealing case study for how a social constructionist view of gender has difficulty with giving a clear rationale for morally evaluating gender across different cultures.[94] It could not be said that the Pitcairn men were *bad men* independent of context, for they were simply behaving according to the definition of masculinity in Pitcairn. Rather, on a social constructionist view, these were men *who were bad*, where the moral valence has to be adjudicated by some standard other than the ones that go into constituting the social kind in question. Again, viewing gender as a context-specific social construct means that the norms and obligations for masculinity are as context specific as the social kind. This is why, on the social constructionist picture, I am a man in the United States, but I would not be a man on Pitcairn. To be an instance of the latter, one must also sexually assault young girls. The men, it could be said, were simply behaving *as Pitcairn men*. Thus, the most that can be said is that the Pitcairn men were bad *people*, not bad *men*. But this is moral blindness. It was the *men* of Pitcairn who gruesomely assaulted the *girls* of Pitcairn, and to relegate the gendered dimensions of the crimes to cultural specificity is to fail to recognize that there was one specific group of people who used their power for wickedness and that there was

92. Marks, *Lost Paradise*, 145–46.
93. Marks, *Lost Paradise*, 158.
94. There are many indications that those involved considered gender to be a social construct, not least of which were their comments that they wanted to judge the men according to the standards of the roles they played on the island.

another class of people who are vulnerable and defenseless and who served as the consistent target of violence and rape. It is of utmost importance to the proper moral evaluation of the situation in Pitcairn that these were not just bad people but *bad men*; they were bad men who preyed on young girls, using their unique social position to destroy vulnerable lives, and no amount of cultural specificity can circumvent that. Sadly, the trials failed to see that.[95]

For two reasons, then, I conclude that the social construction of gender is an inadequate theory. First, the theory makes it impossible to say anything about men, women, or any gender *as such*; rather, since social kinds are context specific, then the cultural differences between genders means that there are as many men, women, and otherwise as there are cultures. This is a counter-intuitive outcome, since I assume that I am the same kind of thing as my grandfather and that I can encourage my daughter to emulate great women of the past. But it also has theoretical problems. If we take into account the constantly differing necessary conditions for these kinds, it is impossible to say anything about men or women *simpliciter*, resulting in a gender-skeptical position.

My second criticism of the social construction of gender, which follows from the first, is that it precludes genders from being morally evaluable.

---

95. Perhaps it can be said that socially constructed kinds can still be morally evaluated but that their moral evaluation must come from standards that exist outside of the kinds themselves. That is, nothing *within* the kind will be morally guiding, but we might have external reasons for constructing things in one way or another. In this sense, a moral norm according to which sexual assault is wrong would, when applied to the case of Pitcairn, accurately condemn the men but not the girls. Theoretically, that would suffice. However, I worry that there are issues with implementing this in a practical political way. This is because the norm must remain gender neutral if it is to avoid begging the question; one cannot say that "it is wrong for men to sexually assault girls," only that "sexual assault is wrong" and these people have done it. History has shown, however, that many moral norms and the protections they entail are not distributed fairly; though the letter of the law might entitle everyone to certain rights and protections, actual practice has often favored those in power.

There are several examples that might be cited, but the Violence Against Women Act of 1994 makes this particularly clear. US Americans always had a legal right to be protected from acts of violence, but addressing the vast amount of violence done *to women* required additional legislation. Thus, though a norm might in theory extend to all people, in practice it is often the case that the vulnerable need to be explicitly named in order to be protected. In cases pertinent to gender, especially to women, explicit naming of their gender is often necessary to remind citizens that these rights extend to them as well. In theory, there should be no need for an additional law to specify that women should not be the recipients of violence and to accord them specially named rights, like the right to sue their assailants. But actual practice reveals that gender specificity is required in a number of our moral and legal norms in order for the vulnerable to be recognized as properly included within them. This kind of specificity, however, is exactly what cannot be had on the view that gender is a social construct.

There are no ultimately satisfying answers to Linda Martín Alcoff's questions, "What can we demand in the name of women if 'women' do not exist and demands in their name simply reinforce the myth that they do? How can we speak out against sexism as detrimental to the interests of women if the category is a fiction?"[96] The answers, it would seem, are "nothing" and "we cannot." Nevertheless, though I reject the social construction of gender for these two reasons, I do not think that the only alternative is biological essentialism or that there is nothing within the view that is worth affirming. Before I say what might be worth affirming, let us consider one final attempt in the literature to salvage the view by affirming that both gender and sex are socially constructed.

2.4 The Social Construction of Sex: Judith Butler

The work of Judith Butler stands tall among other gender theorists. Butler's books are found in both airport bookstores and theological syllabi, indicating just how influential their[97] views have been.[98] Part of their remarkable influence is drawn from the bold assertion that they are willing to make—namely, that both *sex* and *gender* are social constructs, taking the position beyond any of the theorists we have considered so far. For Butler, maleness and femaleness, categories often taken to be biological facts, are themselves components of a broad constructionist understanding of reality. Acknowledging them as such, they claim, is the proper response to the fact that "the notion of a generally shared conception of 'women' . . . has been . . . difficult to displace."[99] According to Butler, social constructionists should not defend themselves against the arguments I have put forward in the previous section; they should recognize that the cultural diversity among women is sufficient to show that, because gender is a social construction, there are necessarily multiple, disparate kinds

96. Alcoff, *Visible Identities*, 143.

97. Butler's preferred pronouns, as indicated in places like their faculty page: https://vcresearch.berkeley.edu/faculty/judith-butler.

98. Butler has had an influence on many theologians. For a nuanced theological engagement of Butler, see Daniel R. Patterson, *Reforming a Theology of Gender: Constructive Reflections on Judith Butler and Queer Theory* (Eugene, OR: Cascade, 2022). See also the creative combination of Butler and Aquinas in Eugene F. Rogers Jr., *Aquinas and the Supreme Court: Race, Gender, and the Failure of Natural Law in Thomas's Biblical Commentaries* (Malden, MA: Wiley-Blackwell, 2013), chap. 9. For a theological view supporting the social construction of sex, though not necessarily with recourse to Butler, see Adrian Thatcher, *Redeeming Gender* (New York: Oxford University Press, 2016).

99. Judith Butler, *Gender Trouble* (New York: Routledge, 1990), 5.

rightly labeled "women." Where they diverge, of course, is that they are willing to bite the bullet on the matter. Instead of attempting to rehabilitate the concept of "women" with a new, unifying definition, Butler looks to show that feminism flourishes best "only when the subject of 'women' is nowhere presumed."[100] Feminism succeeds, Butler maintains, when it allows for a greater diversity and openness of gendered terms in an effort to lift the cover of the complex power relations that constitute them.

If there is a heuristically helpful starting point to Butler's views, it must be what they term the "heterosexual matrix," which is a "hegemonic discursive/epistemic model of gender intelligibility that assumes that for bodies to cohere and make sense there must be a stable sex expressed through a stable gender (masculine expresses male, feminine expresses female) that is oppositionally and hierarchically defined through the compulsory practice of heterosexuality."[101] In other words, the heterosexual matrix is the dominant, if not ubiquitous, grid in which concepts of sex and gender are produced and rendered intelligible. The concepts produced then go on to regulate how many genders there are, how many sexes there are, what the conditions are for inclusion within each and which relations are appropriate between them (in the heterosexual matrix, of course, only heterosexual relations between exactly two corresponding sexes and genders are possible). It is itself not only a cultural product but the grid through which culture is interpreted, and anything produced by it is appropriately considered to be socially constructed. The heterosexual matrix, therefore, supplies concepts necessary for sex and gender: "The institution of a compulsory and naturalized heterosexuality requires and regulates gender as a binary relation in which the masculine term is differentiated from a feminine term, and this differentiation is accomplished through the practices of heterosexual desire. . . . The categories of female and male, woman and man, are similarly *produced* within the binary frame."[102] It is precisely this heterosexual matrix that Butler's theory of gender is meant to debunk.

Butler goes on to claim that it is only *within* the heterosexual matrix that sex appears to be a natural and preconceptual given, something that is what it is apart from our discursive practices. But it appears to be so only when viewed

100. Butler, *Gender Trouble*, 8.
101. Butler, *Gender Trouble*, 208n6.
102. Butler, *Gender Trouble*, 31 (emphasis added). To clarify, I take the "binary frame" to be the same as the "heterosexual matrix" in Butler's thought.

from within its grid. Just as in a soccer game it only *seems* natural that there are a certain number of positions, so also within the heterosexual frame it only *seems* natural that there are just two sexes and that they are precultural realities. But this is all part of the game and would not make sense without it. Moreover, just as it would make no sense to ask where the shortstop plays in a soccer match, so also do certain configurations of gender (such as drag) and of sex (such as intersex/DSD individuals) fail to make sense within this matrix.[103] Yet, when one begins to inquire about the particular conditions required to be counted as of one sex or another, one finds that such conditions are no less the product of a history than of the cultural conditions for gender. Thus, Butler regularly queries *why* it is *these* genotypical and phenotypical traits that make a male while it is *those* traits that make a female, for these decisions are no less a conceptual product within the heterosexual matrix than the cultural concepts of gender.[104] It is no less socially constructed to make the possession of certain genitalia constitutive of one sex than it is to make the possession of certain social cues constitutive of a certain gender. Butler takes considerable trouble, especially in *Bodies That Matter*, to show that these decisions themselves have a history and could have been otherwise. "Sexual difference," then, "is never *simply* a function of material differences which are not in some way both marked and formed by discursive practices. . . . The category of 'sex' is, from the start, normative; it is what Foucault has called a 'regulatory ideal.'"[105] Or again, "If the immutable character of sex is contested, perhaps this construct called 'sex' is as culturally constructed as gender."[106] In short, both sex and gender are concepts derived from the heterosexual matrix, which reveals that both are social constructs.

Butler, toward the end of *Gender Trouble* and in their subsequent volume, *Bodies That Matter*,[107] seeks to make the metaphysical underpinnings of their view clear. Against critics who allege that Butler denigrates the materiality

103. See Butler, *Gender Trouble*, 23–24: "The notion that there might be a 'truth' of sex, as Foucault ironically terms it, is produced precisely through the regulatory practices that generate coherent identities through the matrix of coherent gender norms. . . . The cultural matrix through which gender identity has become intelligible requires that certain kinds of 'identities' cannot 'exist'—that is, those in which gender does not follow from sex and those in which the practices of desires do not 'follow' from either sex or gender."

104. For examples of such queries, see Butler, *Gender Trouble*, 156; and Judith Butler, *Bodies That Matter* (New York: Routledge, 1993), xii.

105. Butler, *Bodies That Matter*, xi.

106. Butler, *Gender Trouble*, 9.

107. For further specifications, one might also look to Judith Butler, *Undoing Gender* (New York: Routledge, 2004).

of the body, they insist that they are happy to affirm it. "Materiality" and "body," however, will have to be revised heavily. For Butler, "matter" is "*a process of materialization that stabilizes over time to produce the effects of boundary, fixity, and surface we call matter.*"[108] Thus, to say something falls under the category "matter" is not to say that it is a physical substance or something of that sort. Rather, Butler takes the term as a verb: it is not that things *are* matter; it is that they *matter*, where the first is taken descriptively and the second verbally. The concept of matter is no less a component of the heterosexual matrix than sex and gender; for something to have materialized is for it to obtain the semblance of fixed and stable boundaries over its history within the matrix. Only then, by definition, has it "mattered." By extension, bodies also matter: "The body is not a 'being,' but a variable boundary, a surface whose permeability is politically regulated, a signifying practice within a cultural field of gender hierarchy and compulsory heterosexuality."[109] For bodies to matter, then, is not what we typically mean by that combination of words. Bodies matter when they have been adequately described as having a stable and fixed boundary through their history. The primary mechanism by which this occurs, according to Butler, is through *reference*, but even here the concept must be understood differently:

> The linguistic capacity to refer to sexed bodies is not denied, but the very meaning of "referentiality" is altered. . . . To "refer" naively or directly to such an extra-discursive object will always require the prior delimitation of the extra-discursive. And insofar as the extra-discursive is delimited, it is formed by the very discourse from which it seeks to free itself. This delimitation, which often is enacted as an untheorized presupposition in any act of description, marks a boundary that includes and excludes, that *decides as it were, what will and will not be the stuff of the object to which we then refer.* . . . What will and will not be included within the boundaries of "sex" will be set by a more or less tacit operation of exclusion.[110]

There are significantly ambiguous wrinkles in the above statement, and they will be ironed out shortly. For now, note that the process of materialization is

108. Butler, *Bodies That Matter*, xviii. See also xxiii: "The process of that sedimentation or what we might call *materialization* will be a kind of citationality, the acquisition of being through the citing of power, citing that establishes an originary complicity with power in the formation of the 'I.'"
109. Butler, *Gender Trouble*, 189. More simply: "Materiality will be rethought as the effect of power, as power's most productive effect" (Butler, *Bodies That Matter*, xii).
110. Butler, *Bodies That Matter*, xix–xx (emphasis added).

one in which the boundaries of an entity are recognized or made stable, and the process by which those boundaries are fixed is our ability to refer, particularly to perform speech acts that bring about the stuff and the boundaries of the entities to which they refer, analogous to God's declaration, "Let there be light."[111]

These considerations, if true, are sufficient to prove that sex, along with bodies, natures, and anything that is material, is socially constructed. Though there are further twists and turns to Butler's admirable view, the sketch above exposits the main points they aim to make. Butler's view, to conclude, is that "'the body' is itself a construction, as are the myriad 'bodies' that constitute the domain of gendered subjection."[112] Or again, "language constructs the categories of sex."[113] Yet, there are significant ambiguities inherent to Butler's presentation. In fact, I will now suggest that there are *two* ways to interpret their main claim that "sex is socially constructed." Both, I will show, are untenable and irremediably problematic. The first is a more modest reading, yet it fails to support the proposals they actually advance; the second is more radical, yet it fails on metaphysical, ethical, and theological grounds.

The first reading of Butler's views is that they are putting forward an *epistemic* thesis regarding the *concepts* we use to describe criteria for membership in a gender, sex, and so on. This is a permissible reading of Butler, for they often make reference to the epistemic importance of their views and seem to be describing categories and concepts.[114] On this reading, it is the *concepts* and *categories* of sexed bodies and gender that are socially constructed, not sex and gender themselves. This is a comparatively modest view. Since concepts and categories are not identical to the things of which they are concepts and categorizations, to say that the former are socially constructed is not the same as saying that the latter are. My concept of my wife is not the same thing as my wife, and my concept was formed by social processes and is itself a social product resultant from years of interaction with my wife. In the same way, our concepts of sex and gender have a long and diverse history, and they have been revised whenever we have seen them to be inadequate, giving us the impression that they are remarkably fluid. If this is Butler's view (and it sometimes sounds like it is), then it does not prove the thesis they set out to prove—namely,

---

111. Butler's own example. See *Bodies That Matter*, xxi.
112. Butler, *Gender Trouble*, 12.
113. Butler, *Gender Trouble*, xxxii.
114. See Butler, *Gender Trouble*, xxiv: "*What are the categories through which one sees?*" This is the reading that Mikkola takes of Butler. See Mikkola, *Wrong of Injustice*, 39–40.

that sex is a social construct. The social construction of *concepts* is perfectly compatible with a strongly essentialist account of sex and gender that they so ardently criticize. My concept of my wife has also undergone revision; I have been mistaken about things that I thought were true about her, causing me constantly to revise the concept. But this does not disprove that my wife has no mind-independent features. This is simply how concepts work: if we have any notion of our epistemic limitations, we recognize that our concepts are always corrigible and revisable according to the adequacy of their representation of the conceptualized object. Our revisions, though, do nothing to alter the objects themselves. If Butler is claiming that the *concepts* of sex and gender are socially constructed, then their view will have no objectors, for it is a fairly obvious view.[115] Concepts are perfectly suitable means of acquiring knowledge about the world, just as glasses help me to see out my window and cell phones allow me to hear the voices of those far from me.

Perhaps this is not what Butler means. Other interpreters have taken a *metaphysical* reading of Butler, according to which it is not the concepts of sex and gender that are socially constructed but sex and gender *themselves*. On this reading, our concepts of such things do not *bring to light* their basic features; they *bring about* those basic features.[116] This interpretation, then, sees Butler as a kind of creative anti-realist. Butler's "picture is not that our thought and practices conform to how the world is, but that, at least sometimes, the world conforms to our thought practices."[117] Of course, several of the quotes above suggest a view in which there are no features of the world independent of human thought and reference. Rather, things are what they are, have the boundaries they have, and relate in the ways they relate because of human practices, linguistic, mental, or otherwise. Sex and gender will then be situated within a broader metaphysical anti-realist picture in which cultural practices construct not only concepts and cultural artifacts but all material objects (which, for Butler, exhausts all that exists). To say that sex is a social construct, on this reading, is to say that humans have the capacity, through their referential practices, to make their world, of which sex is a part.

---

115. For a further development of this line of thought, along with a contextualization of its history going back to Kant, see Nicholas Wolterstorff, "Does the Role of Concepts Make Experiential Access to Ready-Made Reality Impossible?," in *Practices of Belief: Selected Essays*, vol. 2, ed. Terence Cuneo (New York: Cambridge University Press, 2010), 41–61.

116. This phrasing is taken from Nicholas Wolterstorff, "Living within a Text," in *Faith and Narrative*, ed. Keith E. Yandell (New York: Oxford University Press, 2001), 207.

117. Ásta, *Categories We Live By*, 67.

Creative anti-realism, one type of metaphysical anti-realism, is a recognizable philosophical view. It has representatives in Hilary Putnam and Nelson Goodman,[118] and Butler's views have remarkable similarities to the former. The view maintains that "for any kind of thing, a condition of the existence of that kind of thing and of things belonging to that kind is that some human being [has] formed the concept of that kind."[119] Typically, arguments put forward in its favor look to point out how two inconsistent propositions both truthfully describe some aspect of the world. Though it has some notable representatives, metaphysical anti-realism has also suffered from some severe criticisms.[120] On the erstwhile strategy, apparently conflicting propositions are easily harmonized when clarified or set in proper context. Butler, however, does not put forward this kind of argument. The only detectable argument for creative anti-realism in Butler's work is their observation that the criteria for sex, gender, bodies, materiality, and so forth seem to have a history that shows they have always shifted. But creative anti-realism does not follow from these premises, for a realist can easily affirm this observation if by it we mean that our concepts have a history, epistemically understood. Were Butler to insist that it is not the concepts that have a fluid history but bodies themselves, this would amount to arguing for creative anti-realism about bodies by assuming its truth in one of the argument's premises (in other words, it would amount to question begging). One might inquire further into Butler's views. Do humans really have the ability to produce entities *ex nihilo* like that, in a way analogous to God? Christians have particularly good reason to think not, but so would anyone who does not believe in a God who created all things. (If there is no God with this capacity, why think there are humans who have it?) Even more basically, what reason do we have for thinking that something like the heterosexual matrix is true and can sovereignly produce reality?

It is far more intuitive, absent a strong argument to the contrary, to maintain a realist stance on the world, even if it is a version of critical realism.[121] For instance, for a long time, scientists and museum curators had a concept of a

118. See Hilary Putnam, *Representation and Reality* (Cambridge, MA: MIT Press, 1991); Nelson Goodman, *Ways of Worldmaking* (Indianapolis: Hackett, 1978).

119. Nicholas Wolterstorff, "The World Ready-Made," in *Practices of Belief: Selected Essays*, vol. 2, ed. Terence Cuneo (New York: Cambridge University Press, 2010), 24.

120. For some of the most exacting criticisms, see Wolterstorff, "World Ready-Made," and Alvin Plantinga's classic "How to Be an Anti-Realist," *Proceedings and Addresses of the American Philosophical Association* 56, no. 1 (September 1982): 47–70.

121. For more on critical realism, see Janet Martin Soskice, *Metaphor and Religious Language* (Oxford: Clarendon, 1985), chap. 7.

dinosaur as something similar to what we see in the early *Jurassic Park* films. Since then, they have discovered that, in all likelihood, dinosaurs had feathers. What changed in this scenario? Did our concept of a dinosaur change in order better to fit what they were in reality, or did those very beings that lived seventy million years ago sprout feathers upon the revision of our concept? The critical realist will side with the former, all while sustaining the corrigibility of her use of language. So it is with bodies and their fundamental features. The concept of a male is now, at least in scientific terms, very different than what it was 1,500 years ago. But male bodies have not changed: our concepts of them have. Wolterstorff summarizes this stance well:

> To saw a board is to alter it. To count some segment of reality as a rabbit is not to alter it. It is to give it a certain role in our lives. It is to make it possible for us to think and talk about it in a certain way. Counting a segment of reality as a rabbit is not like counting the hitting of a ball over a fence as a home run. In the latter case, the ball's being hit over the fence is not sufficient for its *being* what we call "a home run": there must also be in effect a certain social arrangement which brings it about that *by* performing one action, a person performs the other. In the former case, everything necessary and sufficient for being what we call "a rabbit" is provided by external reality, wholly apart from social arrangements.[122]

So it is with bodies, sexes, and matter. Our conceptualization of them does not constitute what they are, for our linguistic and conceptual capacities are categorically different from God's declaration of "Let there be light." Rather, we conceptualize sex and gender so as to understand better the role they play in our lives. The second reading of Butler, then, is untenable.

There are further worries. If bodies are socially constructed, and if there are no normative ways in which sex and gender ought to be constructed,[123] then what prevents a wicked society from constructing the female body as something fit to be violated by men bent on assaulting them? A wicked society may very well bring it about that female bodies are those that are fitting recipients of abuse and rape, and there is nothing normative within Butler's view to preclude that (witness once again the case of Pitcairn, where this is precisely

122. Wolterstorff, "World Ready-Made," 35.
123. Something Butler maintains; see *Gender Trouble*, viii. Butler does have a concept of gender normativity, but it is used only to describe the norms that prescribe the performances pertaining to a gender within the heterosexual matrix. See *Gender Trouble*, xxi–xxii. This is not *moral* normativity.

what happened). On that view, discursive practices have simply constructed these bodies to be treated in this way. This is problematic for any view that hopes to facilitate feminist goals and ambitions, as Butler's does. Additionally, Christians have specific reasons for rejecting Butler's proposals. One outcome of Butler's views is that there is no such thing as a human nature, for these too are socially constructed within the heterosexual matrix. The distinction between cultural and natural is itself produced by ambits for power, as is the notion of a human nature. The conditions for being human are as much "historically revisable criteria of intelligibility" as those for sex and gender that can easily "vanquish bodies that matter."[124] It seems to me, however, that Butler's position makes the incarnation impossible. If nothing else, the doctrine of the incarnation affirms that the Son of God, the second person of the Trinity, assumed a *human nature* in addition to the divine nature already possessed. Such language is meant to capture scriptural affirmations like "Therefore he had to become like his brothers and sisters in every respect" (Heb. 2:17) and that the Son "emptied himself, taking the form of a slave, being born in human likeness" (Phil. 2:7). Even if one considers "nature" language to be ill-suited to express what these passages are saying, *some* concept is needed to specify what the Word assumed in order to be like us in every respect, excepting sin.[125] Butler's view, it seems to me, precludes this very possibility. Any attempt to specify just what is human and what is not is a grab for power, looking to exclude those who do not fit into the category "human." This is a problem not only for our attempts to define humanity but for the very task of defining itself. Thus, if one adopts Judith Butler's views, one will have considerable difficulty in affirming one of the central confessions of Christianity. If we have no resources for saying that the Son became one of us, in what would Christian hope lie?

Butler's views, for all their sophistication and wide acceptance, are riddled with insuperable problems. It is not obvious whether one should read Butler epistemically or metaphysically, but on either read, they fail to accomplish what they set out to do. Apart from a highly problematic account of creative anti-realism, their claim that sex is a social construct is metaphysically

124. Butler, *Bodies That Matter*, xxii. They also say that the gendered matrix is "prior to the emergence of the 'human'" (xvii). See also *Bodies That Matter*, xiv, as well as Butler, *Gender Trouble*, xxxi, 51, and 151, for further substantiation.
125. Even Adrian Thatcher, whose metaphysical intuitions about gender differ greatly from my own, concurs: "We need to speak of a human nature because Jesus had one" (Adrian Thatcher, *Gender and Christian Ethics* [New York: Cambridge University Press, 2021], 105).

unsustainable. Moreover, if one is committed to the core Christian doctrine of the incarnation, then one is forced to either reject Butler's project or face significant challenges to one's Christian confession. As an attempt to rescue the view that gender is socially constructed by maintaining that sex is socially constructed, then, Butler's view does not succeed.

2.5 Conclusion

I have attempted to outline and critique the view that gender is a social construct in this chapter. I have done so because the view is, by all accounts, the most popular in the philosophical and theological literature. It has an admirable history, stretching at least as far back as the seventeenth century, and brilliant representatives in both philosophical and theological guilds. All the same, it is liable to significant objections. It cannot account for the diversity within gender of differing times and cultures in a theoretically satisfying way, and it cannot morally evaluate those genders in a consistent manner. One might attempt to rehabilitate the view, along with Judith Butler, by claiming that sex is also socially constructed. This view faces even more unconquerable challenges, requiring a highly dubious metaphysical anti-realism to succeed as an argument. Social construction, I conclude, is an inadequate way to describe the fundamental features of gender.

All the same, I should not be taken to say that there is nothing to commend the view. Certain features of the social construction of gender, particularly in its earlier, more epistemic guise, are highly suggestive. For instance, the emphasis on our epistemic limitations in being able to say just what gender is explains very well why so many have difficulty in laying out the conditions for being a man or a woman. Additionally, the *purpose* of the view—that is, to empower conceptions of gender relations that are conducive to human flourishing and justice—should be maintained. Finally, the resistance to saying that social identities are reducible to biological facts is well motivated, and the recognition of the need to build a conceptual bridge between having a certain kind of body to acting in certain gendered ways uncovers the central issue in question. In part 2, I shall attempt to craft a broad metaphysical and theological account of gender that, though not a social construction view, retains all of these favorable elements of the social construction approach.

PART 2

* * * * * *

The Constructive
Proposal

* * * * * *

THREE

"What God Has Joined Together, Let No One Separate"

Bodies and Culture in the Metaphysics of Gender

In the first chapter, I introduced two bifurcations encountered in the literature on gender. The ontological bifurcation observes a division between gender as social construct and gender as (biological) essence. In the second chapter, I argued against the view that gender is a social construct, the most prominent view held among feminist theorists and theologians. Yet, it must be remembered that I am rejecting the aforementioned bifurcation as a whole; so, while I have rejected one side of it, I am not therefore accepting the other side. Better concepts are needed to make headway on the ontology of gender. This chapter takes a first step in providing a constructive view by putting forward four theses for a metaphysics of gender. I will show that these theses, drawn from two theorists of gender, are theologically warranted.

3.1 Expanding What We Mean by Culture and Nature

Is gender a social construct, or is it an essence? What is meant by these terms in the first place? In the previous chapter, the view that gender is a social construct was shown to be, in point of fact, a plurality of views that are diverse in their commitments, though they share some fundamental features in common. Judith Butler's views are not the same as Kathryn Tanner's, but they do have some structural similarities. Even so, we saw that it was precisely in those similarities, specifically the context-boundedness of social constructs, that the position revealed its flaws. If one investigates a little more, other latent commitments in the debate emerge, commitments that shape the way its key terms are understood—specifically, a common deflation of the terms "culture" and "nature" or "biology." Often, a fairly reductionist picture of bodies is implicit in social constructionist views, a picture that maintains that no norms can be derived from bodies and their sexes since they are merely biological entities. On this understanding of the body, it makes complete sense as to why biological essentialism is hopeless as a view. Robin Dembroff, on a rare occasion where this assumption is made explicit, says,

> For all the huffing about how gender is just body parts, no one *in practice* holds the identity [i.e., biological essentialist] view of gender. If gender is just reproductive features and *nothing more*, it makes no more sense to insist that people must look, love or act in particular ways on the basis of gender than it would to demand that people modify their behaviour on the basis of eye colour or height.
>
> Even if reproductive traits are correlated to personality, physical capabilities or social interests, such correlations don't equate to norms. As David Hume has taught us, *is* doesn't make *ought*. Having feet is correlated with walking, but I can walk on my hands if I want to. Having a tongue is correlated with experiencing taste, but who cares if I decide to drink Soylent every day? Once we recognise that gender categories mark how one *ought* to be, and not only how one's body *is*, the identity view unravels. *To build in the "oughts" is to admit that gender is more than just body parts.*[1]

According to Dembroff, no gender-relevant "oughts" can be derived from biological facts alone. If one identifies gender with biology, one's view of gender cannot account for those different cultural expressions typically associated with gender. For Dembroff, and for many others who hold to a social construction

---

1. Robin Dembroff, "Why Be Nonbinary?," *Aeon*, October 30, 2018, https://aeon.co/essays/nonbinary-identity-is-a-radical-stance-against-gender-segregation (with the exception of the final sentence, emphasis is original). See also Louise Antony, "Natures and Norms," *Ethics* 111, no. 1 (2000): conceptions of human nature cannot "generate reasons for accepting ethical propositions about what human beings should or should not do" (15).

view of some sort,[2] biology is inadequate simply because of its perceived inability to build an explanatory bridge to social behavior.

Others, however, have risen to defend the side of biology. On their view, gender terms like "man" and "woman" are biological terms meaning "adult human male" and "adult human female," respectively.[3] In response to a charge like Dembroff's, Tomás Bogardus rightly observes that most people do not have such a normatively impoverished account of the biology of adult humans and their sexes:

> If all you know of a thing is that he is an adult human male, you are in a position to know various normative facts about him; those normative facts are knowable solely by reflection upon one's concepts. You're not left wondering, for example, whether this adult human male ought to be enslaved; you're in a position to know he shouldn't be, given only the information that he's an adult male human. And likewise with females. This shows that there *are* a priori entailment relations between our concepts of adult human females and males, on the one hand, and our moral concepts, on the other, presumably because there are entailment relations between the relevant mind-independent properties, and we're tracking these with our concepts.[4]

Bogardus and others rightly resist the normative deflation of natural or biological concepts, and we have some initial theological reasons for the plausibility of this view: "Every sin that a person commits is outside the body; but the fornicator sins against the body itself. Or do you not know that your body is a temple of the Holy Spirit within you, which you have from God, and that you are not your own?" (1 Cor. 6:18–19). There are certain things, Paul maintains, that the body cannot do *qua* body and that should not be done to the body *qua* body. This latter question was, of course, directly phrased in response to sexual immorality in the Corinthian church. Bodies, so it seems, are not so conceptually deflated as social constructionists seem to think.

2. See also, e.g., Adrian Thatcher, *Gender and Christian Ethics* (New York: Cambridge University Press, 2021): "The body, whether male or female, cannot be the basis for making discriminatory judgments *of any kind*, whether about its status, worth, or role. Rather it is prior beliefs about superiority and inferiority with regard to gender that shape how bodies are read and what unjustified burdens are *imposed* upon them" (27, emphasis added).

3. See, e.g., Tomás Bogardus, "Evaluating Arguments for the Sex/Gender Distinction," *Philosophia* 48, no. 3 (2020): 873–92; Tomás Bogardus, "Some Internal Problems with Revisionary Gender Concepts," *Philosophia* 48, no. 4 (2020): 45–75; and Alex Byrne, "Are Women Adult Human Females?," *Philosophical Studies* 177, no. 12 (2020): 3783–803.

4. Bogardus, "Evaluating Arguments for the Sex/Gender Distinction," 885.

All the same, there is a significant cost to accepting the responses offered by these latter thinkers. Whereas social constructionists like Dembroff
deflate notions of nature and biology to the point where they can bear
no normative weight, those interested in recovering traditional biological
definitions of manhood and womanhood must deflate notions of cultural
gender expression to the point where they are irrelevant to manhood and
womanhood. Cultural goods like what kinds of clothes one wears and
whether one shaves one's legs, for instance, have much to do with gender
in the minds of ordinary individuals, but these goods become irrelevant
stereotypes arbitrarily associated with, but not in any sense definitive of,
gender.[5] If being a woman is identical with being an adult human female,
then it does not matter for gender's definition whether a woman shaves her
legs, wears certain kinds of clothes, or performs any other kind of social
activity. This, it seems to me, is a steep price to pay on account of the high
import virtually all humans place on some kind of cultural activity for their
genders. On this traditional view, therefore, culture is deflated and made
irrelevant to gender.

In the debates orbiting around the bifurcation of culture and essence, then,
there is a common tendency to reduce the concepts of the other side to the
point where they have no explanatory weight. On one side of the debate are
those who rightly see the relevance and importance of cultural expressions
of gender while deflating the importance of the body; on the other side are
those who rightly see the pertinence of the body and of sex while denying
any role to cultural expression. But why should one accept the terms of the
debate as they have been laid out? What persuasive reason do we have to
continue insisting on this bifurcation where each side is eager to let the air
out of its competing opposite? Is there a view consistently maintaining the
importance of both? As many culturally relevant debates attest, it is much
easier to sustain a bifurcation between "us" and "them" when those on the
opposite side are considered only artificially—culture wars thrive on super-
ficiality, like bacteria in a warm and damp environment. It is the task of the
remainder of this project to find a better alternative. This chapter takes the
first step by offering a rudimentary theological ontology of gender that resists

5. This is the tendency, in my opinion, in much of the work being done in "gender-critical
feminism." When one looks beyond the frequent, politically oriented, and obscure appeals
to "reality," one sees a general suspicion raised toward the definitional role played by cultural
goods, a role that fuels the sex/gender distinction. See, e.g., Kathleen Stock, *Material Girls:
Why Reality Matters for Feminism* (London: Fleet, 2021).

the simplification just illustrated. This will be accomplished by positing four theses that will be extracted from a survey of two thinkers attempting to craft a better way forward—namely, the feminist theorists Charlotte Witt and Mari Mikkola. From an amalgamation of their views, four characteristics of my proposed ontology of gender will emerge, and these are the four theses. I take these to be something like a set of common denominators for tenable theologies of gender:

1. Gender is an essence, though this is not reducible to or identical with biological determinism or biological essentialism.
2. The complexity of gender, the noetic effects of sin, and the current conditions of oppression complicate our epistemic access to gender's essence. All the same, we can be assured that issues surrounding gender will be rectified in the eschaton.
3. Any theory or theology of gender must be consistent with and supportive of the cultivation of justice.
4. Gender is concerned with selves or identity and with the way selves organize social goods pertaining to their sexed bodies.

This chapter will consist of arguments for these theses, arguments that will draw from explicitly theological premises. In doing so, a picture will emerge that begins to unite those elements typically kept separate: social attributes and nature, theology and gender.

3.2 Charlotte Witt and Mari Mikkola on the Ontology of Gender

Charlotte Witt and Mari Mikkola are two contemporary theorists who have provided salutary, original, and refreshing accounts that seek to accomplish the expansion of terms necessary for a successful ontology of gender. Witt, for instance, rejects the "distinction between biological criteria and social criteria, or between nature and culture" because they are "too sharp and simplistic . . . to be useful."[6] Gender cannot be reduced to biology; neither can one maintain that gender is "purely cultural," for there is no "plausible way of thinking about gender that is entirely detached from bodily, biological existence even if . . . those biological processes, or sexual and reproductive

---

6. Charlotte Witt, *The Metaphysics of Gender* (New York: Oxford University Press, 2011), 34.

functions, are complex and culturally mediated."[7] For her part, Mikkola resists the temptation to "understand the term 'woman' as a purely social gender term" because the term includes many types of traits: "one's appearance (clothing, hairstyles, makeup); behavioral patterns; social roles; self-ascription; anatomical and bodily features (body type, shape, size, amount of body hair, how one 'carries' one's body)."[8] Both Witt and Mikkola see the benefit of expanding understandings of culture and biology to the point where gendered terms are defined by both, an act that joins what social construction and essentialism intend to separate. Attending to their views, then, is a vital step in accomplishing the intent of this chapter.

3.2.1 Charlotte Witt

Charlotte Witt, in her innovative book *The Metaphysics of Gender*, argues for gender essentialism, though the ways in which the terms "gender" and "essentialism" are understood make all the difference. Witt's work has, for a long time, been committed to disabusing feminist theory of its intellectual biases against certain catchwords like "essence."[9] Her motivation for retaining the language of essence derives from what she perceives as "the centrality of gender in our individual lived experiences," something she believes is missed by simple social constructionist views.[10] Gender, for Witt, is a major component (indeed, *the* chief organizing component) of our social self-understanding, and her view is meant to be an articulation of something she takes to be already true of most people's beliefs about themselves.

The particular kind of essentialism for which she advocates is called "unification essentialism" or "uniessentialism."[11] Uniessentialism, claims Witt, is about "the unity and organization of material parts into a new individual."[12]

---

7. Witt, *Metaphysics of Gender*, 36. The notion of cultural *mediation* will be important for my proposal.

8. Mari Mikkola, *The Wrong of Injustice: Dehumanization and Its Role in Feminist Philosophy* (New York: Oxford University Press, 2016), 128.

9. See, e.g., Charlotte Witt, "Anti-Essentialism in Feminist Theory," *Philosophical Topics* 23, no. 2 (1995): 321–44; Charlotte Witt, "Gender Essentialism: Aristotle or Locke?" in *Powers and Capacities in Philosophy: The New Aristotelianism*, ed. Ruth Groff and John Greco (New York: Routledge, 2012), 308–18; Charlotte Witt, "What Is Gender Essentialism?," in *Feminist Metaphysics: Explorations in the Ontology of Sex, Gender and the Self*, ed. Charlotte Witt (New York: Springer, 2011), 11–25.

10. Witt, *Metaphysics of Gender*, xiii.

11. See Charlotte Witt, *Ways of Being: Potentiality and Actuality in Aristotle's Metaphysics* (Ithaca, NY: Cornell University Press, 2003).

12. Witt, *Metaphysics of Gender*, 6.

What makes bits of wood, glass, shingles, and so on a house? For Witt, what makes these material parts a house is their particular organization around a function. The function of a house is to provide shelter, and the successful organization of material parts for the effective performance of that function makes that entity a house rather than some other entity. This function, claims Witt, is essential to the house because it would not be a house without it; that is, for these material parts to be a house, it is necessary that its parts are organized in such a way as to perform this function. A "functional essence," then, is "an essential property that explains what the individual is for, what its purpose is, and that organizes the parts toward that end."[13] This function is not simply what the individual object *does*; it is what the object "*ought* to do" if it is going to be that kind of object.[14] An entity's having a function of this kind is the same as saying it bears a *functional property*, and it bears this property essentially. Another way to understand Witt's uniessentialism is to see it as an essentialist mereology: to bear a functional property essentially is "explanatory; it explains the existence of the new individual as a unity and not just a sum of material parts."[15] Without this function there would be no house at all, just a heap of material parts. The function makes this individual *what* it is.

Witt's argument is that gender is uniessential to social individuals, where this latter concept is technically defined. First, however, it is important to see how gender is anything like a functional essence. For Witt, though there is no "bright line distinction to be drawn between what is natural/biological and what is cultural in relation to the distinction between sex and gender," there is nevertheless a conceptually and heuristically helpful gap to be observed between natural phenomena and their socially mediated counterparts. Important for her view are the phenomena of reproduction and engendering. Reproduction is a natural phenomenon, and engendering is the socially mediated counterpart to reproduction. The difference between the former and the latter has to do with which goods are organized according to the function. Witt provides a very helpful illustration to make the difference clear.[16] She invites us to consider the difference between feeding and dining. Feeding is,

13. Witt, *Metaphysics of Gender*, 14.
14. Witt, *Metaphysics of Gender*, 17.
15. Witt, *Metaphysics of Gender*, 30. And later: "Uniessentialism . . . is the view that [an object's] essence unifies a heap of parts into a new individual" (75).
16. See Witt, *Metaphysics of Gender*, 37.

on her terms, a strictly biological function, requiring only organs like mouths, stomachs, digestive systems, and so on. Dining, by contrast, is like feeding and is even dependent on it to some extent, but as a cultural practice, it has different norms to which diners are responsive and under which they are evaluable. The conditions for feeding are strictly biological, but it is "elaborated" into dining when new norms are introduced. In certain cultures, dining is governed by norms like strictures for which hand is fit for eating, bans against the consumption of certain foods, required practices for hygiene, and so on. Not observing these norms in their operative cultures disqualifies one from dining, but not from feeding. Both of these, however, are functions. Feeding organizes bodily elements and food for a biological purpose (say, maintaining life in an organism), while dining organizes these *along with additional cultural goods for a cultural purpose* (say, bringing friends together for a celebration).

Witt, as a means of upholding the relevance of biology while maintaining its space from cultural expression, claims, "Engendering is to reproduction as dining is to feeding."[17] Reproduction is explained by strictly biological processes. Engendering, by contrast, operates according to different material conditions, conditions that will be specific to different cultures.[18] It is impossible to generalize, but such conditions will include the norms pertaining to the perceived roles associated with conceiving, bearing, begetting, and parenting children, along with the vast social organization that accompanies such roles.[19] The reproductive function organizes the biological conditions required for bearing children, while the engendering function will include in its organization the roles and structures pertaining to and stemming from reproduction. This allows Witt to offer a definition of gender: "My definition of gender—being a woman and being a man—ties these social positions to engendering; to be a woman is to be recognized to have a particular function

17. Witt, *Metaphysics of Gender*, 37.

18. This element of Witt's view, for which I am not advocating, leads me to believe that it is still liable to the objections made in chapter 2, specifically regarding the number of genders created by cultural diversity.

19. Witt's position is somewhat vague on this point, but she insists that it is necessarily so: "The social norms include, but are not limited to, those attaching to different gestational roles and to different parenting roles. Because gestational roles and parenting roles themselves are manifested in very different ways in different cultures, and in different historical periods, there is no useful way to fill in the blank. . . . The actual content of the social roles is variable, just as what counts as a good meal varies widely from culture to culture" (Witt, *Metaphysics of Gender*, 40).

in engendering, to be a man is to be recognized to have a different function in engendering. . . . To be a woman is to be recognized as having a body that plays one role in the engendering function; women conceive and bear. To be a man is to be recognized as having a body that plays another role in the engendering function; men beget."[20]

It is important to clarify that Witt's position is not that gender is identical to playing a certain role in reproduction, biologically understood. Rather, her view is that gender is defined according to certain *perceived* roles in the cultural expression of reproduction known as engendering. This means that one can be a man or a woman without ever having reproduced, so long as one is perceived as having some relation to the cultural norms of engendering (and it may be something as simple as having the perceived capacity of playing a role in engendering but never actually doing so in the duration of one's life).[21] This is her attempt to make her view trans*-inclusive, for possessing a perceived role in reproduction does not actually require the kind of body that is able to perform that role. The relevant function for defining gender is the engendering function, which is about the organization of biological and cultural goods having some relation to reproduction.

Gender, on Witt's proposal, is uniessential to *social individuals*, and social individuals are composed of social positions, which are themselves defined by social roles. Clarifying definitions are in order here. A *social position* is something an individual occupies that is created by a social function she or he performs. Someone might occupy the social position of being a medical doctor in virtue of the social function of treating patients or a parent in virtue of the social function of raising a child, for these are functions one must perform in order to be that kind of thing. (A doctor who has never been involved, in any way, with the treatment of patients would be hard to imagine.) *Social roles* are the "norms associated with a social position," to which the individual in a social position is responsive and under which the individual is evaluable.[22] If someone is in the social position of being a doctor, say, then

20. Witt, *Metaphysics of Gender*, 39–40.
21. Yet Witt makes an important concession: "If human offspring were cloned, and gestated in laboratories, and there was no binary division of engendering function and associated gender norms, then no individuals would satisfy my definition. In that society there would be no women and no men (according to my definition of these social positions), although there would be female and male human beings" (Witt, *Metaphysics of Gender*, 39).
22. Witt, *Metaphysics of Gender*, 29. Regarding this nomenclature, Witt says, "The term 'responsive to' is intended to cover the full range of possible reactions to a norm on the part of those individuals to whom that norm pertains: from compliance to critique. To say that

there will be certain social norms that govern her actions (even if she does not necessarily comply with them) and by which she can be evaluated as either a good doctor or not. Once again, these will be tied to the function definitive of the position—if the function of a doctor is to treat patients, then she will operate according to the norms required for the successful performance of that function and her quality as a doctor will derive from those norms. On Witt's uniessentialist picture, everything just mentioned will be essential to the individual insofar as she occupies that social position. It is essential for the individual who is a doctor that she is at some point functioning, in some way or other, in the treatment of patients, and accompanying this function is a social position and a set of norms.

A *social individual*, finally, comprises various social positions and their attendant social roles: "By social individuals I mean those individuals who occupy social positions such as a parent, a professor, a contractor, or a refugee. Most (perhaps all) social individuals occupy multiple positions simultaneously; we are all multitaskers! The norms that pertain to a social individual are determined by that individual's social position occupancies."[23] An individual is a *social* individual, then, because she occupies various social positions. Not only that, but she acts in and through that position as an agent: "Agents are individuals who are capable of entertaining goals (singly and in groups) and figuring out how to achieve them, and are capable of acting from a standpoint or perspective."[24] Occupying certain social positions as a social individual allows one to act from the unique point of view of that position and will have goals specific to that point of view, as well as the ability to find appropriate means to achieve those goals. They have causal potential not simply in opening up new avenues for action but also in coloring the particular ways in which acts are undertaken. A social individual who is a doctor will thereby have the opportunity to treat patients, something not available to someone who does not occupy that social position, and the doctor will come to see her function in a way familiar only to other doctors. Social individuals, then, are those agents who occupy and act through various social positions.

With these pieces in place, we may now arrive at Witt's conclusion that gender is uniessential to social individuals. She summarizes it as follows: "A

---

an individual is 'evaluable under' a social norm is to say that the individual is a candidate for evaluation by others in relation to that norm" (33).

23. Witt, *Metaphysics of Gender*, 54.
24. Witt, *Metaphysics of Gender*, 60.

social individual (or agent) occupies many social positions simultaneously (and many more diachronically) but its gender unifies the sum of social position occupancies into a new social individual. Its gender (being a man, being a woman) is uniessential to the social individual."[25] Recall the following: (1) uniessentialism is a form of essentialism according to which certain goods are organized and unified around a function defining a new individual; (2) gender is defined according to the engendering function, which organizes the perceived goods of reproduction as they are culturally manifested; and (3) a social individual is someone who occupies social positions governed by social roles. Witt's point, then, is that gender unifies and organizes all the other social positions constituting the individual, thereby grounding the existence of a single social individual. This is because gender is a social individual's "*mega social role*," which goes on to serve as "a principle of normative unity for social individuals or agents."[26] And if it does this, then it is uniessential to the social individual; it is what makes the individual cohesive rather than a random assortment of social positions. But what reason do we have to think that gender is really this supremely organizing social position that brings together all others into a social individual? Witt argues that gender either directly implicates all of the positions one occupies (in cases where the positions are gender specific, like husband, mother, sister, midwife) or indirectly creates norms within social positions that reflect perceived roles in engendering (such as when a masculine doctor is associated with competency while a feminine doctor is associated with compassion, as studies have shown).[27]

For social positions that have an obvious gender index, gender organizes them by making them available or not available according to the individual's gender. Gender creates normative restraints on whether an individual can become, say, a mother. These are social positions available only to those already occupying the social position of "woman." However, for social positions with no obvious gender indexing, Witt maintains that gender nevertheless exercises considerable influence. Thus, certain jobs are said to be gendered, like teaching young children (which has been considered a predominantly feminine job). And men and women sometimes hold identical positions but with different normative forces. For example, as mentioned above, both men and women can become doctors, but studies cited by Witt show that their

25. Witt, *Metaphysics of Gender*, 18.
26. Witt, *Metaphysics of Gender*, 85 (emphasis original).
27. See Witt, *Metaphysics of Gender*, 95.

experience of being a doctor will be different insofar as they are expected to be characterized by different virtues, like compassion or competency. Gender, as an arch social position, colors and organizes all of the other positions we occupy. This view, she believes, gives due attention to the testimony of many who say that gender is central to their identities, and yet it resists any notion that gender is fixed or timeless.

Is Witt's view a social constructionist view or an essentialist view? This question no longer makes sense. Witt has provided a view that does not fit into any of the poorly defined sides of the bifurcation between construct and essence. Yes, it takes into full account the various social roles one plays; but on this view, gender is still essential to our social selves. Before seeing how Witt's view lends itself to the desiderata for a metaphysics of gender mentioned in the introduction, let us turn to another thinker whose proposals are equally stimulating.

3.2.2 Mari Mikkola

Mari Mikkola structures her innovative book *The Wrong of Injustice* around the two objections I leveled against the social constructionist position in the previous chapter. To summarize those objections: the social construction of gender is untenable because it results in the view that there are no women and men *as such*, but only women and men constricted to the particular cultures that establish the necessary conditions for membership in their constructs. This is unintuitive and renders feminist theory and theology inoperable since both presume that there is such a category as "woman." Following from this, a social constructionist position makes gender morally unevaluable insofar as we cannot say of a particular culture that it has good or bad men or women. This is because just as the necessary conditions for gender are culturally specific, so are the moral norms attached to those genders. There are no "bad men" or "virtuous women," only men and women specific to those cultures.

In parallel fashion, Mikkola identifies two puzzles within feminist theory:

Semantic puzzle: Given that ordinary language users tend not to distinguish sex and gender (treating "woman" largely as a sex term, or a mixture of social and biological features), what precisely are feminists talking about when they talk about women? What are the necessary and sufficient conditions that the concept *woman* encodes, if any such conditions exist to begin with?

Ontological puzzle: How should we understand the category of women that is meant to undergird feminist political solidarity, if there are no necessary and sufficient conceptual conditions underlying our gender talk? Do women make up a genuine kind, or simply a gerrymandered and random collection of individuals? What kinds of entities are gender and sex anyway? Are there *really* women and men, if gender is (in some substantial sense) socially constructed?[28]

These puzzles parse out, in semantic and ontological terms, the two objections in their substantial and moral dimensions. According to Mikkola, they have also set the agenda for feminist theory for at least the past fifty years. Whether looking for the conditions for when to refer to someone as a man or a woman or inquiring about just which conditions classify individuals as members of such categories, feminists have attempted to avoid (or justify accepting) the diffusion of gender terms to their cultures and have sought to show how doing so is consistent with feminist political aims. Mikkola capably recognizes the real-life import of these ambitions: "If our metaphysics is too radically constructivist in the service of those with social power, feminist politics will be undermined" because nothing said about women as a category can consistently be employed.[29] This state of affairs and broad research project Mikkola labels "the gender controversy."

Realizing what is at stake, Mikkola's overall claim is that we should give up the gender controversy.[30] Feminist theory needs a new charter and should no longer find itself beholden to these puzzles. Accomplishing this would require showing how and why the feminist theorist can be relieved of the duty to solve the semantic and ontological puzzles by positing new ontological categories and conditions for applying gender terms like "men" and "women." This is precisely what Mikkola sets out to do. One of the basic tenets of feminism is that "feminist politics should be organized around women, understood as a gendered social kind," but Mikkola thinks this was its earliest mistake.[31] Though the sex/gender distinction, the social construction of gender, and their accompanying commitments served the initial purposes of feminism, they have proven theoretically insufficient and require reworking. Mikkola suggests that the more fitting base for feminist political ambitions is not the concept "woman" but the concept "human" and the legitimate interests held

28. Mikkola, *Wrong of Injustice*, 3–4.
29. Mikkola, *Wrong of Injustice*, 127.
30. See Mikkola, *Wrong of Injustice*, 6: "I argue for giving up the gender controversy."
31. Mikkola, *Wrong of Injustice*, 104.

by human beings.[32] Nevertheless, her view is a type of humanist *feminism* that grounds the necessary moral norms in humanity but recognizes that it is specifically *women* who have not been treated as human beings.

Mikkola begins with some helpful terminology. A *gender realist*, she states, is not a biological essentialist. Rather, gender realism maintains that "women as a group are assumed to share some characteristic feature, experience, common condition, or criterion that defines their gender and makes them women (as opposed to, say, men)."[33] This feature or set of features thereby serves as the necessary and jointly sufficient conditions for being a member of the kind "woman" (and, *mutatis mutandis*, any other gender). A gender realist can, on the face of it, be a feminist as well as a social constructionist on her view, because nothing in the definition precludes that condition from being a social property, and the property can be one conducive to the liberative interests of women. Indeed, it is fair to assume that most feminists *are* gender realists, for another way of being a gender realist is simply to commit oneself to the view that there *are* women and men. That is, there is some property that renders the category "women" stable and that serves as a condition for inclusion within it. This is a modest form of essentialism, which Mikkola calls "classificatory essentialism," and it does not commit one to any views about biology. All it commits one to is the view that there is such a category as "women" (and "men," and any other genders one might wish to include).

The alternative to gender realism, as Mikkola and others note, is *gender skepticism*. This is the view that denies "the existence of a single unified social kind of women," committing the holder to the notion that women make up "a merely unbound and gerrymandered collection of individuals."[34] A gender skeptic is not someone who questions the epistemic access humans have to gender's nature. Rather, a gender skeptic is someone who denies that gender exists by denying that there are sufficient conditions relative to the kind, or

---

32. Unpacking this claim is the burden of part 2 of her book, particularly what "dehumanization" amounts to and how women are subject to dehumanizing forces. To put it another way: it is not gender that grounds ethics but humanity. See Mikkola, *Wrong of Injustice*, 151: "The damage done by patriarchy is not to women qua gendered beings, but to women qua human beings." For more on this, see also Mikkola, *Wrong of Injustice*, 164, 197, 237–40.

33. Mikkola, *Wrong of Injustice*, 28. I should add that it does not have to be *one* feature, such as experience, but it may be a *set* of features.

34. Mikkola, *Wrong of Injustice*, 32–33. For more on gender skepticism, see Mari Mikkola, "Gender Sceptics and Feminist Politics," *Res Publica* 13 (2007): 361–80. See also the earlier work of Susan Bordo, *Unbearable Weight: Feminism, Western Culture, and the Body* (Berkeley: University of California Press, 2003), 216–17.

someone who maintains that the conditions that make up the genders with which we are familiar are groundless, arbitrary or a mere expression of power. Elizabeth Spelman and those persuaded by her arguments are an example of the first kind of skeptic, especially if no generalizations about women (even within unique contexts) are possible.[35] An example of the second kind of skeptic is Judith Butler, who argues that "any effort to give universal or specific content to the category of women, presuming that that guarantee of solidarity is required in advance, will necessarily produce factionalization, and that 'identity' as a point of departure can never hold as the solidifying ground of a feminist political movement. Identity categories are never merely descriptive, but always normative, and as such, exclusionary. . . . The very term becomes a site of permanent openness and resignifiability."[36] For Butler, no conditions can *rightly* identify women because such conditions will always bear with them normative commitments, and those normative commitments will always be exertions of power. "Women," at this point, becomes a fluid and undefinable category. Mikkola summarizes the posture of gender skeptics: "So the mistake is not that feminists provided the incorrect elucidation of *woman*. Rather, their mistake was to attempt to define womanhood at all."[37] A gender skeptic like Butler, then, maintains that "the term 'woman' has no definite meaning, and given the normativity of identity categories, it would be politically dangerous to try to define the term in a way that picks out the class of women for feminist and political representation."[38]

Mikkola is not a gender skeptic, but she brings up the view to show how an unnecessary captivity to the gender controversy results in deeply counter-intuitive and politically ineffective conclusions. If gender skepticism is the view that gender terms like "woman" have no stable meanings, and feminist theory has been organized around the term "woman," then it would follow that feminist theorists have based their projects (theoretical and political) on a concept whose grounding is at best shaky and at worst already morally problematic. In order to avoid this unwelcome result, Mikkola must provide an account that shows why the semantic and ontological puzzles do not need

35. For this, see Uma Narayan, "Essence of Culture and a Sense of History: A Feminist Critique of Cultural Essentialism," *Hypatia* 13, no. 2 (1998): 86–106.

36. Judith Butler, "Contingent Foundations: Feminism and the Question of 'Postmodernism,'" in *Feminists Theorize the Political*, ed. Judith Butler and Joan W. Scott (New York: Routledge, 1992), 15–16.

37. Mikkola, *Wrong of Injustice*, 35.

38. Mikkola, *Wrong of Injustice*, 37.

answering. This forms the bulk of her constructive proposal, where she "deflates" the semantic and ontological puzzles. First, she tackles the semantic puzzle, which revolves around requirements for the right reference of gender terms. Mikkola asserts:

> I contend that we need not know "what it is to be a woman" or to define *woman* in order to identify and explain gendered social inequalities or in order to say why patriarchy damages women. Let me clarify: feminists must be able to refer to women, and our language use must pick out women's social kind. If we genuinely cannot distinguish women from other ordinary objects, feminism has lost its viability. But holding that unless we solve the semantic puzzle, we will simply be *unable* to talk about women does not follow. Feminism need not give up gender talk tout court in the absence of a thick conception of *woman*—a minimal conception will do.[39]

Mikkola's basic point is that the bar set by the semantic puzzle is too high. To use a term well, she claims, one does not need to know the content or definition of the object of the term. If so, then referring to women does not require defining "women" or having ready to hand the necessary and sufficient conditions for being a woman. Moreover, if she is correct that a gender term like "woman" is "easy to apply . . . but hard to account for its application," then an account of how gender terms refer that does not require specification of gender's definition will usefully resonate with everyday usage.[40]

In what way does Mikkola suggest this deflated understanding helps with the right use of gender terms? She begins with a distinction between two ways these concepts function, an *extensional* function and a *semantic* function. A gender concept's extensional function guides its right deployment, while its semantic function provides insight into the concept's content.[41] As an illustration, Mikkola considers the concept "water." In order to deploy the term correctly, we can refer to a colorless, odorless, and clear liquid in a glass, but we do not need to know, say, its chemical composition, which would be a requirement for its semantic function.[42] The difference between extension and semantics reveals how the conditions for *applicability* and *reference-fixing* are not the same. To correctly fix a reference, an extensional function is all

39. Mikkola, *Wrong of Injustice*, 105–6.
40. Mikkola, *Wrong of Injustice*, 106.
41. Mikkola, *Wrong of Injustice*, 106.
42. Mikkola, *Wrong of Injustice*, 106.

that needs to be exercised, while applicability requires justification from the concept's content. Once again: I can refer to the water as "water," but if asked what makes that term a right fit for that entity, conditions beyond mere referencing are required. Appropriately appreciating this difference makes sense of why parents celebrate a child's first use of a word like "water," while the child almost certainly does not know that the thing to which she is referring is composed of two molecules of hydrogen and one of oxygen. She can fix the reference, but not account for its applicability. The point to these distinctions is to say that gender terms are perfectly employable in an *extensional, reference-fixing* way: "We need not precisely specify what it takes for someone to count as a woman . . . in order to make good our reference fixing. Thus, my proposal is that in order to retain gender talk for politically relevant social explanations, we can merely rely on the reference-fixing extensional intuitions."[43] In other words, to use the term "woman," one does not need to specify all of the conditions necessary for being a woman.[44]

What *does* one need for the extensional reference-fixing of gender terms? Here Mikkola is happy to resort to the intuitions of ordinary speakers; in everyday life, when one leaves the feminist theory classroom, one simply does not have trouble using terms like "man" and "woman" coherently. Taking a "predoxastic" view of intuitions,[45] Mikkola suggests that extensional reference-fixing, since it does not purport to express the *content* of the term being used, can rely on intuitions, "which enables us to make sense of the common phenomenon that ordinary language users find it easy to apply gender terms, but they struggle to elucidate the grounds for their applications."[46] In the course of a day, we encounter many people, and usually (though not always) we can reliably refer to them by means of the gender terms on offer. These intuitions are little more than pre-reflective notions, which means that though they can guide the extensional application of a concept, they cannot

43. Mikkola, *Wrong of Injustice*, 106.
44. This insight, I believe, makes a crucial contribution to debates regarding gender pronouns. If the reference-fixing function of our gender terms, of which I take pronouns to be an instance, do not require strong commitments about the applicability of the metaphysics of the gendered individual, then no reason is left not to use preferred pronouns, if for no other reason than a desire to love the individual in question. On Mikkola's view, there is no metaphysical cost for doing so.
45. See Mikkola, *Wrong of Injustice*, 107–8: "Intuitions are predoxastic experiences. . . . Roughly, intuitions are like immediate 'gut feelings.' . . . When I have an intuition that Jill is a woman, I judge or have the inclination to judge *that* Jill is a woman."
46. Mikkola, *Wrong of Injustice*, 109.

tell us the content of the concept employed (i.e., they cannot answer the question "What is a woman?"), and they allow for a great deal of corrigibility. Nevertheless, they are sufficient for reference-fixing. Keeping this in mind, Mikkola concludes,

> Focusing on ordinary language users' willingness to apply "woman" is enough to pick out women's type, and this is sufficient to answer the representation problem (how to fix feminism's subject matter). . . . But, unlike other descriptive analyses, my project goes no further: it does not take the step to examining what our extensional intuitions disclose about the content of the concept *woman*. Rather than trying to get at conceptual content via use, my proposal simply attends to the use of "woman" without drawing (or aiming to draw) any conclusions about conceptual content. My view is that this suffices for fixing women's social kind.[47]

To summarize: Mikkola's solution to the problem of how gender terms appropriately refer to individuals is to lower the requirement to extensional, reference-fixing usage, not semantic, applicability usage. To say that someone is a woman (and is thereby included in certain political ambitions), one does not need to know *what* a woman is. Instead, all one needs are predoxastic intuitions that guide the reference but say nothing about the content of the term.

Having deflated the semantic puzzle, Mikkola proceeds to the ontological puzzle, whose pieces consist of gender's fundamental properties: Are there women and men? What makes them what they are? Once again, Mikkola suggests redrafting the terms doing the explanatory work. She argues that "we should give up the underlying sex/gender distinction" in feminist debates, opting instead for a framework that employs "traits" and "norms." Descriptive traits are "traits of which there are 'facts of the matter,'" while evaluative norms are "normative reactions to descriptive traits."[48] Notice, however, that the distinction is *not* between the social and the biological. Descriptive traits may include physical/anatomical traits (like chromosomes), appearance (like clothing and amount of body hair), and roles (like caretaking in the home).[49] Evaluative norms have more to do with "stereotypical reactions and judgments: whether one is viewed or judged to be, to appear, and/or to act in feminine, masculine, or neutral ways. The attributed evaluations include

47. Mikkola, *Wrong of Injustice*, 110–11.
48. Mikkola, *Wrong of Injustice*, 117.
49. See Mikkola, *Wrong of Injustice*, 129.

explicit judgments, but they also capture implicit social values and cultural norms that form the basis of further explicit cognitive attitudes."[50] On the basis of a descriptive norm, then, one forms an evaluative judgment: "having ovaries" or "wearing makeup" count as "feminine."[51] Mikkola's point is that these traits "covary" with norms, where the covariance relation amounts to us taking "certain traits to be of a certain kind."[52] When a culture views certain traits evaluatively so as to count certain individuals within a certain gender, then covariance has occurred.

Mikkola calls this view "quasi-essentialist," for while the evaluative norms create conditions for gender membership, "they merely *purport* to capture some facts about the world . . . when they do not."[53] Rather, the ones making the evaluative judgments on the basis of the descriptive norms "congeal" them into a pair without capturing "any genuinely essential definitional relation."[54] At this juncture, it seems to me that Mikkola's project fails. What "facts about the world" do the evaluative gender norms fail to capture? What genuinely essential definitional relation do these norms *aim* to identify but do so *mistakenly*? For that to be the case, there would have to be a genuine kind, with constitutive necessary conditions, that these norms have failed to capture. But this is not *quasi*-essentialism. It *is* essentialism! It is in principle possible for a culture's norms to identify these conditions correctly, but something about the process of forming these norms hindered them from doing so (the conditions of gendered oppression, the complexity of gender, etc.). Additionally, if classificatory essentialism genuinely allows for both biologically and culturally necessary and sufficient conditions, then there is no reason not to take a culture's evaluative norms as a genuine definitional essence in the classificatory sense (unless, of course, there is a real essence to gender that they have failed to define). Mikkola's proposal is highly suggestive insofar as it allows for a creative blend of cultural and biological categories, yet it does not seem to me to be different than essentialism or gender realism.

In her earlier article "Elizabeth Spelman, Gender Realism, and Women,"[55] Mikkola in fact defended just this kind of gender realism, and I want to

50. Mikkola, *Wrong of Injustice*, 129.
51. Mikkola's own example in *Wrong of Injustice*, 130.
52. Mikkola, *Wrong of Injustice*, 130.
53. Mikkola, *Wrong of Injustice*, 132.
54. Mikkola, *Wrong of Injustice*, 133.
55. Mari Mikkola, "Elizabeth Spelman, Gender Realism, and Women," *Hypatia* 21, no. 4 (2006): 77–96.

propose it as a more satisfactory solution to the ontological puzzle. In her later book, she does not reject the views of the article (in fact, she takes great pains to defend them),[56] but she considers them still too committed to the gender controversy. These earlier arguments, however, provide a clearer and more sophisticated account of the view to which Mikkola seems committed in her book. In the article, Mikkola defends gender realism against the exclusion arguments offered by Elizabeth Spelman (whose main contention is, recall, that definitions of gender are always specific to cultural variabilities, such as race and economic standing, to the point where generalizations about women are impossible). While appreciating Spelman's contributions, Mikkola writes, "I agree that the assumed definition of womanness that women supposedly have in common is clearly wrong and that it is not something women possess qua women. Nevertheless, the recognition that feminist theorists hold a false conception of what women qua women have in common does not give any reason to accept Spelman's conclusion—that there isn't a way to understand womanness such that all women qua women possess this feature. *Rather, Spelman's claim invites us to modify our conception of womanness and to rethink what women by virtue of their gender have (or might have) in common.*"[57] Mikkola's basic point is that the widespread errancy surrounding conceptions of womanhood is not a reason to reject that there is something that all women share *qua* women. In a manner, Mikkola is returning to the older social constructionist view that the problem we have encountered in understanding gender is not with our *metaphysics* but with our *epistemology*. The errors feminists and others have made in defining gender are to be expected for human beings whose epistemic faculties are far from perfect, especially when it comes to understanding highly complex essences like gender. Thus, "although the widespread feminist conception of what women (qua women) share is false, this does not give us any reason to think that there is nothing women by virtue of their gender share. It merely illustrates the need to modify feminist conceptions of womanness and to rethink this notion such that this feature is truly shared by all women (qua women)."[58] Mikkola maintains that gender realism, which holds that there are necessary and jointly sufficient conditions for membership in the kind "woman" that all women have in common, is perfectly consistent with just how wrong and exclusionist we

---

56. See Mikkola, *Wrong of Injustice*, 61–65.
57. Mikkola, "Elizabeth Spelman, Gender Realism, and Women," 83 (emphasis added).
58. Mikkola, "Elizabeth Spelman, Gender Realism, and Women," 84.

have been in defining women. In fact, gender realism is required if we are to know that, in point of fact, we have been wrong, for it provides the standard against which we measure our definitions.

Mikkola goes on to make an even stronger claim, saying not only that gender realism and corrigibility are compatible but also that the following two claims are compatible: "that women share the same feature of woman-ness and that they experience this feature differently from one another."[59] To establish this compatibility, she invites us to consider other universals, like justice. Realists about virtues like justice recognize that alongside the condi-tions that define its essence are other non-necessary accompaniments, such as where, when, and why justice is exercised within particular contexts.[60] What it takes for an act to be just will be the same wherever it is exercised, but just acts admit of variability of experience precisely because of the various ways they are exercised. In fact, the specificity of ordinary life is *necessary* for the universal of justice actually to characterize an action, for there are no such things as universal and context-free actions. Taking a stand against racial injustice and practicing equitable economic practices are both acts of justice, but they are different in their exercise and will be experienced differently by the agent. Mikkola's point is simply that this unity and variability has always been appreciated and recognized by realists about justice. Her idea is to ex-pand it to social entities like gender.

Mikkola captures gender's universal yet particular quality by calling it a "multiply realizable" social entity.[61] She makes a parallel with being an artist.[62] There are certain traits that make an artist (traits that unify Leonardo da Vinci and Vincent van Gogh *as* artists), yet it is in no way difficult to imagine that different artists can experience their artisthood differently on account of their contexts (da Vinci enjoyed considerable success and fame in his lifetime; van Gogh did not). All the same, an artist cannot be an artist apart from the

59. Mikkola, "Elizabeth Spelman, Gender Realism, and Women," 86. The focus on ex-perience derives from Spelman's own argument, which derives the diversity of definitions of womanhood from the diverse *experiences* of womanhood.

60. Mikkola, "Elizabeth Spelman, Gender Realism, and Women," 87, cites Bertrand Russell, who says, "If we ask ourselves what justice is, it is natural to proceed by considering this, that, and the other just act, with a view to discovering what they have in common. . . . This common nature, in virtue of which they are all just, will be justice itself, the pure essence the admixture of which with facts of ordinary life produces the multiplicity of just acts" (Bertrand Russell, *The Problems of Philosophy* [Oxford: Oxford University Press, 1967], 52). This "admixture" is precisely what allows for the diversity of feminine experiences.

61. Mikkola, *Wrong of Injustice*, 62.

62. See Mikkola, "Elizabeth Spelman, Gender Realism, and Women," 89.

particularly cultural ways she expresses her artisthood, even if what it means
to be an artist is not defined by those cultural conditions. In the same way,
to be a woman may still be a universal even if it is experienced in different
ways, which captures the intuition mentioned in the previous chapter that I
am the same gender as my grandfather, despite cultural differences. Mikkola
contends, "Intersectionality makes a difference to which social positions we
in fact end up occupying (and what material resources, say, are subsequently
available to us), but it does not change the underlying constitutive condition
(social position occupancy). Individual experiences alter the constitutive conditions of being a woman or an artist only if experiential considerations are
part and parcel of those conditions. Insofar as some gender realist positions
do not turn on experiential considerations, *these* gender realist positions
are not undermined by Spelman's particularity argument."[63] As long as the
gender realist maintains that there is a way in which particular experiences
and social manifestations are *necessary* for being a gender but not *definitive* of that gender identity (much as particular experiences are necessary
for being an artist but not definitive of "artist"), she can still maintain her
gender realism. I experience being a man in the United States in 2023 rather
differently than my grandfather experienced being a man in Brazil in 1963.
Our culturally particular experiences are necessary for us to be men, yet the
differences between our experiences do not change the fact that we share
masculinity in common.

Mikkola concludes by making recourse to a particular theory of universals
that she sees as having great compatibility with her gender realism—namely,
that of David Armstrong.[64] One of Armstrong's unique contributions was to
challenge the assumption that if something is unanalyzable (i.e., it cannot be
broken down into its constituent parts like necessary and sufficient conditions)
then it must be primitive or simple and therefore *unable* to be broken down
into such parts. By contrast, Armstrong insists that some universals are "epis-
temologically simple" in the sense that they "act . . . upon our sense-organs
in an all-or-nothing way."[65] But this epistemological simplicity need not cor-
relate with an ontological simplicity; rather, some universals are so *complex*
that they cannot but strike us homogeneously. Mikkola suggests that "human

63. Mikkola, *Wrong of Injustice*, 65.
64. See D. M. Armstrong, *A Theory of Universals: Universals and Scientific Realism*, vol. 2
(Cambridge: Cambridge University Press, 1978).
65. Armstrong, *Theory of Universals*, 53–54.

being" is one such universal (listing the necessary and sufficient conditions for being human has, of course, been a white whale to much philosophy); gender terms like "man" and "woman" are another. The complexity and inscrutability of the universal, however, does not disprove its existence. As Armstrong wryly comments, "In philosophy or elsewhere, if it proves difficult to give an account of some phenomenon, somebody is sure to suggest that the phenomenon does not exist"—so it is with gender skepticism![66] Yet Armstrong shows that unanalyzability may be a characteristic feature of many complex universals, making it rather difficult, under our current epistemic conditions, to name their necessary and sufficient conditions. If gender realism is understood in Armstrong's sense, then the "gender realist view would also not require that any necessary and sufficient conditions of womanness be pointed out. . . . Being complex, womanness would be extremely difficult to analyze and the kinds of problems Spelman pointed out would be encountered precisely with such complex features Armstrong discussed."[67] This would not disprove the existence of the universal "woman"; it would only prove the significant epistemic difficulties in specifying the conditions for membership within it.

All the same, Mikkola's theory of reference does not require such specification in order to refer to the kind or its members. All that is needed are the right kinds of intuitions that most speakers seem to have most of the time. To summarize my modified presentation of Mikkola's views: Mikkola is a gender realist who affirms that a highly complex set of necessary and jointly sufficient conditions must obtain in order for a person to be a member of the kind "woman." Mikkola refrains from saying just what these conditions are because we are epistemically disadvantaged from doing so. In this sense, her view is remarkably similar to John Stuart Mill's, but where Mill attributed our epistemic limitations to women's suppressed state, Mikkola adds on the ontological complexity of the kind. This, however, does not block off feminists from the reliable employment of the term. There is a way to fix a reference that avoids its semantic or content-specifying function—namely, by confining one's use to extensional functions. Extensional functions of reference guide the deployment of a term but say nothing about its content or definition. Yet, intuitions guide the user in fairly reliable ways and facilitate feminist political ambitions. In the end, we arrive at a nonbiological, fairly apophatic gender essentialism intended to facilitate feminist aims and ambitions.

66. Armstrong, *Theory of Universals*, 113–14.
67. Mikkola, "Elizabeth Spelman, Gender Realism, and Women," 92.

The purpose of this section's exposition of Witt and Mikkola is to distill four desiderata from their views that I propose chart the most promising way forward. Witt and Mikkola offer accounts of gender that break away from the chief problems afflicting a debate that has reduced to two simplistic options. Like any conversation with only two sides, the chief problems arise on account of the limited options available to its participants. Witt and Mikkola diversify how "essence" is understood, show how there might be epistemic difficulties in understanding such essences, retain moral evaluability, and make a connection between social goods and the sexed body. With views like theirs on offer, the debate cannot exist only between those who think gender is a social entity and those who think it is a biological entity. These four theses identify the most salient elements of their approaches.

3.3 Four Theses on the Metaphysics of Gender and Their Theological Grounding

3.3.1 Thesis 1: Gender is an essence, though this is not reducible to or identical with biological determinism or biological essentialism.

I begin with what, on the face of it, is the most controversial of my four theses. Essentialism has faced almost universal rejection within feminist theory, and if someone claims to espouse it, that is regularly seen as sufficient reason to dismiss their view. Often, this is justified, for many attempts to define "the nature of women" have in fact only served to prop up harmful stereotypes. Yet, if one moves beyond surface appearances, one sees that while gender essentialism *can* mean that, there are in fact at least four varieties of essentialism, some of which have the unsavory features just mentioned while others prove to be of immediate aid in theologies of gender. The one I propose here is a modest essentialism, the alternative to gender skepticism. First, however, let us disambiguate what has become a highly contested concept.

The first type of gender essentialism can be termed *biological essentialism*. This is usually the essentialism to which feminist literature objects and is the counterpoint to the social constructionist position. Typically, biological essentialists about gender either conflate sex and gender (such that gender is nothing but the properties that differentiate biological males from biological females) or partner sex with a theory of human action according to which social behavior is entirely or mainly derived from biological facts. On this view, characteristic gender traits are reducible to the biological features that distinguish males from females (like genes and gonads), and the accompanying theory of action is meant to bridge biology and social activity. One proponent of such a view is the Harvard evolutionary psychologist Steven Pinker, who maintains that the "single difference between the sexes" is a man's "greater desire for multiple partners" as a result of his evolutionary impulse to propagate his genes as widely as possible.[68] By contrast, women desire to secure resources from their mates, such as time and wealth, since their opportunities to reproduce are restricted.[69] The gendered behavior we witness in our world is derived from these evolutionary desires. Another example of this view from a very different corner of the theological ecosystem comes from recent complementarian theology that attempts to ground gendered authority relations in natural law.[70] In short, a biological essentialist holds that sex, specifically the biological features that differentiate males from females, fully account for gendered behavior.

There are many reasons to think that this is a highly problematic view, chief of which is its liability to repeat the mistake of attempting to infer natural traits from universal ones (a mistake that, as we have seen, was objected to as early as the seventeenth century). Often, appeals to what counts as "natural" behavior rely on the putatively "universal" observations of the one making the argument, yielding a view that is not only culturally parochial but also depends on an inference that is invalid. Even if it could be shown that some gender trait is universally demonstrated throughout all times and places, it still would not be the case that this trait can be assumed to be *natural*. Consider

68. Steven Pinker, *How the Mind Works* (1997; reissue ed., New York: Norton, 2009), 479.

69. Pinker, *How the Mind Works*, 479.

70. See, e.g., Steven Wedgeworth, "Good and Proper: Paul's Use of Nature, Custom, and Decorum in Pastoral Theology," *Eikon* 2, no. 2 (Fall 2020): 88–97. Apart from the criticism below, the appeal to natural law to make sense of gender seems rather doomed to me. Apart from general critiques of natural law, one might also point out the obvious fact that men and women have the same natures, making it unable to be the kind of thing that can ground gendered differences. To avoid this conceptual error, Thomas Aquinas, to whom these views appeal, held the view (derived from Aristotle) that the human nature women possess is a defective form of the human nature possessed by men, a view I hope these new natural lawyers will want to avoid. For further detail, see Francisco J. Carrasquillo and Hilaire K. de Romero, "Aquinas on the Inferiority of Woman," *American Catholic Philosophical Quarterly* 87, no. 4 (2013): 685–710; and Michael Nolan, "The Aristotelian Background to Aquinas's Denial That 'Woman Is a Defective Male,'" *Thomist* 64, no. 1 (January 1, 2000): 21–69. Wedgeworth, in particular, seems also to repeat the mistake of attempting to derive natural properties from universal properties.

a trivial counterexample:[71] It is universally the case that every human baby has not been born on the moon. Yet, if a baby was born on a space station on the moon, would that baby not possess a human nature? Of course it would, because universal properties and natural properties are not the same. This is precisely why biological essentialism often ends up baptizing culturally particular (and very often sexist) assumptions about men and women and inscribing them into "the law of nature," when at most they are merely universal. This is a point that very few biological essentialists seem to recognize, much less address.

The biological essentialist view is rightly rejected in most circles. But this is not the only way gender essentialism is understood. The second kind of gender essentialism encountered in theologies of gender is often referred to simply, and pejoratively, as *essentialism*. Here, the label "essentialist" is ascribed to views one perceives to be wrongheaded, and the negative connotations associated with the term are meant to persuade others away from supporting the view to which it is being ascribed.[72] In this parlance, "essentialist" is a word like "fundamentalist": remarkably difficult to define but with such negative overtones that surely one would not want to be one.[73] I also want to distance myself from this employment of the term, for it almost always serves only to increase heat, not light.

If these first two ways of understanding gender essentialism are unfit for Christian theology, how else might one understand the concept, and perhaps more beneficially? There are two remaining gender essentialisms that I believe are defensible and entirely consistent with active interests in justice, equality, debunking oppression, and the like. The third in the list is gender *kind essentialism*. Kind essentialism simply maintains that "there is a property or properties definitive of membership in that kind."[74] A kind is a category,

---

71. Borrowed from Thomas Morris, *The Logic of God Incarnate* (1986; repr., Eugene, OR: Wipf & Stock, 2001), 63.

72. This use of "essentialist" is widespread in the literature on gender and theology. With any amount of exposure, one will encounter it. It is also a distinctive feature of queer theology. See Patrick Cheng, "Contributions from Queer Theory," in *The Oxford Handbook of Theology, Sexuality, and Gender*, ed. Adrian Thatcher (New York: Oxford University Press, 2015), 156: "Queerness . . . resists and challenges this essentialist way of thinking about sexual and gender identities." In context, "essentialist" means "immutable," something Cheng perceives to be a deleterious feature of a view.

73. On the charge of fundamentalism, with which this use of "essentialism" shares structural parity, see Alvin Plantinga, *Warranted Christian Belief* (New York: Oxford University Press, 2000), 244–45.

74. Witt, "What Is Gender Essentialism?," 12.

and in order to be included within the kind, an entity must exhibit a set of properties definitive of the kind. So, in order to be a member of the kind "pine tree," something must be coniferous, be green all year round, have needles, have a particular smell, and have all the other traits that make something a pine tree. Applied to gender, kind essentialism maintains that "women (and men) are kinds whose members share a defining property" or properties.[75] This is identical with what Mikkola calls "classificatory essentialism" or "gender realism," and it is minimally required of anyone who denies gender skepticism.

It is important to offer some clarifications. Gender kind essentialism is a metaphysically modest view. All it claims is that there is *something* necessary for membership in gender kinds. That *something* does not need to be biological, as the theorists above have shown. One might be a social constructionist and maintain that the processes of social construction are what provided the conditions necessary for gender kind membership. If one thinks a man is someone characterized by certain social features (such as wearing these clothes and not those), one is a kind essentialist about gender. Those things define what it is to be a man. This shows that *kind essentialism should not be equated with biological essentialism*. While biological essentialists hold that the conditions for gender membership are biological (and ascribe to a theory about human action according to which particular social behaviors follow from particular biological traits), kind essentialists are open to the possibility that the conditions for gender membership may be non-biological.

Moreover, the *something* necessary for gender kind membership does not need to be specifiable by the person holding the view. The affirmation that women share in common *qua* women something that is constitutive of the kind does not require one to say with certainty what it is. Perhaps it is just beyond a human's ability to know what it is (see thesis 2). This is Mikkola's earlier view: there is something that makes men *men* and women *women*, but for various reasons, we cannot say what it is. Like the early social constructionists who pointed to social oppression as a cloud masking the nature of women, Mikkola maintains that there *are* women and men but that denoting with clarity their necessary and sufficient conditions is something beyond human epistemic capacities. Guided by certain intuitions and moral concerns, we can say what gender is *not*, but it would be too ambitious to claim to know with precision the necessary and jointly sufficient conditions for such a complex kind as gender.

75. Witt, "What Is Gender Essentialism?," 13.

Serene Jones, in her book *Feminist Theory and Christian Theology*, has defended a position similar to this, yet from a distinctly Christian theological vantage point. Jones calls the position "eschatological essentialism."[76] It begins with an affirmation of a modest kind essentialism that "finds positive value in making essentialist claims about human nature in general and women's nature in particular," believing claims like this to be important for collective action in support of human and women's rights.[77] Yet these claims are situated within a particular picture of human epistemic and moral capacities and are seen to be always corrigible and in need of revision and improvement: eschatological essentialism "stays open to critique and hence continually revises its 'universals.'"[78] Revision occurs not because the universals do not exist but because the human capacity to know them is compromised. This is because "feminist theology affirms that sin—a fundamental fault line running through humanity—twists thought and distorts the vision of humanity."[79] For this reason, eschatological essentialism maintains that it is only when these epistemic deficiencies are cured that we will have unproblematic access to gender's essence. Because of sin, eschatological essentialism, this side of the consummation of all things, "recognizes the need for constant revision and critique of the vision it proclaims."[80] Jones's move is elegant in its simplicity. It recognizes the need for a modest essentialism in order to avoid gender skepticism and the moral sterility it lands in, yet it remains sensitive to the abuses and limitations of essentialist claims.

Christians must realize that statements about human beings and their genders are always indexed to the particular time they occupy in the economy. Jones's view recognizes that we do not yet enjoy the full benefits of the resurrection and that, at present, creation still creaks and groans under the reign of death in anticipation of the return of its King (Rom. 8:22). Yet she is willing to emphasize the importance of God's creation of humankind in God's image, for "male and female he created them" (Gen. 1:27). Gendered creation is not something to be shrugged off or eradicated, as the theological implications of

76. It is worthwhile to note that Jones fits neatly with the theorists above in her belief "that the divide between essentialists and constructivists fails to capture the complexity of daily experience" (Serene Jones, *Feminist Theory and Christian Theology: Cartographies of Grace* [Minneapolis: Fortress, 2000], 44).

77. Jones, *Feminist Theory and Christian Theology*, 45.

78. Jones, *Feminist Theory and Christian Theology*, 46.

79. Jones, *Feminist Theory and Christian Theology*, 52.

80. Jones, *Feminist Theory and Christian Theology*, 54.

gender skepticism suggest, but it would be overly ambitious to say that we can return to the garden as though sin had never entered the picture. Christians confess a redemption ultimately fulfilled in the eschaton, where what it means to be women and men will be seen and experienced in the way it ought to be. As Carla Swafford Works testifies, "The male-female dichotomy—which was created by God—will not be erased, but *redeemed*. Gender is not removed; the relationship between the genders is rectified. God is not a creator of uniformity, but diversity."[81] Jones's eschatological essentialism—which maintains that there are properties the bearing of which is sufficient for kind membership but that our ideas of those properties must be constantly revised as we recognize our errors—is a fitting way of maintaining the balance between the stability needed to avoid gender skepticism and the corrigibility demanded of the age between Christ's advent and parousia.

There is, finally, a fourth type of gender essentialism: the type commonly called *individual essentialism*. On this view, "there is a property or properties that make that individual the individual that it is."[82] Here the concern is not about kinds but about what picks out an individual—that is, what makes you the very individual that you are rather than someone else. There are certain things that could have been different about a person without changing the fact that they are still that same person. I could have been born blond, for instance. However, certain other properties are not like that; if I lacked these properties, I would not be the very same individual that I am, numerically speaking. Applied to gender, being a woman or being a man is individually essential to a person in that they would be a different individual if they were a different gender.[83] A test case for individual essentialist intuitions can be drawn from *Doctor Who*. The first through the twelfth Doctors were men, but the much-anticipated thirteenth Doctor regenerated as a woman. Are Doctors one

---

81. Carla Swafford Works, *The Least of These: Paul and the Marginalized* (Grand Rapids: Eerdmans, 2020), 85. While Works refers to sexed bodies in the quote, on her reading of the Pauline epistles the same conclusion applies to gender.

82. Witt, "What Is Gender Essentialism?," 12. For more on its metaphysics, see Alvin Plantinga, *The Nature of Necessity* (New York: Oxford University Press, 1974); and Saul Kripke, *Naming and Necessity* (Malden, MA: Blackwell, 1981).

83. For an example of this view, see Anthony Appiah, "'But Would That Still Be Me?' Notes on Gender, 'Race,' Ethnicity, as Sources of 'Identity,'" *Journal of Philosophy* 87, no. 10 (October 1990): 493–99. For Appiah, gender is not individually essential to a person but to what he calls an "ethical self," such that being a different gender entails being a different ethical self. For a theological example that relies on Scotus's account of essentialism, see Daniel Horan, "Beyond Essentialism and Complementarity: Toward a Theological Anthropology Rooted in *Haecceitas*," *Theological Studies* 75, no. 1 (2014): 94–117.

through twelve the same individual as the thirteenth Doctor? An individual essentialist would say no. Of course, the decision one comes to regarding individual gender essentialism will have implications for questions about issues like trans* identities, and I do not intend to settle such matters at this point. I simply highlight this as a fourth viable version of gender essentialism.

Gender essentialism, understood as kind essentialism, is, I conclude, a position worthy of assent. By it one avoids gender skepticism and leaves appropriately open the question of whether the conditions for kind membership are social or biological or both (and the question of whether we have identified the correct ones). It allows one to resist the bifurcations persisting in theological gender debates while still affirming a robust, if modest, metaphysical position. All the same, this position requires a broader epistemic picture in order to understand why we are limited and just how much access one might have to gender's essence. Let us turn to that now.

3.3.2 Thesis 2: The complexity of gender, the noetic effects of sin, and the current conditions of oppression complicate our epistemic access to gender's essence. All the same, we can be assured that issues surrounding gender will be rectified in the eschaton.

Mikkola's presentation has shown us that certain universals (or, in the nomenclature of the last section, kind essences), like "human being," might be so complex that they cannot help but strike us in an all-or-nothing way. It is difficult for minds like ours to break down such universals into their constituent parts because of their remarkable intricacy. She went on to claim that gender terms like "man" and "woman" are universals of this sort, and for this reason it is hard to specify just which conditions are necessary and jointly sufficient for membership in gender kinds. Moreover, in the previous chapter, John Stuart Mill's view that the unnatural conditions of subjection obscure the nature of women was introduced—for such an unnatural state cannot help but complicate our discernment of what is natural and what is simply universal. Some gender traits, he maintained, might just be ubiquitous without defining the *nature* of gender. I wish to uphold these affirmations for theological reasons.

Though the complexity of essences and current states of oppression are two powerful reasons to show epistemic restraint, I want now to suggest that Christians have unique reasons to deny that we have unproblematic or complete access to gender's definition or that we experience gender in the way it ought to be experienced. In discussing Serene Jones's eschatological essentialism, we have already seen that we ought to allocate certain epistemic capacities and incapacities to different moments in the economy.[84] In creation, humanity knew God and one another and it was good (Gen. 2:20–24). Upon the introduction of sin, "they knew that they were naked" (Gen. 3:7), yet here knowledge is acquired in direct disobedience to God, introducing into all creation the reign of sin and death, a reality implicating the proper function and harmony of all things, noetic faculties included. As a result, Paul describes fallen humanity as "futile in their thinking" (Rom. 1:21) and "darkened in their understanding" (Eph. 4:18). Even redeemed individuals are considered epistemically *immature* (Eph. 4:11–13) and vulnerable to sway in this direction or that. This is because, to cite a familiar verse, "now we see in a mirror, dimly, but then we will see face to face. Now I know only in part; then I will know fully, even as I have been fully known" (1 Cor. 13:12). It is only when the beatific vision is bestowed upon Christians that the world will be seen in its clearest light (see 1 John 3:2).

All of this means, of course, that we will understand humanity and gender only from the perspective of our resurrection. As Alan Torrance reminds us, we must "conceive of human nature *eschatologically* . . . and thus neither naturalistically nor in some transcendentalist manner that fails to center its thinking on God's promise of new creation for all things. . . . Properly functional human nature, therefore, requires to be conceived first and foremost eschatologically. Only 'retrospectively,' therefore, in the light of the promised consummation of God's creative purposes, can we perceive the telos that defines our 'natures.'"[85] The sheer complexity of gender, the oppressive conditions that prevent us from seeing it clearly, and the epistemic effects of sin will be overcome when we are raised again, and only then will we see gender clearly.

But does this mean that we can say nothing about gender here and now? Not at all. First, a commitment to corrigibility does not require a commitment to silence or relativity. It *does* require a dedication to epistemic humility among other epistemic virtues, but one can still venture claims about gender

84. For a clear exposition of these different epistemic capacities along the biblical storyline, see Dru Johnson, *Biblical Knowing: A Scriptural Epistemology of Error* (Eugene, OR: Cascade, 2013).

85. Alan J. Torrance, "Is There a Distinctive Human Nature? Approaching the Question from a Christian Epistemic Base," *Zygon* 47, no. 4 (December 2012): 912.

and evaluate their truth or falsehood. It is precisely *because* we know that there is a standard against which we measure our claims that we have the confidence to make them. Accountability increases confidence in our theological work; it does not diminish it. That is why, when discussing a doctrine like divine simplicity, Oliver Crisp suggests that what theologians do is offer "models," where a model is a "theoretical construction that only approximates to verisimilitude, offering a simplified account of a particular data set or (in this case) cluster of theological doctrines."[86] A model of an airplane is not the same as the airplane itself, but it reliably represents features of the airplane it aims to depict. This does not mean that models are not true; they are truth-apt and can guide the theologian in proper reasoning about lofty matters. Crisp maintains that this posture "comports with an intellectual humility on the part of the theologian: it may be that we are unable to capture the truth of divine simplicity because we are incapable of understanding it as finite creatures or do not have the epistemic access to comprehend the doctrine, which is part of the divine nature."[87] If gender is a complex subject that pushes us to the edges of our noetic abilities, the complexity only increases when we turn to divine simplicity! Nevertheless, the theologian is able to offer models that aim to capture some truth of the matter, and such models can be evaluated. Additionally, we already have in place a means by which gender references can be fixed without fully, completely, or incorrigibly knowing their definitions. By drawing on Mikkola's views, we can carry on the task of model building, knowing that fixing the reference of gender terms does not require specifying their applicability.

By what standard, however, can one measure such models? Though one ought to show appropriate reservation in making claims about gender, certain parameters are available to guide theological reflection. God's canonical self-disclosure in Holy Scripture is surely one such means (indeed, the *primary* means, on my view), but one must also develop the ability to read Scripture well. Additionally, it seems to me that the theologian of gender, given other facts she knows about God and God's activity, can be guided by certain *moral* facts. Chiefly, as will be stated in the third thesis, any theologically viable account of gender will be able to support the cultivation of justice.

86. Oliver D. Crisp, *Analyzing Doctrine: Toward a Systematic Theology* (Waco: Baylor University Press, 2019), 54. See also William Wood, "Modeling Mystery," *Scientia et Fides* 4, no. 1 (2016): 39–59.
    87. Crisp, *Analyzing Doctrine*, 55.

3.3.3 Thesis 3: Any theory or theology of gender must be consistent with and supportive of the cultivation of justice.

"But let justice roll down like waters," Amos 5:24 famously states, "and righteousness like an ever-flowing stream." Micah 6:8 likewise affirms in superlative terms: "He has told you, O mortal, what is good; and what does the Lord require of you but to do justice, and to love kindness, and to walk humbly with your God?" God's *mishpat*, or justice, is mentioned at least 421 times in the Hebrew Bible, and verses such as these have undergirded the crucial importance of justice for Christian moral theology.[88] Justice has meant many different things in the writings of those interested in gender, and a fuller discussion of its properties must await chapter 7. Nevertheless, it is uncontroversial to state that a *perfectly just state of affairs* is not one where harm, wrong, oppression, malice, wickedness, and all other kinds of evil persist. It is equally uncontentious to claim that God's purposes for creation, fulfilled in the eschaton, will be distinctly characterized by justice (see Isa. 32:16; Rev. 19:2; 21:4, 8). Taken together, these claims are sufficient to prove that God has not intended gender to be characterized by injustice and that proposals about gender that fail to support the cultivation of justice fall outside of the possibilities for theological consideration.

This is another way to state the second charge made against social constructionist views of gender in the previous chapter. Because gender, on that position, becomes morally unevaluable, it cannot sustain the moral weight required to pursue justice. Gender skepticism, because it denies that there are stable meanings to gender terms, is not a robust enough view to sustain the requisite pursuits of justice in which Christians ought to be engaged. If we cannot say with clarity that there are women, then it becomes impossible to say that women are the disproportionate recipients of certain injustices and that it is they (and not some other category of people) who have been denied certain rights. Thus, though I advocated for epistemic restraint in the previous thesis, this restraint cannot result in a position where certain moral truths about gender are no longer possible to advance. Our accounts of gender must be definite enough to support the pursuit of justice, and we can be assured, by other things we know about divine action, that no account that fails to be so is true.

One way, then, to adjudicate theological proposals about gender from within an appropriate epistemic context is to ask whether they are able to

---

88. For a fuller development of my own account, see Fellipe do Vale, "Justice, Grace, and Love: A Theological Commendation," *Trinity Journal* 42 (2021): 185–200.

sustain and promote the cultivation of justice. If one's theology of gender is unable to pick out instances of gendered oppression with consistency and provide the appropriate categories to make sense of them, then there is a serious flaw with it. The upshot is, then, that no theology of gender that cannot challenge male dominance, misogyny, sexual assault, violence against women, or any other kind of gendered injustice is fit for Christian assent. A fuller discussion of the relationship of grace, justice, and gender will be undertaken in chapter 7. For now, I am attempting to restate the negative argument from chapter 2 and articulate a positive, constructive desideratum. Gender should not be morally unevaluable. Theories of gender should be aimed at justice.

3.3.4 Thesis 4: Gender is concerned with selves or identity and with the way selves organize social goods pertaining to their sexed bodies.

I began this chapter by noting that those who uphold the bifurcation between social construction and nature have a tendency to deflate the component opposite to their view; that is, social constructionists tend to treat the body as a mere object unable to generate moral norms, while biological gender essentialists tend to regard the social components of gender as irrelevant stereotypes that need not figure into their accounts of gender. By contrast, Witt and Mikkola have shown that resisting the bifurcation allows one to see the importance of the body *and* its social manifestations. By producing the concept of a "social self" and by noting the ways in which biological processes take on social significance when they are situated in a context that adds to them further social conditions, Witt helps us see how certain roles and positions are socially *manifested*, even if they are not socially *constructed*. Mikkola's point that social properties and biological properties are both *descriptive* and *evaluative* helps us see how both can play a role in a theory of gender. The claim I would like to make now, and to unpack in greater detail in the next two chapters, is that gender cannot be neatly categorized as either social *or* biological. Rather, gender is about the appropriation of social goods that pertain to our biologically sexed bodies, an appropriation that enables sexed bodies to acquire social meaning.

When Scripture appears to discuss gender as something more than the biological differences in question, it does so by giving prescriptions on wise negotiation of social goods that are relevant to those sexed bodies. This, in fact, is one of the overarching claims of Cynthia Westfall's major work *Paul and Gender.* Westfall argues that when Paul makes statements about gender, he is attempting to keep in balance two motivations. First, he is describing ways in which the gospel challenges and subverts regnant first-century cultural paradigms about women and men, paradigms that run against the things for which the church ought to be known. Second, he is remaining sensitive to the Greco-Roman culture in which his churches are located and providing for them norms that will allow the mission to the gentiles to go on without significant obstacles from the outside. Thus Westfall: "In order for Paul's gentile mission to succeed, the behavior of Christian women would need to be consistent with what was practiced by women in the broader first-century Greco-Roman world. Therefore, Paul's gender concerns were often missional when he addressed gender roles in the church and the home, and his intention was for believers to fit into the culture while remaining ethically pure."[89] Simultaneously, "Paul in fact subverted the Greco-Roman household codes by reframing the basis, purpose, and motivation for the behavior of social inferiors, and by adjusting and restricting the privileges of those who have power."[90] Overall, with regard to both the broader society and the distinctly countercultural norms of Christianity, Paul was concerned that "the word of God may not be discredited" (Titus 2:5). Or, as Westfall puts it, Paul's missional goal was "to make the gospel attractive," to highlight the important ways in which the gospel was noticeably countercultural while avoiding or correcting misconceptions about the churches that would make them appear dangerous to outsiders.[91]

This means that, for Paul, gender was about the wise organization of social goods, where that wisdom consisted in recognizing the gendered goods one encounters in one's world and finding ways to conform those nuances with the norms appropriate to being united to Christ. This is perhaps clearest in his discussion of veiling in 1 Corinthians 11:4–16. What is he doing there? Is he advocating for a public symbol that kept a woman in her place—that is, lower than the unveiled men in the house church gathering? Understanding

---

89. Cynthia Long Westfall, *Paul and Gender: Reclaiming the Apostle's Vision for Men and Women in Christ* (Grand Rapids: Baker Academic, 2016), 13.

90. Westfall, *Paul and Gender*, 163.

91. Westfall, *Paul and Gender*, 163. For a similar analysis of Paul's approach, see John M. G. Barclay, "What Makes Paul Challenging Today?," in *The New Cambridge Companion to St. Paul*, ed. Bruce W. Longenecker (New York: Cambridge University Press, 2020), 299–318. Shively Smith captures this sentiment well in her monograph on 1 Peter: "The author commands submission not because it was God's way but because it was his way of mitigating the conspicuousness of his community and keeping members alive" (*Strangers to Family: Diaspora and 1 Peter's Invention of God's Household* [Waco: Baylor University Press, 2016], 165).

the veiling practices of the first-century Greco-Roman world suggests, in fact, that this was not at all the case. Veils, by and large, were worn by women with the greatest privilege to demonstrate their wealth, modesty, sexual cleanliness, respect, and piety.[92] The discussion about the Eucharist that immediately follows indicates the presence of a power imbalance,[93] which suggests that veil wearing was a sign of privilege that was playing far too significant a role in the Corinthian church, and that this cultural structure needed to be reckoned with. Veils were indicators of social capital, and it is crucial to observe that the most dignified and powerful women in the ancient world "were those who had *the right* to wear a veil in public."[94] By contrast, those who lacked social capital were prevented from wearing a veil. If someone was deprived of the status of a Roman wife, was accused of adultery, or was a prostitute (which often meant being enslaved and forced into such occupation), then they were seen as lacking the requisite dignity to wear a symbol depicting lofty status. What's more, because exposed hair was perceived as sexually arousing, women who did not veil were judged to be sexually available and were therefore vulnerable to the desire of men. Westfall's verdict on this sordid state of affairs is that "keeping certain classes of women unveiled was considered to be in the interests of men as a group, and laws were made and enforced that prevented women who were deemed without honor from veiling, which included prostitutes, slaves, freedwomen, and women in the lowest classes. This not only signaled that such women were sexually available, but also maintained the social order and a distinction between classes."[95] So, veiling was indeed part of a sexist cultural practice that disadvantaged women, but not because it was a sign of dishonor. Rather, a veil was a sign of privilege and sexual purity, and being deprived of the right to wear one placed a woman in a position of lower worth, which made her vulnerable to sexual attack.

Consider, then, going up to pray in a church service as a Corinthian woman with an uncovered head. It would be advertising sexual availability in a context where the sacrifice of Christ is being remembered. In this light, Paul's exhortation for *all* women to veil takes on a far more liberative and equalizing

92. See, for example, Sarah Ruden, *Paul among the People: The Apostle Reinterpreted and Reimagined in His Own Time* (New York: Pantheon, 2010), 86–87.

93. For this claim, see Gerd Theissen, *The Social Setting of Pauline Christianity*, ed. and trans. John J. Schütz (Edinburgh: T&T Clark, 1982).

94. Works, *Least of These*, 61 (emphasis added).

95. Westfall, *Paul and Gender*, 33. See also 97: "An uncovered head told them whom they could solicit for sex without consequences."

tone. It no longer mattered that one was divorced or a slave-prostitute; such symbols of worth are rendered obsolete in Christ. Divorcees and prostitutes can receive sexual protection in a Pauline church by wearing a veil, according to Paul. Westfall powerfully concludes, "Paul's support of *all* women veiling equalized the social relationships in the community; inasmuch as such veiling was in his control, he secured respect, honor, and sexual purity for women in the church who were denied that status in the culture."[96] Works agrees: "Paul's advice here—for *all* women to pray and prophesy with a covering— would be countercultural. It would grant status to women who, outside the church, could never hope to be treated with the respect granted a Roman wife. . . . Donning the veil treated all women with human dignity and respect."[97] Finally, Ruden calls us to imagine looking at the assembled congregation and noting how, with all women veiled, one could not tell who had power and prestige and who was elsewhere looked at lasciviously on account of their low social status.[98] Paul's command, while sensitive to the regnant cultural practices, flew in the face of the sinful, oppressive, and sexist world in which the churches found themselves.

What does this show about how Paul approaches gender? It shows that Paul would not have been content to dismiss veil wearing as a mere cultural stereotype that made no difference to gender. It mattered deeply for those women whose inability to wear a veil in everyday life made them appear to be items for sexual consumption, and therefore it mattered deeply for Paul. Social expressions of our created givenness as males and females needed to be interpreted and taken up into right Christian practice, for the sake of the gospel. In other words, Paul is concerned about the right organization of goods pertaining to our sexed bodies. The allusions to Genesis 1 and 2 (1 Cor. 11:8–9, 12) reveal that Paul considers created sexual embodiment as relevant, but relevant because of the social goods attached to those bodies when they are socially mediated. Created females were those who, in Corinth, needed to consider how best to use the cultural symbol of a veil. It was not created males who needed to be concerned about this, for their maleness afforded them the privilege of not worrying about *this* social good (though the system of which veiling was a part granted to them considerable power by comparison to women, particularly power for doing violence). It was gender, expressed

96. Westfall, *Paul and Gender*, 33–34.
97. Works, *Least of These*, 62.
98. Ruden, *Paul among the People*, 88.

in distinct right or wrong social manifestations, that was the object of Paul's
concern, along with how males responded to those manifestations in a Christ-
like manner.[99] Discerning the right expression of social goods that pertained
to the sexed body, ultimately, was Paul's approach to gender.

As will become clearer later, this relieves the church of the need to make up
gender out of thin air. The theological task is not to *define* gender, prescribing
traits and roles apart from considerations of context, as though gender existed
in isolation from the concrete experiences of people in particular times and
places. The theological task, rather, is this: to discern, and subsequently to
morally evaluate, those gendered goods we already find ourselves encountering
simply by participating in a world where others exist. Paul was not *defining*
gender when he commended the women of Corinth to wear veils; rather, he was
taking stock of the concrete gendered goods *already* constituting the church's
life and providing a robust moral evaluation of them by drawing out the implications of the gospel. Gender does not need to be defined by theologians. It
needs to be filtered through the lens of what must not "be rejected, provided it is
received with thanksgiving" (1 Tim. 4:4) and what must be rejected as evil (Ps.
36:4). The theologian's responsibility lies with this task of moral discernment,
not with pronouncements of what gender must be, as though we were not all
already gendered and simply waiting for abstract "gender roles" to perform.

More needs to be said about how this occurs. The thesis I hope to have
advanced is merely *that* gender is about the way we attach ourselves to certain social goods as a means of socially mediating our sexed bodies. *How*
this happens—that is, how these social goods become attached to us in such
a way that they form *who* we are—will be explored next, and it will have
everything to do with the nature of love. For now, though, I conclude that
for Paul, and for many of the theorists considered in this chapter, gender is
neither *merely* social (as though the body were just an inert object on which

---

99. One might raise the objection that, because of my emphasis on sex, I am building into
my definition of gender conditions that would preclude at the outset transgender and trans*
affirmation. I do not think the view I am proposing precludes such affirmation, because more
would need to be said to yield a position on the matter. In fact, I think it is compatible both with
full trans* affirmation as well as the vast range of other approaches available on this complex
issue. To affirm trans* identities using this understanding of gender, one would simply have to
add that what is at issue is *perceived* biological traits, that an individual need only be *perceived*
as having a certain sexed body to be truly of a certain gender (whether or not their body is, in
fact, so sexed). This is a standard move in feminist theory, as attested to by Witt's position. All
this is to say that, in the end, my view does not decide the matter one way or another; rather,
it addresses a question conceptually upstream of these considerations.

social meanings are constructed) nor *merely* biological (as though the social goods we encounter daily had nothing to do with it). Our having been made female and male is a matter for social manifestation insofar as we organize social goods relevant to being sexed.

3.4 Conclusion

By way of conclusion, allow me to summarize the central claims of this chapter. In an effort to move beyond the bifurcation in the literature on gender between essences and social constructs, I have examined the views of Charlotte Witt and Mari Mikkola, two feminist theorists who are attempting to provide fresh accounts of gender. Both are essentialists who incorporate social aspects into their essentialism. For Witt, gender is a social position that organizes all the other social positions that a social individual occupies, and it is a position constituted by the engendering function, which is what reproduction looks like when it is taken up into the social realm and attached to other social responsibilities. For Mikkola, a minimal kind of essentialism is necessary in order to avoid gender skepticism, a position many feminists worry undermines the political ambitions of their work. Nevertheless, she argues that we do not need to be able to specify the necessary and jointly sufficient conditions for a gender kind in order to refer to it or to know that it is an essence.

From their positions, I extracted four theses for a theory of gender. They were:

1. Gender is an essence, though this is not reducible to or identical with biological determinism or biological essentialism.
2. The complexity of gender, the noetic effects of sin, and the current conditions of oppression complicate our epistemic access to gender's essence. All the same, we can be assured that issues surrounding gender will be rectified in the eschaton.
3. Any theory or theology of gender must be consistent with and supportive of the cultivation of justice.
4. Gender is concerned with selves or identity and with the way selves organize social goods pertaining to their sexed bodies.

I posited that genders must be essences if we are to avoid gender skepticism but that we should think of them, more specifically, as kind essences (while still rejecting biological essentialism). Also, if genders are essences, it does not follow that we have clear, uncomplicated, or complete access to the conditions that compose them. In fact, the complexity of the essence, the current conditions of oppression, and the noetic effects of sin make that rather difficult. This ought to commend to us epistemic humility in defining gender, but it does not mean that we must be entirely silent. Theologians may be guided by certain moral norms of whose truth they are assured—for example, no model of gender is theologically viable if it cannot sustain the cultivation of justice. All the same, Christians must be keenly aware, as the apostle Paul was, of the importance of the right organization of social goods. Gender is tied to our created, sexed embodiment, but discipleship consists in knowing how to make use of and attach ourselves to cultural goods in ways consistent with the gospel.

This overview surely leaves questions unanswered. In particular, the final thesis raises the important question of the relationship between the body and its social manifestation. How is it that we become who we are through the social lives we live? In particular, how does one acquire a gender identity by means of cultural goods to which one attaches oneself? Very often, gender discussions orbit around the notion of *identifying* as a member of a particular gender kind. This is made obvious when one hears "I identify as man" or "Some people don't identify with any gender." Unfortunately, little to no theological attention has been given to the notion of identification. This is particularly disappointing when one realizes how richly the Christian tradition has spoken about human identity. The view for which I argue in the remainder of this work will take seriously such comments. Already mentioned is a shorthand definition of gender that I find acceptable; it is the appropriation of cultural goods pertaining to the sexed body by means of which the sexed body is socially manifested. "Appropriation," however, will be a theologically important term, for the way goods are appropriated will go on to shape gender identity. Specifically, in the next two chapters I shall argue that gender identity has primarily to do with what one *loves*, for loving is the shaping force in making us who we are. In chapter 4 I shall develop an Augustinian theology of human love, and in chapter 5 I shall put the pieces together to argue that gender is a species of human love: love, which is *both embodied and social*, is the means by which we appropriate social goods and manifest our sexed bodies. A picture of gender identity will emerge that, drawing on the four foundational theses established above, has deep roots in our identity as creatures and has a clear connection to our social lives.

FOUR

An Augustinian Theology
of Human Love

Chapter 3 introduced four theses that constitute the foundations for my proposal. The fourth of these claimed that gender is concerned with the way selves organize social goods pertaining to their sexed bodies. In this chapter, I go into further detail about how individuals appropriate social goods to themselves, thereby forming their identities. Human beings, I claim, are what they love in the sense that the objects of their love shape their identity. Human beings are created to love God above all else and to love created goods in God, all while becoming conformed to these objects of love. Love requires an order and is easily disfigured into a lust for selfish power and domination. Love also has the capacity to form humans into social communities wherein identities are shared and goods are held in common. All of these claims, which will guide us in this chapter, stem from the theology of human love advanced by Augustine. By the end, a framework for how social goods are identity forming will have been provided, in order to set up the following chapter's claim that gendered social goods are formative for gender identity, while neglecting neither created nor social dimensions.

4.1 Love, Identity, and an *Apologia* for Augustine

Within conversations about gender, it is common to hear the language of "identity." For example, the DSM-5 defines "gender identity" as "a category

111

of social identity and refers to an individual's *identification* as male, female, or, occasionally, some category other than male or female."[1] The DSM's treatment stands as a representative statement that identity and identification language is fairly standard in current approaches to gender. Theologians, by contrast, have been critical of identity language, often because of the particularly "modernist" overtones of contemporary articulations.[2] Senses of identity after the sexual revolution, it is alleged, are far too individualistic, internalist, and voluntaristic. Christians should, therefore, reject attempts to characterize gender in such terms.

My point here is simply to show that while modern identification language is widely accepted, it tends to be rejected within theology, even when no better alternative is offered. Perhaps the conflict in question arises from the all-or-nothing approach of those disparaging the claims of individuals to identify as members of a certain gender, failing to see that perhaps there is a "precious clue"[3] woven into such claims. After all, the Christian tradition has had a great deal to say about the nature of identity and what is fundamentally true about human beings, even if such approaches are markedly different from identity language used today. The theological motivation to think about identity has come from texts like 1 Samuel 16:7: "Do not look on his appearance or on the height of his stature, because I have rejected him; for the LORD does not see as mortals see; they look on the outward appearance, but the LORD looks on the heart." Our identities are, so it seems, our *hearts*, or that place from which our love proceeds.[4] The full rejection of articulations of "gender identities," then, may not be sufficiently nuanced to craft a salutary way forward.

In the previous chapter, I argued that gender has a great deal to do with personal identities, particularly the way social goods are attached to selves. I claimed, from Paul's treatment of veiling, that gender is defined by the

---

1. *Diagnostic and Statistical Manual of Mental Disorders*, 5th ed. (Washington, DC: American Psychiatric Publishing, 2013), 451 (emphasis added).

2. See, e.g., Carl Trueman, *The Rise and Triumph of the Modern Self: Cultural Amnesia, Expressive Individualism, and the Road to the Sexual Revolution* (Wheaton: Crossway, 2020). For a critical analysis of this approach, see Fellipe do Vale, "Book Review: The Rise and Triumph of the Modern Self," *The London Lyceum*, April 27, 2021, https://www.thelondonlyceum.com /book-review-the-rise-and-triumph-of-the-modern-self/.

3. In the words of Sarah Coakley, *God, Sexuality, and the Self: An Essay "On the Trinity"* (Cambridge: Cambridge University Press, 2013), 309.

4. For a perceptive exploration of the heart as the center of the human person, a very fitting complement to the claims of this chapter, see Robert C. Roberts, "Situationism and the New Testament Psychology of the Heart," in *The Bible and the University*, ed. David Lyle Jeffrey (Grand Rapids: Zondervan, 2007), 139–60.

social goods we appropriate to ourselves as sexed beings. Gender, therefore, is importantly related to our identities and the way social goods are appropriated to them according to the standards and norms established by Christ. This attenuated sense of identity, I want to suggest, is a helpful clue provided by contemporary discussions about gender. If gender is something like an identity, how do we identify as women and men? Already we have seen how a scriptural argument can be made *that* gender is an identity concerned with social goods and deep links with our creation. In this chapter, I will articulate a vision for *how* such identities are formed, broadly speaking, by means of retrieving the theology of human love expounded by Saint Augustine of Hippo. This, I believe, will provide a broader framework for understanding how social goods and created categories interweave to form our identities, including our gender identities. In this way, a very ancient figure will provide help with a pressing question of contemporary concern. In short, this chapter will furnish a theological framework that makes sense of what it means to have an identity, broadly speaking. The next chapter will then situate gender within that framework, resulting in a theological account of gender. This will be a constructive account of human identity that takes seriously the contemporary discussions about gender identity while appreciating the need for a radical theological reorientation.

What, then, is the rendering of human identity provided by Augustine? Augustine consistently maintains that we are what we *love*. In one of his earliest works, he plainly asserts that "one becomes conformed to that which one loves."[5] Augustine speaks of the sum of a person's character, moral virtues, personality, and social roles as defined by one's loves. What it means to be *you*—in a natural, moral, *and* social sense—is a matter of what you love. Augustine's conception of human love, as John Burnaby puts it, forges in the lover "the unsatisfied longing of the homesick heart."[6] Nevertheless, one's homesick love does not preclude one from loving creaturely goods and other people, but it does *reframe* the fundamental relations of love that obtain between the lover and her beloved objects. This formatively relates the lover both to God and to the world, and the crucial contribution this can make for

---

5. Augustine, *De moribus ecclesiae Catholicae et de moribus Manichaeorum* 1.21.39 (hereafter cited as *De mor.*). English translation from "The Catholic Way of Life and the Manichean Way of Life," in *The Manichean Debate*, trans. Roland Teske, vol. I/19, The Works of Saint Augustine: A Translation for the 21st Century (Hyde Park, NY: New City, 2006).

6. John Burnaby, *Amor Dei: A Study of the Religion of St. Augustine* (1938; repr., Eugene, OR: Wipf & Stock, 2007), 96.

our understanding of gender is that it makes human identity *both* shaped by categories supplied at creation *and* irreducibly social. For, as Augustine maintains without compromise, there is "nothing more *social* by virtue of its *nature*" than human beings, a claim that in one breath resists the bifurcations latent in much feminist theory.[7] In the Augustinian understanding of human identity, for which love is the central point, there is no clear division between what is natural and what is social. As lovers, our identities are accountable both to features with which we are naturally equipped and to those we acquire by loving social goods. Eric Gregory, another author who sees the potential benefits of an Augustinian retrieval for contemporary social life, summarizes Augustine's picture of human identity nicely:

> Here is the Augustinian story. In contrast to standard liberal anthropology, Augustinians think human beings are best understood as bundles of loves. Mortal creatures are lovers constituted by loving, and being loved by, others and God. These primordial relations are neither essentially conflictual nor simply aggregate, foreclosing any possibility of a peaceful intersubjective social ontology. They also do not immediately pit autonomous action or feeling over against publicly shared action or feeling. . . . A self always stands in relation to the world, including the political world, in terms of her loves. . . . Human loves are various and in conflict. In a fallen world, they are disordered, misdirected, and disproportionate. Their operations are diverse and often self-defeating. Love has multiple directions and is beset by many potentially pathological corruptions that disrupt an original justice. . . . The life of charity is only progressively realized, always in danger of being corrupted by prideful self-possession.[8]

Unpacking this in all of its Augustinian complexity will be the burden of this chapter. Human identity is a bundle of many loves, and included in that bundle are the complex social identities we bear, like gender. Therefore, having a grasp on human identity enables us to acquire a better sense for what a theology of gender identity requires. That is the claim, anyway, of

7. Augustine, *De civitate Dei* 12.28.27 (hereafter cited as *De civ.*). English translation from Augustine, *The City of God*, ed. Boniface Ramsey, trans. William Babcock, vol. I/7, The Works of Saint Augustine: A Translation for the 21st Century (Hyde Park, NY: New City, 2012). Emphasis added. Recall from chapter 2 that theorists defending the social construction of gender see what is social as incompatible with what is "natural" or "biological."

8. Eric Gregory, *Politics and the Order of Love: An Augustinian Ethic of Democratic Citizenship* (Chicago: University of Chicago Press, 2008), 21–22.

this chapter and the next. My main proposal for this chapter is that in order to understand gender, especially if a major part of it is the way we appropriate social goods to form our identities, we need a theology of how human identities are formed in relation to created natures and to social goods. Augustine will be our guide, showing us how this happens primarily through our loves.

Before diving into Augustine's theology of human love, however, a few clarifications need to be made, especially in an academic climate where the retrieval of historical figures for understanding contentious human identities is suspect.[9] First, why retrieve Augustine's thought on love? A complete answer to this question will have to await the end of the chapter, for my rationale for selecting Augustine's theology of human love must be evaluated on the basis of what it contributes to our understanding of human identity and the adequacy of my presentation. But some preliminary reasons can be stated. I am persuaded that Augustine has the best account of human love in the Christian tradition and that this account is apposite for understanding the complexities of human identity, like gender. It does not exclusively prioritize the intellectual aspects of humanity but gives adequate explanatory weight to noncognitive dimensions of human life. It does not make a harsh distinction between what is natural and what is social, a key desideratum for the accounts of gender promoted so far. It retains a mooring in creation, while also taking into account the corruption of sin and the work of Christ to redeem, indicating a sensitivity to the narrative indexing of human nature mentioned in the first chapter.

But isn't Augustine a representative of the worst of Christianity, oppressing women and the marginalized, promoting violence and privilege? Doesn't he have a reprehensible account of gender, according to which women are not made in the image of God?[10] I cannot answer all of the objections posed to Augustine here, nor do I desire to defend Augustine on all points, especially on what he has to say about gender. Augustine *did* have a problematic

---

9. I have sought to explore this issue in greater detail in Fellipe do Vale, "Gender and Theological Tradition: On How to Retrieve the Irretrievable," *Journal of Reformed Theology* (forthcoming). My argument is basically that there is a way to be theologically consistent with the Christian tradition on issues such as gender and race without being concretely committed to anything the tradition has said about those topics as long as what is being retrieved are the doctrines that *implicate* gender and race.

10. Many of these objections can be found in Kim Power, *Veiled Desire: Augustine on Women* (New York: Continuum, 1996).

account of gender, but it is usually not for the reasons his most adamant critics avow.[11] It seems to me that Augustine's explicit reflections on gender, however, are conceptually separable from what he has to say about human love, for endorsement of the latter does not commit one to the former, nor does the latter *entail* the former. Thus, I intend to put forward a particular *aspect* of Augustine's reflections on humanity, namely what he has to say about love and its shaping force on human identity.[12] Many have found that the Augustinian insights unfolded in this chapter have been successful in clarifying many difficult human issues facing the church today, issues that Augustine may not have experienced himself or treated directly in any of his works, like eating disorders and racial identity.[13] Thus, despite his shortcomings on the theology of gender, Augustine can still be of immense help in understanding human identity. Whether this is true can be adjudicated only by considering the concrete claims made by Augustine himself. So perhaps it is best to treat

11. For instance, it is simply not true that he thought women were not made in the divine image, as most Augustinian scholarship now recognizes. The issues with Augustine's theology of gender have to do with a complex account of mental symbolism he puts forward in places like *De Trinitate* 12.8.13, according to which different aspects of the mind symbolize maleness and femaleness. Both males and females have *both* mental aspects, leading them to have one biological sex while having both mental genders, a curious conclusion to say the least. For reliable expositions of Augustine on this question, see David Vincent Meconi, "*Grata Sacris Angelis*: Gender and the *Imago Dei* in Augustine's *De Trinitate* XII," *American Catholic Philosophical Quarterly* 74, no. 1 (2000): 47–62; and John M. Rist, *Augustine: Ancient Thought Baptized* (Cambridge: Cambridge University Press, 1996), 115.

12. A further point can be raised in defense of Augustinian retrieval. Influential readers of Augustine like Rowan Williams have noted how there has been a shift in Augustinian scholarship since the 1980s with respect to how he is interpreted, a shift that has been much more sympathetic to his contributions while still clearly acknowledging his shortcomings. While those unfamiliar with the most recent Augustinian scholarship still recycle some tired biases about the saint, the "extravagances of these charges is usually in inverse proportion to any writer's direct acquaintance with the detail of Augustine's texts" (Rowan Williams, foreword to *The Theological Epistemology of Augustine's "De Trinitate,"* by Luigi Gioia [New York: Oxford University Press, 2008], vii). More careful attention to what Augustine has actually said and greater availability of the diversity of his writings in English have made it "harder to repeat clichés about Augustine's alleged responsibility for Western Christianity's supposed obsession with the evils of bodily existence or sexuality" (Rowan Williams, *On Augustine* [New York: Bloomsbury, 2016], vii). My intention is for this chapter to be seen as a contributor to this more sympathetic—yet still clear-eyed—reading of Augustine.

13. See Joanna Leidenhag, "Forbidden Fruit: Saint Augustine and the Psychology of Eating Disorders," *New Blackfriars* 99, no. 1079 (January 2018): 47–65. J. Kameron Carter, additionally, found in Augustine's insistence on human development according to a narrative a powerful resource against Christianity's complicity in the development of whiteness. See J. Kameron Carter, *Race: A Theological Account* (New York: Oxford University Press, 2008), 261–66. For a fuller exploration of Augustine and race, see Matthew Elia, *The Problem of the Christian Master: Augustine in the Afterlife of Slavery* (New Haven: Yale University Press, 2023).

Augustine's views in the same way as he treated Scripture in his conversion: *tolle lege*, take and read, in an effort to derive what benefit we can.

What follows, then, is a retrieval of Augustine's theology of human love. It will provide a broad framework for understanding human identity, of which gender will later be shown to be a component. Through this chapter, my aim is to show Augustine to be a much more nuanced and beneficial theologian than is often assumed and an example of "the generosity of a great mind putting itself at the service of real people in their intellectual perplexities"[14]—of real people, that is, who are gendered and in need of a theological guide to understanding the complexities of human life.

4.2 Augustine on Human Love

Throughout his career, Augustine maintained that a person is fundamentally identified by what they love. "A person's love," he perorated in a homily on 1 John 2:16–17, "determines the person's quality."[15] Or again, in a sermon from 416 or 417, he states succinctly, "Most people are somehow like the loves that drive them."[16] Forming our identities by our loves is nonnegotiable for Augustine, for there is "no one of course who doesn't love, but the question is, what do they love? So we are not urged to love, but to choose what we love."[17] Identity-forming love is both universal and natural for human beings, so the real question he drives his congregation to ask is, "Do you want to discern the character of a person's love? Notice where it leads."[18] It is not controversial to say, then, that on Augustine's view, we are what we love, loving is an inescapable activity definitive of being human, and the quality of the objects

14. Margaret R. Miles, *Augustine on the Body* (1979; repr., Eugene, OR: Wipf & Stock, 2009), 117.

15. Augustine, *Tractatus in Epistolam Ioannis ad Parthos* 2.14 (hereafter cited as *Tr. in Ep. Io.*). English translation from Augustine, *Homilies on the First Epistle of John*, trans. Boniface Ramsey, vol. III/14, The Works of Saint Augustine: A Translation for the 21st Century (Hyde Park, NY: New City, 2008).

16. Augustine, *Sermones* 96.1 (hereafter cited as *Serm.*). English translation from Augustine, *Sermons 94A–150*, trans. Edmund Hill, vol. III/4, The Works of Saint Augustine: A Translation for the 21st Century (Hyde Park, NY: New City, 1992).

17. *Serm.* 34.2. English translation (slightly altered) from Augustine, *Sermons 20–50*, trans. Edmund Hill, vol. III/2, The Works of Saint Augustine: A Translation for the 21st Century (Hyde Park, NY: New City, 1991).

18. Augustine, *Enarrationes in Psalmos* 121.1 (hereafter cited as *En. in Ps.*). English translation from Augustine, *Expositions of the Psalms, 121–150*, trans. Maria Boulding, vol. III/20, The Works of Saint Augustine: A Translation for the 21st Century (Hyde Park, NY: New City, 2004).

of our loves has a deep impact on *our* quality. How are we to understand such claims, and what are the mechanisms at work in our identity-forming love?

4.2.1 Love as a Component of Human Nature

All love, for Augustine, begins with God and ends with God, for love is not simply a divine attribute, but also something that characterizes the person of the Holy Spirit.[19] Though 1 John 4:7–8 clearly affirms that God is love, Augustine is keen to point out that it also claims that love is "of God [*ex Deo*]."[20] This observation leads Augustine to conclude: "The Holy Spirit is, therefore, something common, whatever it is, between the Father and the Son. But this communion is itself consubstantial and coeternal . . . [and] it is more aptly called love."[21] Therefore, the main mission of the Holy Spirit is to indwell our hearts in love, derived from Romans 5:5, one of the passages cited most frequently by Augustine.[22] Thus, late in life, he affirms: "Love, then, which is from God and is God, is properly the Holy Spirit, through whom the charity of God is poured forth in our hearts, through which the whole Trinity dwells in us."[23] As a result, Augustine is able to preach, again on the basis of Romans 5:5, "Let us love God with God. Yes indeed, since the Holy Spirit is God, let us love God with God!"[24] All of this is important because, when we turn to love in creatures, we must have a clear grasp of the trinitarian basis for God's motivation of love in creating them: divine love shed forth in the creation of

19. For a critical perspective on this claim from an Orthodox perspective, see Andrew Louth, "Love and the Trinity: Saint Augustine and the Greek Fathers," *Augustinian Studies* 33, no. 1 (2002): 1–16.

20. For reflections on "Augustine's view that names taken from the temporal economy should be applied to the Holy Spirit in his eternal procession," see Matthew Levering, "The Holy Spirit in the Trinitarian Communion: 'Love' and 'Gift'?," *International Journal of Systematic Theology* 16, no. 2 (April 2014): 137.

21. Augustine, *De Trinitate* 6.5.7 (hereafter cited as *De Trin.*). English translation from Augustine, *The Trinity*, trans. Stephen McKenna, vol. 45, The Fathers of the Church (Washington, DC: Catholic University of America Press, 1963). For further detail on the Holy Spirit as the "gift" within the divine life, see Lewis Ayres, *Augustine and the Trinity* (Cambridge: Cambridge University Press, 2014), chap. 10; and Gioia, *Theological Epistemology of Augustine's "De Trinitate,"* chap. 6.

22. Carol Harrison estimates that he references this passage more than 200 times to make this point. Carol Harrison, *Augustine: Christian Truth and Fractured Humanity*, Christian Theology in Context (New York: Oxford University Press, 2000), 96.

23. *De Trin.* 15.18.32. The influence of 1 John 4:7–8 is strong here in the language of the Holy Spirit being *from* God while nonetheless *being* God.

24. *Serm.* 34.3.

all things is what enables creatures themselves to love.[25] Specifically, the ability to love was an aspect of the trinitarian creation of human beings, something humans were able to do even before they entered into any social relationships.

Augustine maintains that humans are therefore lovers by nature. In order to understand this claim, we must turn to Augustine's central conviction, derived from Wisdom 11:21, that "all things were ordered in measure, number and weight."[26] As Carol Harrison maintains, these categories "constitute the unity of existence under God and lie at the basis of Augustine's metaphysics," for without them, "nothing could be good, indeed nothing could *be*."[27] Measure, number, and weight provide Augustine with the basic categories for analyzing the properties of all created entities, such that for anything that exists, it is what it is in virtue of its measure, number, and weight. Measure "sets a limit to everything," number "gives everything its specific form," and weight "draws everything to rest and stability."[28] For our purposes, a focus on weight is sufficient. An entity's weight establishes its teleology, what it tends toward when it does that for which it was designed and what it culminates in when it has done what it ought to according to its design. This is what Augustine means by its "rest"—a stone rests as gravity pulls it downward, and oil rests when it rises above water when mixed with it. That is what it does when it is performing its proper function in its suitable context.

Weight is central for an Augustinian account of love, for as Augustine makes clear, *the weight of human beings is their love*. Thus, in a famous passage from the *Confessions*, he states, "My love is my weight [*pondus*]; wherever I am carried, it is love that carries me."[29] It is important to pause in order to appreciate the precise point Augustine is making here. He is not

25. Augustine's homilies on the Gospel of John are particularly emphatic on this point. See, e.g., *In Iohannis euangelium tractatus* 17.6: "Where does love come from? From the grace of God, from the Holy Spirit. We should not, after all, get it from ourselves, as if we could make it ourselves. It is a gift of God, and a great gift too!" English translation from Augustine, *Homilies on the Gospel of John 1–40*, trans. Edmund Hill, vol. III/12, The Works of Saint Augustine: A Translation for the 21st Century (Hyde Park, NY: New City, 2009).

26. In Augustine's Latin version: "Omnia in mensura, et numero, et pondere disposuisti."

27. Carol Harrison, "Measure, Number and Weight in Saint Augustine's Aesthetics," *Augustinianum* 28 (1998): 592. See also Jared Ortiz, *"You Made Us for Yourself": Creation in St. Augustine's "Confessions"* (Minneapolis: Fortress, 2016), 20–22.

28. Augustine, *De Genesi ad litteram imperfectus liber* 4.3.7 (hereafter cited as *De Gen. ad litt.*). English translation from Augustine, *On Genesis*, trans. Edmund Hill, vol. I/13, The Works of Saint Augustine: A Translation for the 21st Century (Hyde Park, NY: New City, 2002).

29. Augustine, *Confessiones* 13.9.10 (hereafter cited as *Conf.*). English translation from Augustine, *Confessions*, trans. Carolyn Hammond, vol. 2, Loeb Classical Library (Cambridge, MA: Harvard University Press, 2016). Here and in other quotations, I have altered Hammond's

merely illustrating the importance of love with the metaphor of weight; he is making the precise metaphysical point that human beings have an objective telos established at their creation and that they arrive at this telos by means of loving. This is why it makes perfectly good sense that in that very same quote, illustrations from the natural world are invoked: "Under its own weight a body gravitates to its proper place; that weight is not always downward, but rather to that proper place. Fire's natural path is upward, that of stone is downward: they have their own weights, they make for their proper place. When oil is poured under water, it rises above the water's surface; when water is poured into oil, it sinks below the oil: they have their own weights, they make for their proper place. What is out of its proper place is restless; once in its proper place it finds rest."[30]

The love of a human being is its weight in just the same way that fire's natural trajectory is upward, and a stone's is downward. This is what these entities do *by nature*, what they were equipped to do at their creation and what provides their rest when they have acted according to their natures. Human beings were created with the capacity to love, and it is by loving that humans do what they were designed to do.[31] As Rowan Williams states, just as weight "continually guarantees an overall balance, so that there is not, in the natural order, a chaos of conflictual agencies," so also "it is love that draws us back to our proper place, that pulls us back to stability and harmony."[32] Measure, number, and weight provide the dimensions for all of creation, and the fact that the weight of human beings is their love is a metaphysical fact about creation that enables them to tend toward their true end and rest.[33]

There is a point of great consequence that is worth making here with respect to discussions about gender. Recall from the previous chapter that there is a reductionist tendency in those who insist on the bifurcation of gender as either a social construct or a biological essence. For both, the nonsocial side of the bifurcation is *biological*, in the sense of the word associated with the academic discipline. If something is not social, in other words, it is biological. Augustine's account of creation reveals that there is actually significant

---

"gravitational force" simply to "weight" for *pondus*, for while there is a gravity metaphor being employed, it obfuscates the technical terms Augustine is using.

30. *Conf.* 13.9.10. For a further statement of this, see *De civ*. 11.28.

31. See *De Gen. ad litt*. 4.4.8: "There is a weighing for the will and for love."

32. Williams, *On Augustine*, 65.

33. See Joseph Torchia, "'Pondus Meum Amor Meus': The Weight-Metaphor in St. Augustine's Early Philosophy," *Augustinian Studies* 21, no. 1 (1990): 163–76.

conceptual space available between these two poles. For instance, the human capacity to love is *natural* to human beings (even before any considerations about particular instances of loving relationships). But to say that this is biological because it is not necessarily a social category is to make an unsustainable claim. The natural sciences have not been able to establish that human beings love, and they may be unable to do so. At best, evolutionary accounts maintain that human beings altruistically *cooperate* against a backdrop of evolutionary violence, but this is a far cry from a robust claim about our natural ability to love, especially if love is understood by the standards of Christian theology.[34] This should lead us to conclude that calling something *natural* to human beings is not the same thing as calling it *biologically* human—the divine image, for instance, can be seen as the former but not the latter. In fact, there are good reasons to think that "biological," "natural," and "embodied" are not identical categories. Biological considerations are restricted by methodology, but Christian theology and metaphysics are under no such restrictions. This is a further reason to resist the biological/social bifurcation and to adopt a more variegated vocabulary. The claim here, though, is that Augustine maintains that human beings love by *nature*, even if that is not a posit of biology (and it is not limited to the body). Part of the definition of "human," in other words, includes the capacity to love, along with many other nonbiological properties (and possibly nonembodied ones too). A person who lives exactly one second is still naturally a lover, as is the person who lives one hundred years.

So, God created all things with measure, number, and weight by nature, and the weight of human beings is their love. We are pulled to our place of rest by our love, our weight. But what is that place of rest? Anyone with a passing familiarity with Augustine's thought will know: "You have made us for yourself, and our hearts are restless until they rest in you."[35] Again, Augustine is not *just* making a poetic point; the poetry communicates something with profound metaphysical and theological significance. As Ortiz ventures, "This

34. For explorations of this claim, see Sarah Coakley and Martin Nowak, eds., *Evolution, Games, and God: The Principle of Cooperation* (Cambridge, MA: Harvard University Press, 2013). For an argument for the high bar set by a Christian account of love, see Kent Dunnington, "Is There a Christian Duty to Love?," in *Love, Divine and Human: Contemporary Essays in Systematic and Philosophical Theology*, ed. Oliver D. Crisp, James M. Arcadi, and Jordan Wessling (New York: T&T Clark, 2020), 199–214.

35. *Conf.* 1.1.1. English translation from Augustine, *Confessions*, trans. Carolyn Hammond, vol. 1, Loeb Classical Library (Cambridge, MA: Harvard University Press, 2014).

famous sentence, I would argue, sums up all the fruits of Augustine's exegesis, metaphysics, and ethics at this point in his life, and moreover, contains the whole of the *Confessions*."[36] Augustine is maintaining that by nature of our creatureliness, we are designed to love God and to be in union with God, and that when this obtains, we are at rest, which is to say that we have arrived at the perfection of what it means to be human, the only way human beings can find stability and integration.[37] Because our weight—what pulls us to our ultimate end or rest as human beings—is our love, and we were created to have God as our rest, we are created to love God above all.

Augustine actually makes even stronger claims than these, revealing his commitment to eudaimonism. Because we were created to love God above all, it is only in loving God that we are truly happy. Though some Platonic and Stoic influence may account for aspects of this opinion, Augustine's motivations are primarily scriptural. He regularly cites Psalm 73:28—"For me, to cling to God is the good"[38]—and the elaboration of the greatest commandment in Matthew 22:37: "You shall love the Lord your God with all your heart, and with all your soul, and with all your mind." This supreme love for God is the only source of human happiness: "The pursuit of God, therefore, is the desire for happiness, but the attainment of God is happiness itself. We pursue him by loving."[39] Augustine confesses, "I grieve for those who want more. What more can you want, brothers and sisters? When we see God face to face there will be nothing whatever that can be better for us than to hold fast to him."[40] God's rest on the seventh day of creation, Augustine exposits, testifies to the fact that we too must rest in God: "What we are meant to rest in, surely, is a certain unchangeable good, which is

36. Ortiz, *"You Made Us for Yourself,"* 121. He goes on to say, "The idea of rest is inseparable from the idea of place and weight. All things have their proper place, toward which they tend by their weight, and when they are in their place they are at rest. For human beings, their weight is their love, that is, they move toward or away from God according to the disposition of their heart" (123).

37. Augustine specifically maintains that this obtains in the beatific vision. See, among many other places, *De Trin*. 2.17.28: "For it is this very sight, which everyone who endeavors to love God with his whole heart, his whole soul, and his whole mind yearns to contemplate."

38. The Vulgate reads, "Mihi autem adhaerere Deo bonum est" (Ps. 72:28). The original Latin lends itself to a eudaimonistic reading more easily, with its absence of the definite article with *bonum* and a substantival reading of *adhaerere*. Thus my translation: "For me, to cling to God *is* [*est*] the good."

39. *De mor*. 1.11.18.

40. *En. in Ps*. 72.34. English translation from Augustine, *Expositions of the Psalms, 51–72*, trans. Maria Boulding, vol. III/17, The Works of Saint Augustine: A Translation for the 21st Century (Hyde Park, NY: New City, 2001).

what the one who made us is for us," for God "swings everything whatever that comes from him back to himself."[41] All of these assertions indicate that there is a fundamental wiring of human beings to flourish, find beatitude, and sustain genuine happiness only in God. Though all humans desire happiness, and though they *appear* to have found happiness in various temporal goods, the claim that we are happy only when we love God is not dependent on our phenomenological experiences of happiness. It is *natural*, a posit of creation that remains true even in the face of credible claims of happiness. Yet Augustine maintains that there is experiential evidence available for our exclusive mirth in God, for in our happy earthly experiences there are "bitter elements even with these innocent pleasures, so that even in them we experience distress."[42] No earthly good can provide an unqualified happiness; this is space occupied by God alone. Above all, however, the plausibility of this claim will stand or fall with one's convictions about teleology in general and scriptural claims that at God's "right hand are pleasures forevermore" (Ps. 16:11). We are created to love God insofar as that is our weight, and since our weight pulls us to the only place of true rest, stability, and mirth, such things can be found only in loving God.

4.2.2 The Human Love of Earthly Goods

Does all of this mean that Augustine's theology of objective human love is reducible to God alone? If we love the Lord with our whole heart, does it follow that we have no more heart left with which to love creatures? As we will see, none of these conclusions follow, but Augustine sometimes is taken to be saying as much. The problem acquires a sharper edge in light of Augustine's tendentious claim that some things are to be enjoyed while others are to be used: "Things that are to be enjoyed make us happy; things which are to be used help us on our way to happiness, providing us, so to say, with crutches and props for reaching the things that will make us happy, and enabling us to keep them. . . . Enjoyment, after all, consists in clinging to something lovingly for its own sake, while use consists in referring what has come your way to what your love aims at obtaining. . . . The things therefore that are to be enjoyed are the Father and the Son and the Holy Spirit, in fact the Trinity,

41. *De Gen. ad litt.* 4.17.29, 4.18.34.
42. *En. in Ps.* 40.5. English translation from Augustine, *Expositions of the Psalms, 33–50*, trans. Maria Boulding, vol. III/16, The Works of Saint Augustine: A Translation for the 21st Century (Hyde Park, NY: New City, 2000).

one supreme being, and one which is shared in common by all who enjoy it."[43]
This set of claims has instigated a tremendous amount of literature. Some,
like Hannah Arendt and Anders Nygren, find them entirely objectionable,
largely because of their alleged failure to see anything worth loving except
God.[44] As Gregory memorably phrases objections like these, the worry is that
love on this account is "always looking over the neighbor's shoulder to God."[45]
Other more sympathetic Augustinian interpreters have said that while this
way of thinking is indeed objectionable, it was nevertheless abandoned by
Augustine later in his career.[46] Oddly, however, this is not how the distinction
between use and enjoyment has been interpreted in the reception history of
Augustinian thought. Since at least Peter Lombard's immortalization of it in
his *Sentences*, which became the standard textbook for medieval theological
training, it was seen as a helpful aid to moral theological thought.[47] It was
then upheld even by figures like John Calvin and John Wesley.[48] While much of
the tradition would not have had the luxurious access to Augustine's corpus

43. Augustine, *De doctrina Christiana* 1.3.3–1.4.4 (hereafter cited as *De doct.*). English
translation from Augustine, *Teaching Christianity*, ed. John E. Rotelle, trans. Edmund Hill,
vol. I/11, The Works of Saint Augustine: A Translation for the 21st Century (Hyde Park, NY:
New City, 1996).

44. See Hannah Arendt, *Love and Saint Augustine*, ed. Joanna Vecchiarelli Scott and Judith
Chelius Stark (Chicago: University of Chicago Press, 1996), where Augustine's theology of love
is said to make "a desert out of this world" (4). Nygren, by contrast, objected to the possibility
of love as in any way self-interested, which Augustine's eudaimonism is, if nothing else. See
Anders Nygren, *Agape and Eros: The Christian Idea of Love*, trans. Philip S. Watson (New
York: Harper and Row, 1969), 453.

45. Gregory, *Politics and the Order of Love*, 44.

46. This was the basic thesis forwarded by Oliver O'Donovan in *The Problem of Self-Love
in St. Augustine* (1980; repr., Eugene, OR: Wipf & Stock, 2006) and in "*Usus* and *Fruitio* in
Augustine, *De Doctrina Christiana* I," *Journal of Theological Studies* 33 (1981): 361–97. This
reading, however, was challenged almost as soon as it was proposed. See, e.g., William Riordan
O'Connor, "The *Uti/Frui* Distinction in Augustine's Ethics," *Augustinian Studies* 14 (1983):
45–62; and Helmut David Baer, "The Fruit of Charity: Using the Neighbor in 'De doctrina
christiana,'" *Journal of Religious Ethics* 24, no. 1 (1996): 47–64. I will not assume O'Donovan's
reading here, taking it to be rather contentious. Instead, I follow what I take to be the best reading of the *uti/frui* distinction, that of Sarah Stewart-Kroeker, who maintains that O'Donovan's
division of ontological and eschatological elements in Augustine's theology of love is artificial
and fabricates the results he intends to find in Augustine (Sarah Stewart-Kroeker, *Pilgrimage as
Moral and Aesthetic Formation in Augustine's Thought* [New York: Oxford University Press,
2017], 223).

47. See Severin Valentinov Kitanov, *Beatific Enjoyment in Medieval Scholastic Debates: The
Complex Legacy of Saint Augustine and Peter Lombard* (Lanham, MD: Lexington Books, 2014).

48. See John Calvin, *Institutes of the Christian Religion*, ed. John T. McNeill, trans. Ford
Lewis Battles (Philadelphia: Westminster, 1960), 3.10; John W. Wright, "'Use' and 'Enjoy' in John
Wesley: John Wesley's Participation within the Augustinian Tradition," *Wesley and Methodist
Studies* 6 (2014): 3–36.

enjoyed by readers in the twenty-first century, it would be surprising to see so many uncritically take on a concept so foundationally flawed. Perhaps there is a better way to understand the ideas at stake.

First, it must be remembered that Augustine is working with complex and technical Latin vocabulary, employing words that would not have had the negative connotations that they do in the English language. To repeat the claim of *De doctrina Christiana* 1.3.3, those things that must be enjoyed (*illae quibus fruendum est*) make us happy (*nos beatos faciunt*). But to be "happy" here refers to Augustine's broader eudaimonistic framework, according to which happiness is qualitatively different than that feeling I get when my daughter hugs me or when Liverpool wins a match (feelings that are still good and pleasurable). This kind of happiness is an unchanging, irremovable, and singular mirth obtained only at the rest achieved when creatures are pulled by their weight to their proper rest. Moreover, to "use" someone or something (*aliae quibus utendum*) is not to objectify them as a fungible receptacle that is easily discarded. Rather, the word translated as "use" here, *uti*, is more like "treat"—as in "You treated him well."[49] There are theological considerations to take into account as well. First, a detail that is almost always missed: *both use and enjoyment can be ways of loving something rightly.* On the one hand, some things that are used can be used with love: "Not all things, however, which are to be used are *also* to be loved, but only those which can be related to God."[50] That an act of use can *sometimes* also count as an act of love shows that it is not the act that is problematic but, rather, a particular way of going about doing it. On the other hand, *some* instances of use *are* sinful, but only when loved to the exclusion of the love for God: "Sin consists not in the things themselves, but in the unlawful *use* of them. Now the use of things is lawful when the soul remains within the bounds of God's law and subject to the one God in unqualified love and regulates other things that are subject to it without greed or lust."[51] The picture that emerges is *not* that enjoyment is love while use is not really love. Rather, both are forms of love,

49. See Rist, *Augustine*, 163–64: "That is merely a standard Latin locution—found also in earlier English, e.g. 'He used him well'—indicating how people [and things] are to be 'treated'; the notion of 'exploitation' is not to be read into it."

50. *De doct.* 1.23.22 (emphasis added).

51. *De Gen. ad litt.* 1.1.13 (emphasis added). There is a complex background to this claim regarding whether the moral status of an entity is one of its intrinsic properties or whether it lies in its use. Augustine, it seems to me, thinks both, but that *most* goods obtain their moral valence through their use. Coffee is good, but if I develop an addiction to it, it becomes bad for me. There is no good way, however, for an atomic bomb to be used. For more on this question,

and their evaluation must come from external considerations about how one relates to the beloved and the divine intentions necessary for informing the proper relation. Sometimes, instances of use are rightly ordered and count as godly love; at other times, instances of use are sinful and do not count as godly love. So it goes, *mutatis mutandis*, for enjoyment, which can be turned toward creatures rather than God. Charles Mathewes, then, is right to conclude, "The contrast between 'enjoy' and 'use' does not divide what should be loved from what should not be loved; rather it is a guide to how one should love things. Augustine is not Kant's sap; his use of 'use' means to forbid us to expect things to be God, to forbid us from acting as if we deserved from them some sort of ultimate happiness."[52]

Ultimately, Augustine is not offering a means/ends calculus when putting forward the use/enjoyment distinction. Rather, he is prescribing wisdom for the best practices of love when it comes to God, neighbor, self, and temporal goods.[53] What, then, *is* that practice? Augustine is clearly committed to the view that all creatures are substantially good and therefore worthy of love. In a remarkable passage, Augustine even defends the beautiful creation of maggots:

> Most of them, you see, are either bred from the sores of living bodies, or from garbage and effluents, or from the rotting of corpses; some also from rotten wood and grass, some from rotten fruit; and we cannot possibly say that there are any of them of which God is not the creator. All things, after all, have in them a certain worth or grace of nature, each of its own kind, so that in these minute creatures there is even more for us to wonder at as we observe them, and so to praise the almighty craftsman for them more rapturously than ever.[54]

Such words could not be spoken, and such caring attention could not be given, by someone who thinks creatures are not to be loved. Augustine is famously committed to the view that evil is a *privation*, a lack of what ought to be in

---

see Joseph Clair, *Discerning the Good in the Letters and Sermons of Augustine* (New York: Oxford University Press, 2016), chap. 1.

52. Charles Mathewes, "A Worldly Augustinianism: Augustine's Sacramental Vision of Creation," *Augustinian Studies* 41, no. 1 (2010): 341–42.

53. Thus Stewart-Kroeker claims that the use/enjoyment distinction "does not restrict [love's] scope, in principle, but it impacts its practice. Lovers must know where to place their ultimate hope, whom to follow and whom to lead, what limits to draw, and so on" (Stewart-Kroeker, *Pilgrimage as Moral and Aesthetic Formation*, 208).

54. *De Gen. ad litt.* 3.14.22.

a substance, never a substance in itself.[55] Instead, "God is the highest good, and the things that he made are all good, though they are not as good as he who made them is,"[56] thereby creating a hierarchy of valued goods, at the top of which is the source of all good, God. The bottom of the hierarchy is not to be spurned, however. All things have been created by God and by virtue of their creatureliness are valuable and lovable. Augustine is very careful and clear about this. When 1 John 2:15 commands us, "Do not love the world or the things in the world," he does not take the opportunity to show why creatures are unfit objects of love. Rather, he qualifies: "What is the world? When it is understood in a bad sense, it is the lovers of the world [i.e., those who love to the exclusion of loving God]. When it is understood in a praiseworthy sense, it is heaven and earth and works of God that are in them."[57] The latter are fit objects of love, when recognized in the proper hierarchy of love.

As early as 395, Augustine was citing his edition of Song of Songs 2:4, "Order love in me," in his writing and preaching.[58] The ordering of beloved objects was crucial for Augustine, and preserving this order was precisely that for which the use/enjoyment distinction was intended. Thus, shortly after introducing the distinction, he says, "Living a just and holy life requires one to be capable of an objective and impartial evaluation of things; to love things, that is to say, in the right order, so that you do not love what is not to be loved, or fail to love what is to be loved, or have a greater love for what should be loved less, or an equal love for things that should be loved less or more, or a lesser or greater love for things that should be loved equally."[59] In fact, such a recognition is a sensible thing to suggest. If I buy a new car and

55. See *De mor.* 2.2.2 and 2.4.6: "Evil itself, then . . . is a falling away from being and a tending toward non-being . . . for it is most truly spoken of not as an essence but as a privation."

56. *De mor.* 2.4.6. See also *De Natura Boni* 1: "Every nature insofar as it is a nature is something good, no nature can be made except by the highest and true God." English translation from Augustine, "The Nature of the Good," in *The Manichean Debate*, ed. Boniface Ramsey, trans. Roland Teske, vol. I/19, The Works of Saint Augustine: A Translation for the 21st Century (Hyde Park, NY: New City, 2006).

57. *Tr. in Ep. Io.* 5.9. See also 2.12 and 4.4. It is worthwhile to note that some Augustinian scholars have claimed that Augustine's confidence in the incarnation and resurrection of Christ further affirms material goods and other embodied people as fitting objects of love. Thus Stewart-Kroeker, *Pilgrimage as Moral and Aesthetic Formation*, 28: "Augustine roots his affirmation of embodiment in Christ's incarnation." See also Rist, *Augustine*, 109: "It is clear that as soon as Augustine began to give serious consideration to the dogma of the Resurrection of the body, he found good reasons to conclude that . . . the Platonists . . . were wrong, and even begin to look 'Manicaean,' when they wish to be rid of the body so far as possible."

58. The earliest occurrence, in 395, is in *Serm.* 100.2.

59. *De doct.* 1.27.28.

love it more than I love my wife and kids, I would be desperately mistaken about the order of my loves. If I love anything at all above God, I am an idolater, trading a creature for the Creator (Rom. 1:25). Now, there might be epistemically complicated instances where ordering one's beloved objects is not altogether clear. This is perfectly compatible with the broader principle being advanced. Augustine provides a very memorable and epistemically uncomplicated example of disordered love:

> If a bridegroom made a ring for his bride, and she loved the ring that she had received more than her bridegroom, who made the ring, in the same way wouldn't an adulterous soul be detected in the bridegroom's very gift, even though she loved what the bridegroom gave her? To be sure, she loved what the bridegroom gave her. Yet, if she said, "This ring is enough for me; now I don't want to see his face again," what sort of person would she be? Who wouldn't detest this woman whose loves were disordered? Who wouldn't convict her of an adulterous mind? You love gold instead of the man, you love a ring instead of your bridegroom.[60]

Augustine then summarizes the point succinctly: "*God doesn't forbid you to love these things*, but you mustn't love them in the expectation of blessedness. Rather, you must favor and praise them in such a way that you love the creator."[61] So we are called to love, and love abundantly, but never forgetting that our objects of love are gifts of a much greater Lover, the source of all that is good: God.

The engagement ring analogy reminds us that all our objects of love are gifts from God, for as Paul wrote, "What do you have that you did not receive?" (1 Cor. 4:7). And with all gifts, it is the liberty of the giver to specify the conditions under which the gift is to be used as well as the value and worth of the gift itself. Suppose I find an old, broken watch on the sidewalk. I would be entirely within my rights simply to discard it. But if my father, on his deathbed, gives me the old, broken watch he has worn all his life and tells me to wear it only on the most special of occasions as a means of remembering him, suddenly the gift receives an entirely new use and worth, even if the two watches are physically identical. It is these dynamics that Augustine is attempting to preserve, all with an eye on our tendency to turn the objects of our love into

---

60. *Tr. in Ep. Io.* 2.11. I have modified Ramsey's translation from "crazy woman" to "woman whose loves were disordered," since in my judgment that better suits Augustine's broader point while avoiding sexist stereotypes brought about by over-translation.

61. *Tr. in Ep. Io.* 2.11 (emphasis added).

sources of ultimate bliss. The real problem is that such objects of love can never support such intense and unqualified adoration. Thus, expressions of love that use things in their right order prevent us from idolizing them to the point at which they are loved beyond what they can bear. Our "temptation is constantly to project on to the things and persons around us expectations they are unable to fulfil, and so to shrink both them and ourselves," says Rowan Williams.[62] Because of this, he claims,

> The language of *uti* is designed to warn against an attitude towards any finite person or object that terminates their meaning in their capacity to satisfy my desire, that treats them as the end of desire, conceiving my meaning in terms of them and theirs in terms of me. . . . Loving humanly, it seems, must be a love that refuses to ignore the mortality and limitedness of what or whom we love. Forget this, and we are left with an intensity or felt intimacy that ultimately and subtly refuses to "release" the person loved from the bonds of that intimacy.[63]

The order of love, and its recommendation to use some things, is for the mutual benefit of lover and beloved. As Augustine found out too painfully, at the death of one of his friends (see *Conf.* 4.7–8), and as every parent learns as children grow older, to place the hopes of ultimate satisfaction in something or someone who cannot bear it is to harm them, to act in a rapacious manner, and to prioritize one's appetites above the honor and dignity of the creature whose presence in one's life is a gift, not a right. Gerald Schlabach summarizes this Augustinian motivation beautifully: "To love other creatures rightly, a human being must relativize that love—devaluing its object in one way, yet rediscovering its true and stable value in another way. When we love friends or neighbors rightly, the value they lose is their value as a tool of our own egocentric self-interest; the value we recognize in them is their value insofar as God, the source of all things, creates and secures them. To love one's neighbor rightly, in other words, Augustine's abiding conviction was that we must not first love the creature but must first love God."[64] The use/enjoyment distinction, the ordering of love, and all other aspects of Augustine's theology of human love are not *deterrents* to love; rather, they are powerful encouragements to love—to love boldly, to love rightly, to love with integrity, and to love with respect.

---

62. Williams, *On Augustine*, 200.
63. Williams, *On Augustine*, 44, 194.
64. Gerald W. Schlabach, *For the Joy Set before Us: Augustine and Self-Denying Love* (Notre Dame, IN: University of Notre Dame Press, 2001), 37.

4.2.3 You Are What You Love: Internalizing the Beloved

So far, we have been inquiring about what are the proper objects for human love and in what order they are to be loved. How, then, do these various objects of love shape our identities or selves? How is it, after all, that we *are* what we love? For Augustine, love operates as a kind of glue, uniting the lover to the objects of their love and effectively "sticking" them to her. The idea is biblical. Just as Psalm 63:8 states, "My soul has been glued to you" (my trans.),[65] so also Augustine regularly perceives love as a means by which lover is joined to beloved: "What else is love, therefore, except a kind of life which binds or seeks to bind some two together, namely, the lover and the beloved? And this is so even in external and carnal love."[66] Thus, one of the basic features of love is that it is a special kind of union, bringing together lover and beloved in such a way that the lover is shaped by the beloved.[67] There is a basic Pauline thought pattern at play here, for Paul also noticed that acts of love, sexual or otherwise, were essentially unitive (see 1 Cor. 6:16).

To move beyond the metaphor, and to explain how this shaping union occurs, we must explore what Augustine has to say about the nature of human memory. Memory is relevant here because it has the unique capacity both to internalize objects encountered in the everyday and to store those internalizations in the soul:

> The force of love is so great that the mind draws in with itself those things upon which it has long reflected with love, and to which it has become attached by its devoted care. . . . And because they are bodies which it has loved outside of

65. This verse is numbered as Psalm 62:9 in Augustine's Latin Bible, where it reads, "Agglutinata est anima mea post te." See also Joseph T. Lienhard, SJ, "'The Glue Itself Is Charity': Ps 62:9 in Augustine's Thought," in *Augustine: Presbyter Factus Sum*, ed. Joseph T. Lienhard, SJ, Earl C. Muller, SJ, and Roland J. Teske, SJ (New York: Peter Lang, 1993), 375–84.

66. *De Trin.* 8.10.14. See also *En. in Ps.* 62.17: "Where are we to find the strong glue? The glue is charity. Have charity in you, and it will glue your soul into place, following God."

67. It is here that there are significant points of commonality between my Augustinian account and the Thomistic account of Eleonore Stump in *Wandering in Darkness: Narrative and the Problem of Suffering* (New York: Oxford University Press, 2010). For Stump, love consists in two desires, desire for the good of the beloved and for union with the beloved. Union is a matter of personal presence and mutual closeness (109), where the former involves second-personal experience and shared attention (112–16). Lovers share their thoughts and appropriate the mental states of the other, she maintains, and through them they are united. However, this could not account for loving nonpersonal creatures, like clothes (which are very relevant for gender identity). So I think that her account is not false but narrow. I intend a much broader account of union here. In this sense, her view provides depth where mine provides width.

itself through the senses of the body, and with which it has become entangled by a kind of daily familiarity, it cannot bring them into itself as though into a country of incorporeal nature, and, therefore, it fastens together their images, which it has made out of itself, and forces them into itself. . . . And thus it is made like them to some extent.[68]

Through love, humans devote attention to some things, and in such devotion the human memory[69] creates images of those things and stores them up inside itself. As these images linger, they "leave their footprints, as it were, in our mind because we have thought of them so often." He goes on: "These footprints are, so to speak, impressed on the memory when the corporeal things which are without are so perceived that, even when they are absent, their images are present to those who think of them."[70] Augustine should not be taken to be making an overly psychologized point here. Our memories work concurrently with our bodies, our activities, and our other faculties to bring in the most significant objects of our care so that their presence in the deepest recesses of our hearts grants to them an opportunity to "leave their footprints," making us like them.

This point is not so difficult to recognize once it is applied to some concrete examples. For instance, the power of memory to shape us is familiar to anyone who has watched a horror film on a cold, dark October night and has been subsequently afraid to walk down the stairs of their home. Or, in a more serious vein, this claim should be familiar to anyone who has walked alongside someone suffering from dementia or another memory-related illness; as the person's memories begin to go, it can be a great temptation to conclude that the person herself or himself is slipping away, a remarkably painful experience.[71] Or again, victims of great trauma often struggle with

68. De Trin. 10.5.7–10.6.8. For greater detail on this point, see Paige E. Hochschild, *Memory in Augustine's Theological Anthropology* (New York: Oxford University Press, 2012).

69. Though Augustine narrows in on the faculty of memory, he should not be taken to mean that human beings can be compartmentalized into discrete faculties that can be independently analyzed. Memory and love, as the quote indicates, work inseparably, as do all other aspects of human psychology. For a detailed account of the complex and heterogeneous nature of the human mind, see Peter Burnell, *The Augustinian Person* (Washington, DC: Catholic University of America Press, 2005), chap. 2. For a thorough study of Augustinian psychology, see Jesse Couenhoven, "Augustine's Moral Psychology," *Augustinian Studies* 48, no. 1 (2017): 23–44.

70. De Trin. 10.8.11.

71. For a powerful reflection on this phenomenon, see John Swinton, *Dementia: Living in the Memories of God* (Grand Rapids: Eerdmans, 2012). For Swinton, memories can be externalized and "held" by other entities, like photographs or diaries. Most importantly, when our

how best to remember the atrocities done to them. They do not have an option as to whether the incident that caused the trauma will shape them as people; because it lives on in their memories, they must find ways to cope, grasping for ways to heal their memories.[72] Augustine's basic point is this: as we love temporal goods and people, we bring them into ourselves by means of our memories, and they form who we are. This is how they are glued to us, how they leave their footprints on our souls. It is also why the disappearance of those footprints or the dissolving of the glue is such a painful experience for the person experiencing it.

We might extend Augustine's picture of mental appropriation with recourse to a more recent Augustinian thinker—namely, Eleonore Stump. Stump has defended a rich and multilayered account of love in her book *Wandering in Darkness*, elements of which nicely illuminate and expand upon Augustine's point. Stump makes a distinction between what she calls "Franciscan" and "Dominican" knowledge—or more familiarly, personal and propositional knowledge.[73] Propositional knowledge is knowledge *that* something is the case, while personal knowledge is something closer to personal acquaintance. The difference is akin to my giving someone a full description of my wife (propositional knowledge) and that person actually *meeting* my wife (personal knowledge). The latter is a second-personal kind of knowledge, and the best means to communicate personal knowledge is to tell a story.[74] This is because there is an intimate relation between knowing the identity of persons and knowing the narrative of that person's life, such that if we really want to know the person, we delve deeply into the stories that disclose who they are. For Stump, moreover, we are identified by our loves, for "a human being's true self is to be identified with her higher-order desires, because they reflect the all-things-considered judgments of her rational faculties."[75] Who we are consists of these desires, knowledge of which can only be of a Franciscan or personal sort. Personal knowledge, moreover, is inseparable from a narrative construal. Hence, our identities are shaped by the narratives with which we identify by means of our loves. By loving, we appropriate certain stories to

memories begin to evaporate, they are held for us by God, providing a stability to our selves that we could not provide for ourselves.

72. On this point, see Miroslav Volf, *The End of Memory: Remembering Rightly in a Violent World* (Grand Rapids: Eerdmans, 2006).

73. Stump, *Wandering in Darkness*, 41.

74. See Stump, *Wandering in Darkness*, 78–79.

75. Stump, *Wandering in Darkness*, 134.

ourselves, making who we are irreducibly personal and narratival. So, in addition to the memories of the objects of love, we may say that our loves place us in a story the telling of which discloses our true selves and structures the resources from which our memories draw.

Because our objects of love shape us, it follows that if we love good things, we become good, but if we love wicked things, we become wicked. By "lov[ing] God with God," we become *like* God, a crucial insight into sanctification.[76] Loving the beautiful God, Augustine insists, makes us beautifully godly. Yet, this is not automatic. Many have noted the narrative shape of Augustine's theological anthropology,[77] and it has been claimed that the most important part of the narrative has to do with how our loves are healed within the divine economy.[78] This was a central tenet of what I argued was required of a theological account of human beings and affords the appropriate epistemic restrictions in making claims about human nature; we must be aware of the narrative indexing of human beings, knowing that at this point in the narrative, sin still distorts our perceptions of humanity. Augustine, argues Peter Burnell, is committed to the same view: "In specifying human nature Augustine examines practical human experience rather than attempting definition in vacuo; yet he does not think our nature to be fully perceptible in its present condition, either, for that condition has thrown the nature itself into more or less violent disorder. . . . Consequently, he brings into consideration (as therefore we must) the divine *administration* of human life in its three main stages: the Garden, this world, and heaven (or its privation)."[79] So, an economic indexing of the claims made about human

76. See *De mor.* 1.13.21–23: "To him we cling through becoming holy. For, having been made holy, we are ablaze with love that is whole and entire, a love that alone prevents our being turned away from God and makes us conformed to him rather than to this world. . . . Love, then, will see to it that we are conformed to God and, having been conformed and configured by him and cut off from this world, that we are not confused with the things that ought to be subject to us. But this is done by the Holy Spirit." Conversely, the "soul . . . is filled with folly and unhappiness the farther it wanders off from God to things lower than itself not by place but by love and desire." See also *Tr. in Ep. Io.* 9.9: "Our soul, my brothers, is loathsome through wickedness; by loving God it is made beautiful." For a constructive account of sanctification along these lines, see Simeon Zahl, *The Holy Spirit and Christian Experience* (New York: Oxford University Press, 2020), chap. 5.

77. See Matthew Levering, "Linear and Participatory History: Augustine's *City of God*," *Journal of Theological Interpretation* 5, no. 2 (2011): 175–96.

78. A claim made by William Babcock in "Augustine and the Spirituality of Desire," *Augustinian Studies* 25, no. 1 (1994): 179–99.

79. Burnell, *Augustinian Person*, 71. See also the comments made by Ian Clausen: "One reason Scripture floods the narrative in *Confessions* is that its author wants Scripture to claim

nature and its healing is central to an Augustinian account of subjective human love.

As human beings love God and proceed along the different stages of human nature indexed by the divine economy, an internal integration of loves that were once contradictory begins.[80] Sanctification is the slow and painful process of bringing those desires into proper alignment. But Augustine also has a great deal to say about the nature of disordered love, about what love is like for those for whom that ordering has not begun, a misshapen love that still haunts those in whom the Spirit dwells. This warped expression of love goes by many names in the Augustinian corpus—*concupiscentia, cupiditas, libido*—but its basic attribute is "a dark drive to control, to appropriate, and turn to one's private ends, all the good things that had been created by God to be accepted with gratitude and shared with others. It lay at the root of the inescapable misery that afflicted [humankind]."[81] Distorted love is "the universal symptom *par excellence* of all forms of deranged relationships, among demons as among men."[82] It is tempting to multiply names for love in Augustine's thought, but what we are talking about here is not really *another* love than the love that is natural to human beings; rather, it is this love's privation, deformation, and warping.[83] Whereas godly, rightly ordered love sees God in all things, recognizes their worth as gifts from God, and refuses to turn the beloved into an item for consumption and instrumentalization, disordered love is rapacious, lascivious, and selfish. This is due to original sin,[84] and it works only to de-

---

control of his story; he wants it to show him where he is and where he is going" (Ian Clausen, *On Love, Confession, Surrender, and the Moral Self* [New York: Bloomsbury Academic, 2018], 20).

80. The theme of internal integration will be examined in the next chapter. For now, see Rist, *Augustine*, 177, as well as Augustine's own comments in *De spiritu et littera* 34.60; *De nuptiis et concupiscentia ad Valerium comitem* 1.23.25; and *Contra Julianum* 5.3.8.

81. Peter Brown, *The Body and Society: Men, Women, and Sexual Renunciation in Early Christianity*, 20th anniversary ed. (New York: Columbia University Press, 2008), 418.

82. Peter Brown, "Saint Augustine," in *Trends in Medieval Political Thought*, ed. Beryl Smalley (Oxford: Basil Blackwell, 1965), 10.

83. Thus Burnell: "Love, therefore, is in a sense divided, but its division is only into charity and that which wrongfully falls short of charity—charity and the (partial) privation of that virtue" (Burnell, *Augustinian Person*, 102). See also Schlabach, who observes that Augustine's terms for love "probably had more to do with the meter of his sentence, or with the need to retain parallels with other sentences, or with the scriptural allusion or Latin version of the Bible that he had in mind, than with any other factor" (Schlabach, *For the Joy Set before Us*, 200n24).

84. A point rightly elucidated by Jesse Couenhoven: "Augustine's typical picture is that original sin or grace operates in and on us by shaping our beliefs and loves, and that we consent to those beliefs and loves" (Jesse Couenhoven, *Stricken by Sin, Cured by Christ: Agency, Necessity, and Culpability in Augustinian Theology* [New York: Oxford University Press, 2013], 86).

stroy the relations that obtain among lovers. It dominates the beloved as an exercise of power, with the only result being mutually assured destruction, for the beloved is oppressed while the lover becomes more and more dominating and vicious—for this reason Augustine calls it the *libido dominandi*, the lust for domination.[85] It operates at the level of nations, but it also has a hold in interpersonal exchanges, for "there is hardly anyone who is free of the love of wielding power or does not long for human glory," a ruinous love "which creeps like a cancer."[86] It harms the lover *and* their objects of love,[87] even to the point of acts of criminality like rape,[88] and it is the opposite of genuine love, which as a rule requires that a "Christian must live in such a way as not to exalt himself over other people."[89] Sinful, disordered love does just that: it is characterized by Augustine as a prurient, power-hungry *grasping* in contrast to a delighted, equalizing *clinging*.[90]

4.2.4 Natural Love, Socially Expressed

At the end of every kind of love is an object of worship of some kind, and this becomes important for understanding the final component of Augustine's account of human love to be considered here—namely, the power of love to create social bonds and identities. Recall that for Augustine, human beings are social by nature,[91] but the kinds of social identities they bear must

85. See *De civ.* 1.pref.

86. *En. in Ps.* 1.1. English translation from Augustine, *Expositions of the Psalms, 1–32,* trans. Maria Boulding, vol. III/15, The Works of Saint Augustine: A Translation for the 21st Century (Hyde Park, NY: New City, 2000).

87. *En. in Ps.* 105.34: "The plans of men and women are extremely harmful to themselves when they seek their own ends rather than God's." English translation from Augustine, *Expositions of the Psalms, 99–120,* trans. Maria Boulding, vol. III/19, The Works of Saint Augustine: A Translation for the 21st Century (Hyde Park, NY: New City, 2003).

88. The relationship between sexual assault and the *libido dominandi* will be explored in chapter 7, but for now see Melanie Webb, "'On Lucretia Who Slew Herself': Rape and Consolation in Augustine's *De ciuitate dei,*" *Augustinian Studies* 44, no. 1 (2013): 37–58. On criminality in general, see *De civ.* 5.19: "Anyone who wants domination and power . . . will generally seek to obtain what he loves by even the most blatantly criminal acts." English translation from Augustine, *The City of God,* ed. Boniface Ramsey, trans. William Babcock, vol. I/7, The Works of Saint Augustine: A Translation for the 21st Century (Hyde Park, NY: New City, 2012).

89. *Tr. in Ep. Io.* 8.8.

90. For an exploration of Augustine's language of *grasping* in contradistinction to *clinging,* see Schlabach, *For the Joy Set before Us,* 67–68.

91. See *De bono conjugali* 1.1: "Human nature is a social entity." English translation from Augustine, "The Excellence of Marriage," in *Marriage and Virginity,* trans. Ray Kearney, vol. I/9, The Works of Saint Augustine: A Translation for the 21st Century (Hyde Park, NY: New City, 1999).

be understood theologically, whether that is at a basic level or at a complex political level. The most relevant detail of social organization is not primarily geographical location or anything of the like, but rather love, for only love "joins many hearts into one."[92] Thus, "even though there are a great many peoples spread across the world, living under various religious rites and moral customs and distinguished by a wide variety of languages, weaponry, and dress, *there are actually only two types of human society*; and following our Scriptures, we may rightly speak of these as two cities."[93] It is important to note that the cities do not designate concrete cities in the world, like points on a map locating Mexico City or Barcelona, though within any actual cities and organizations of people, there is an "admixture" of members of the heavenly and earthly cities differentiated by their loves. So Augustine famously states,

> Two loves, then, have made two cities. Love of self, even to the point of contempt for God, made the earthly city, and love of God, even to the point of contempt for self, made the heavenly city. . . . In the former the lust for domination dominates both its princes and the nations that it subjugates; in the latter both leaders and followers serve one another in love, the leaders by their counsel, the followers by their obedience. The former loves its own strength, displayed in its men of power; the latter says to its God, *I love you, O Lord, my strength* (Ps 18:1).[94]

In light of the foregoing discussion about the natures of rightly ordered and wrongly ordered love, it should be clear enough to say that the heavenly city (when it is operating as it is supposed to) is inhabited by those with genuine divine love, while the earthly city (when it is operating in its characteristic way) is inhabited by those ruled by the *libido dominandi*.[95] In fact, given what Augustine has to say about creation and election,[96] it is not too much of an

92. *De civ.* 15.3.
93. *De civ.* 14.1 (emphasis added).
94. *De civ.* 14.28.
95. The parenthetical qualifications are meant to avoid the suggestion that members of the earthly city are *always* sinful and members of the heavenly city *always righteous*. Members of the heavenly city who are still on pilgrimage on this earth are continually being made fit for the city, and therefore continually require a transformation of their loves, while members of the earthly city can still approximate virtue (a claim to be explored in chapter 6 with respect to justice).
96. The two cities are spoken about in Augustine's earlier treatments of creation and providence: "These two loves—of which one is holy, the other unclean, one social, the other private . . . were first manifested in the angels, one in the good, the other in the bad, and then distinguished the two cities, one of the just, the other of the wicked, founded in the human race under the

oversimplification to say that the heavenly city constitutes the elect, both humans and angels, and the earthly city constitutes the non-elect, both humans and demons: "Love alone, then, distinguishes between the children of God and the children of the devil."[97] In the end, it seems to me that Rowan Williams articulates correctly that, with respect to the two cities, "their goals are distinct, and so will be their eternal rewards."[98] Or, in Gregory Lee's words, the cities "differ as much as their objects of worship."[99]

A people, then, is "a multitude of rational beings joined together by common agreement on the objects of their love," making it clear that "to discover the character of any people we should take a close look at what it loves."[100] Once again, what appears to be an over-theorized point gains quick familiarity when applied to examples. Augustine provides one himself. Those who love God and are members of the heavenly city will wish to

> bring others to love him together with you. If you were enamored of a charioteer, would you not pester other people to become your fellow-fans? A charioteer's fan talks about his hero wherever he goes, trying to persuade others to share his passion. . . . Do not begrudge God to anyone. Grab someone else, as many people as you can, everyone you can get hold of. There is room for all of them in God; you cannot set any limits to him. Each of you individually will possess the whole of him, and all of you together will possess him whole and entire.[101]

Augustine's point that common objects of love are the most important factor in community formation can be readily observed by anyone who attends a

---

wonderful and inexpressible providence of God as he administers and directs everything he has created" (*De Gen. ad litt.* 11.15.20).

97. *Tr. in Ep. Io.* 5.7. This is a contentious reading, for it does not place an emphasis on the visible church to designate the cities, but on divine election, which does not correspond exactly to the visible church. For an argument for this reading, see James Wetzel, "A Tangle of Two Cities," *Augustinian Studies* 43, no. 1/2 (2012): 5–23.

98. Williams, *On Augustine*, 110.

99. Gregory W. Lee, "Republics and Their Loves: Rereading *City of God* 19," *Modern Theology* 27, no. 4 (2011): 567.

100. *De civ.* 19.24. O'Donovan, in his theological appropriation of this claim, rightly adds, "Every concrete community, then, is defined equally by the things it does *not* love together, the objects it refuses to accept as a ground of its association" (Oliver O'Donovan, *Common Objects of Love: Moral Reflection and the Shaping of Community* [Grand Rapids: Eerdmans, 2009], 22).

101. *En. in Ps.* 72.34. In *De doct.* 1.29.30, Augustine makes the same point using the example of an actor. He says of someone who is a fan of an actor, "If he notices someone is rather cool about him [i.e., the actor], he tries to stir him up by singing the actor's praises, while if he finds someone who takes an opposite view of his favorite actor, he hates and detests that person's dislike of his favorite."

sports match or a concert by a famous artist, where a shared love for a team or singer (or, in his case, a charioteer) can cause strangers to embrace (or to erupt in a fistfight). On another level, however, the cities are socially unique because they are divided by common objects of *ultimate* love.[102]

This ultimate division, however, does not mean that Christians should separate themselves from non-Christians. There is a significant epistemic complication for doing so prior to the eschaton, because only election entails membership in any one city. The church "in these evil days" has many "of the reprobate mixed in with the good. Both are gathered, so to speak, in the nets of the Gospel, and in this world, as in the sea, both swim about without distinction, enclosed in those nets until drawn to shore, where the evil will be separated from the good."[103] There is a distinction to be made, but it is not one to be made by those who live in these evil days, who are still on pilgrimage to God.

So what is the heavenly city to do in the meantime? How should it act during the *saeculum*, the time that begins with "the creation out of nothing of the cosmos as a beautifully ordered whole (*de civ.* II.3–6) and ends with the last judgment that definitively and irreversibly separates the Lord's city from the human city (XX.1, XX.14–30)"?[104] In some ways, Augustine's answer is surprisingly simple. The heavenly city "makes *use* of earthly and temporal goods like a pilgrim."[105] Use, of course, is that aforementioned type of rightly ordered love. So, it "defends and seeks an accommodation among human wills with regard to the things that pertain to humanity's mortal nature. At the same time, however, it directs this earthly peace toward the heavenly peace which is so truly peace that, strictly speaking, it alone is to be considered and called the peace of the rational creature, namely, a perfectly ordered and wholly concordant fellowship in the *enjoyment* of God and of each other in God. . . . By this faith it lives justly when it directs to the attainment of this peace every good act it performs for God."[106] It is true that both cities engage the same goods in the span of time between creation and

---

102. For further explorations on these themes, see Phillip Cary, "United Inwardly by Love: Augustine's Social Ontology," in *Augustine and Politics*, ed. John Doody, Kevin L. Hughes, and Kim Paffenroth (Lanham, MD: Lexington Books, 2005), 3–34.

103. *De civ.* 18.49.

104. Paul J. Griffiths, "Secularity and the Saeculum," in *Augustine's "City of God": A Critical Guide*, ed. James Wetzel (New York: Cambridge University Press, 2012), 34.

105. *De civ.* 19.17 (emphasis added).

106. *De civ.* 19.17 (emphasis added).

consummation—goods like food, government, and familial relations—but they are calibrated to radically different ends and are shaped by entirely different norms of use. Residents of the earthly city will feel free to turn their enjoyment toward creatures, attempting to distort finite goods into objects of ultimate satisfaction and blessedness. This is an expression of the *libido dominandi* insofar as it attempts to turn lovable goods meant to be treated as gifts from God toward private consumption. Residents of the heavenly city, by contrast, will see all beloved goods enjoyed during the *saeculum* as gifts from God, images of God, and ordered according to a hierarchy established with God at its peak, knowing that these goods need not be seized upon for they will perdure into the eschaton. The difference is a matter of the telos. Toward what is the engagement with earthly goods directed, and is that telos the true telos for humanity, union with God? And how does that telos shape the norms by which these goods are loved?[107]

Even so, this teleological separation does not mean the heavenly city should sanctimoniously go about its business with its nose turned up to its earthly neighbor or enemy. Far from it. The heavenly city lives a life of true sacrifice (Rom. 12:1), which for Augustine was a matter of mercy and compassion shown toward those within and without the walls of the church. Augustine claims that "mercy is the true sacrifice" of the heavenly city on pilgrimage and calls upon it to engage in the work of cultural activity to benefit all.[108] So James Lee concludes this about the work of the heavenly city on pilgrimage: "For Augustine, true worship must yield works of mercy toward one's neighbor. A purely spiritual offering does not suffice for true charity, for charity necessarily yields works of mercy that are visible, such as the offering of 'bread to a beggar.'"[109] The task of the heavenly city is to be a compassionate, merciful,

107. Thus Lee: "Augustine's chief task in this text is to address different conceptions of the *summum bonum*, and his basic thesis is that the two cities differ on the *summum bonum* according to their desires for temporal and eternal happiness. . . . He fundamentally rejects their position that the *summum bonum* can be found in this earthly condition" (Lee, "Republics and Their Loves," 568).

108. *De civ.* 10.5. On cultural activity, see *De Gen. ad litt.* 8.9.17: "Voluntary activity comes through the works of angels and human beings. . . . In this other mode signs are given, taught and learned, fields cultivated, communities administered, arts and skills practiced, and whatever else is done, whether in the higher company of the angels or in this earthly and mortal society, in such a way as to be in the interest of the good even through the unwitting actions of the bad."

109. James Lee, *Augustine and the Mystery of the Church* (Minneapolis: Fortress, 2017), 109. He references *Contra Faustum* 20.16. See also Stewart-Kroeker, *Pilgrimage as Moral and Aesthetic Formation*, 186–7: "Augustine has a very expansive view of sacrifice. . . . Christ's sacrifice that elicits the love of believers, who sacrifice themselves to him in response, and,

and beneficial presence to all those in the *saeculum*, independent of their ends, so as to reflect most beautifully the sacrifice of Christ.

The elect will even have an awareness of systemic injustice. Augustine knows that since humans are inescapably social, "all the grinding evils with which human society abounds here in this mortal condition" will also be socially ingrained.[110] The "perverted love with which every son of Adam is born" causes this life to be "so wretched that it is like a sort of hell," and it is the task of the heavenly city to recognize and address these systems.[111] What is privately true of the lust for domination infiltrates human systems like families and governments,[112] and Christians must speak wisely into such organizations in an effort to show mercy to those who have been dominated by the *libido* of others. So, even though there is every bit of difference between the two cities, the heavenly city has no opportunity to be distant—it must be known for its compassion, mercy, and true peace in a world infested by evil.

4.3 Conclusion

"The entire life of a good Christian is a holy desire," Augustine maintained.[113] This is an ambiguous claim; did he mean that a Christian life consists only in those loves that are holy, or did he mean that there is no aspect of a Christian's life, no earthly good she encounters, that cannot be subject to a holy love? It seems to me that he meant both. We are what we love, and Christians are characterized by that love poured forth into their hearts in the Holy Spirit. Moreover, the world has been created good and is suffused with the divine presence and can be the object of love so long as that love is observed in right order.

It will be the task of the next chapter to take what has been said here and situate gender within it. A suggestion in that direction, however, has already been made. If human beings are what they love, and if the objects of their loves leave their footprints on the lover so as to form their identities, then *gender-relevant* goods that are loved will, therefore, form gender identities.

re-formed in the image of God, offer sacrificial acts to God and neighbor, becoming united in fellowship, and offered back up to God as the universal sacrifice of Christ's body."

110. *De civ.* 19.5.
111. *De civ.* 22.22.
112. Cf. *De civ.* 19.5–12.
113. *Tr. in Ep. Io.* 4.6.

What it takes for an object of love to be gender-relevant will be explained, but if the central task of accounts of gender is to explain how it is that social identities are formed and how they might relate to the sexed body, then the pieces have been put into place for a theological account of gender. Love, for Augustine, is natural to human beings prior to any social relations and is also deeply formative of social identities. That I love and form my identity through loving is both deeply rooted in my created nature (my weight) and in my social nature. An account of gender that can situate gender within this framework will be social, natural, and deeply informed by theological concepts.

I will attempt to show how this is so in conversation with the thinker I take to be the leading theologian of gender writing today, Sarah Coakley. For Coakley, gender is fundamentally a *desire*, a claim that will be shown to have remarkable commonality with mine. Yet I take issue with the concept of desire, claiming that the account of love just sketched is a far more promising home in which to locate gender. In any case, it should be clear by now that there is available to the Christian theologian a remarkably rich account of identity that contemporary identity language echoes, even if imperfectly. If someone says, "I identify as X," an Augustinian appraisal will immediately jump to the person's loves. What do they love in order to make sense of such an identification, and to what are those loves ordered? The means by which that identification happens is not mere choice or selfish individualistic expression—or at least it should not be, if that person has rightly ordered loves. For an Augustinian theology of human love, we should not dissuade individuals from identifying with social categories like genders. The problem is not with identification but with the account by which such identifications happen. However contemporary identities are said to be formed, Augustinian Christians will insist that at their center must be the loves of the individual, a love beginning and ending with God. And if this is so, then there is no escaping the theological relevance of the identity being claimed, for all loves must be directed to their ultimate enjoyment: God.

Treating identity in this way has great promise. Identity, on this view, is not mere choice; it is not reduced to biology; it is not the arbitrary product of a culture; it is not the blatant negotiation of power—yet it has important things to say about all of these. It takes all of the important desiderata for claims about identity while retaining a robust theological frame, fit for speaking wisely into Christian discipleship. We are what we love, says Augustine, and we are also gendered. So how does love form our gender?

FIVE

Gender as Love

A Theological Proposal

This chapter presents the central constructive proposal for this work. Specifically, it seeks to show that if gender is concerned with the organization of social goods around selves, and if identities are formed by our loves, then gender is about the formation of identities by means of our love for social goods according to the sexed body. I will introduce this claim by means of a view very similar to it—namely, that of Sarah Coakley, for whom gender is a desire. Though similar to my own, Coakley's vision is susceptible to objections, which I put forward by placing her account alongside Harry Frankfurt's philosophy of love. Love, I conclude, is a better category than desire for understanding gender. I then present the model, arguing that gender is a particular relation of love in which goods acquire social meaning in virtue of being loved because of the lover's sexed body.

5.1 Integrating Claims

To this point, I have argued for an assortment of claims that I now intend to integrate in order to put forward the main constructive proposal of this project. The arguments that will be pieced together can be summarized as follows: In chapter 1, I sought to clarify what identifies a theological account

142

of gender as distinct from (but not independent of) accounts that might be given by other disciplines. In chapter 2, I presented the most widely held family of views that seek to answer the question "What is gender?" These are social constructionist views, and while their historical and present-day proponents have made many highly suggestive claims that I want to retain, the view on the whole is philosophically and theologically problematic and untenable. Chapter 3 began the positive project by discussing two feminist theorists whose views have been charting a unique and salutary way forward—namely, Charlotte Witt and Mari Mikkola. From their views, I distilled four foundational theses for a workable metaphysics of gender:

1. Gender is an essence, though this is not reducible to or identical with biological determinism or biological essentialism.
2. The complexity of gender, the noetic effects of sin, and the current conditions of oppression complicate our epistemic access to gender's essence. All the same, we can be assured that issues surrounding gender will be rectified in the eschaton.
3. Any theory or theology of gender must be consistent with and supportive of the cultivation of justice.
4. Gender is concerned with selves or identity and with the way selves organize social goods pertaining to their sexed bodies.

While in that chapter I argued *that* gender is concerned with identity and the organization of social goods according to the sexed bodies of those bearing such identities, it was in chapter 4 that I specified *how* social goods form identities in general. There I argued, with the help of Augustine, that we are what we love, in the sense that the identities we bear are formed by means of our loves. Now it is time to assemble these claims in an effort to put forward a theological account of gender.

After the presentation of the above four theses, I offered a basic definition of gender: gender is the appropriation of cultural goods pertaining to the sexed body by means of which the sexed body is socially manifested in something like an identity. This is a *minimal definition* of gender, for I believe it applies to any tenable account of gender, of which mine is only one instance. What gives my account its specificity is the means by which "appropriation" occurs, how this appropriation forges our identities, how the social manifestation of the sexed body retains the attenuated essentialism of the first thesis, how the process of appropriation is consistent with the complicated access we have to the right relation to gendered goods, and how the formation of love aids in our ventures toward gendered justice. Expatiating this operation of appropriation is the task of this and the following chapters.

To anticipate, I will argue that there are many things we love in virtue of our sexed bodies. Doing so grants to these beloved objects a social meaning and to us a social role, and this is our gender. More than that, we identify with these beloved goods, for they make us who we are and shape our narratives. Because our chief love is to God, moreover, Christians always have an obligation to evaluate these gendered goods in accord with the moral norms of all properly ordered love.

I will also seek to remain consistent with the principles of theological method set forth in the first chapter. To that end, this chapter will include a theological reading of the Song of Songs, prompted by the chapter's main interlocutor, Sarah Coakley, whose views will serve as an important propaedeutic to my own. Coakley, who maintains that gender is fundamentally a *desire*, has led the discussion among theologians attempting to give adequate theological attention to gender. She occupies an important space in the theological discussion, largely because she has denied, outright and with decades of consistency, the bifurcation between recognizable theological practice and careful reflection upon gender. Thus, to the theologians, she says, "It is perhaps even more common . . . for systematic theologians to be dismissive, even derogatory, about theologians interested in feminism or gender." Yet, even when theologians do rise to the challenge, she says, "they tend to import a gender theory from the secular realm without a sufficiently critical *theological* assessment of it." Therein lies the source of the bifurcation, and the way out is not less theology, but more: "A robustly theological, indeed precisely *trinitarian*, perspective on gender is required, and not one that merely smuggles secular gender presumptions into the divine realm at the outset."[1] I am persuaded that Coakley is correct, and the theological perspective she advances will have similarities with my own, even though some significant differences will be discerned. Paying some attention to this groundbreaking theologian, therefore, will set the stage in a helpful way for my proposal.

1. Sarah Coakley, *God, Sexuality, and the Self: An Essay "On the Trinity"* (Cambridge: Cambridge University Press, 2013), 34.

5.2 Sarah Coakley on Desire and Gender, with a Frankfurt-Style Critique

5.2.1 Desire Is More Basic Than Gender: Sarah Coakley

The focus of my exposition of Coakley will be on her understanding of desire and the way it informs and defines gender, which is no incidental component of her theology. The organizing element of Coakley's thought, as any casual inspection of her work will indicate, is a rich vision of desire that draws unto itself the various aspects of a human being's life, chiefly her relationship to God as Father, Son, and Spirit. She describes her ambitious project as an "ontology of desire": "a vision of God's trinitarian nature as both the source and goal of human desires, as God intends them."[2] Human persons are, for Coakley, fundamentally desirous beings, particularly because they are made in the image of a desiring God; these desires, moreover, are meant to be ordered in such a way as to culminate in desire for God through the Holy Spirit. Such a culmination—which occurs only through the rigorously transformative practices of contemplative prayer—reshapes the individual into that for which she was meant, purging the sin that malforms her. Gender, itself a desire, when subsumed to these divine desires, is itself taken up into the life of God, no longer a source of harm and oppression but a means by which we access the triune God.

I find this a tremendously attractive picture, but while it sets the stage for my own view, it contains some conceptual problems. To anticipate, it is not clear which desires are the ones meant to constitute one's gender. At times it seems like it is strictly *sexual* desire (a narrow subset of the desires a human being experiences); at other times it seems like it is the complex of all desires at play in the social life of a human being. Moreover, the specific way Coakley claims gender is purified from a fallen "twoness" is unclear and does not seem to proceed discernibly from the reasons she provides. Third, and most substantially, Coakley's concept of desire itself needs reworking. While she takes care to qualify how she intends to use the term, there is insufficient conceptual analysis of it to see if it will bear the weight she intends it to bear. Here I will refer to the work of Harry Frankfurt to show that desire language is ill-suited to describe the variegated interplay of volitions at stake in moral psychology—and, by extension, in human identity and gender. I

2. Coakley, *God, Sexuality, and the Self*, 6.

will then demonstrate how the Augustinian vision of the previous chapter is actually a much better candidate to forward the kind of theological account of gender Coakley favors. This will set the stage for my more systematic statement of the view.

As broad as Coakley's theological vision is, any account of it must begin with her claim that "desire is divinely and ontologically basic."[3] Desire is basic, but basic to what? Coakley's position seems to be that desire is basic to any personal being, whether that person is human or divine: "But a *theological* analysis such as I propose puts desire at the root—both anthropologically in the human, and theologically in the divine. Desire, I now suggest again— even fallen desire—is the precious clue woven into the crooked human heart that ever reminds it of its relatedness and its source."[4] Persons are basically beings who desire, whether we are describing the everyday activity of human persons, the relations among persons of the Trinity, or the relationship between God and creatures.[5] For this reason, human desire is the "'precious clue' woven into our created being reminding us of our rootedness in God, to bring this desire into *right* 'alignment' with God's purposes, purified from sin and possessiveness."[6] Our desire is a divine link to the God who has made us in God's image, meaning that desire can be a holy and restorative presence in human beings. At the fundamental level, then, a person is a being who desires, desire being a crucially necessary (though presumably not sufficient) condition for personhood.

As the last quotation suggests, there are two further features of specifically human desire involved in Coakley's vision—namely, the *ordering of desire* and the *purification of desire* from sin. It is important to consider each of these in their turn. First, human beings are not only created with a capacity to have objects of desire that define them, but they also bear the responsibility of undergoing "the godly ordering of desire."[7] We are called into "a *training* of desire, a lifelong commitment to what we might now call the 'long haul' of personal, erotic transformation, and thereby of reflection on the final

3. Coakley, *God, Sexuality, and the Self*, 10.
4. Coakley, *God, Sexuality, and the Self*, 58–59.
5. Drawing on Dionysius, Coakley affirms that the outflowing of divine action, especially in the act of creation, is a form of desire (see *God, Sexuality, and the Self*, 315–16). God, then, desires Godself interpersonally as well as desiring creation.
6. Coakley, *God, Sexuality, and the Self*, 309–10.
7. Sarah Coakley, *The New Asceticism: Sexuality, Gender and the Quest for God* (London: Bloomsbury Continuum, 2015), 30.

significance of all one's desires before God."[8] There is a specifically theological duty to "evaluate and *adjudicate* desires, both sexual and others, and how to live a life of balance and moderation such that desire is negotiated with ascetical realism, and in a mode conducive to genuine human flourishing."[9] But how is the theologian to do this? By what order does she adjudicate human desire? Here Coakley's thought is self-avowedly hierarchical, yet the hierarchy she invokes is not the kind in which the higher attempts to dominate the lower. Rather, she defends a hierarchical order of human desire according to which the chief object is God alone.[10] When the "primacy of *divine* desire" is recognized as the anchor for right order, the deleterious hierarchies that produce oppression in human societies are seen for what they are—namely, aberrations of something made to be a creaturely good. Human beings were made to desire God and to order all other desires by directing them toward God and undergoing the purgation from wickedness that such orientation produces. When our nondivine desires fail to find their proper orientation toward God, or if they are intrinsically *unable* to be directed toward God, it follows that these are sinful desires, twisted, warped, and misapplied instances of something originally meant for good.

Second, Coakley's notion of desire emphasizes the need for its purification. Desire, since it is not exempted from the distorting effects of the fall, is always liable to abject uses and ends. Christian theology, felicitously, has at its disposal the "theological concepts of creation, fall, and redemption," which allow theologians to identify and place desires in accordance with where they are located within the divine economy.[11] Is a given desire good, created by God for human delight? Or is it fallen, an aberration of a good desire? Or has it been redeemed, the realignment of an evil desire that once was good? Or is its realignment incomplete, awaiting a future redemption in which it is completely fulfilled and directed in God? Of course, part of the ordering task results in the purification task; by recognizing the proper order of desire one is given a "map" for the purifying process.[12]

8. Coakley, *New Asceticism*, 30.

9. Coakley, *New Asceticism*, 3–4.

10. See Coakley, *God, Sexuality, and the Self*, 321: "I want to defend this idea of hierarchy in a particular sense in the *human* realm, and argue that we cannot do without it, if we are to *order* our values aright—order them appropriately, 'orient' them, towards God."

11. Coakley, *God, Sexuality, and the Self*, 53–54.

12. Surprisingly, *submission* plays an important role here, though not the submission featured in some theologies of gender where women exclusively submit to men, but the *human* submission to God whereby the human heart is purged and reformed in ways often too deep for words. On

Both of the above claims can be traced back in some way or other to a
Platonist stream of Christian theology that Coakley endorses (and shares with
Augustine).[13] The original move she makes beyond this Platonic heritage is
this: *gender is among those human desires that find their source and completion in desire for God.* Thus Coakley: "I now want to extend that analysis to
the issue of gender, and to hypothesize that *desire is also more fundamental
than gender*; and that the key to the secular riddle of gender can lie only
in its connection to the doctrine of a trinitarian God."[14] There is a "messy
entanglement of sexual desires and desire for God," for "sexual desire finds
[its] final meaning *only* in (the trinitarian) God."[15] Coakley summarizes the
proposal in this way: "Physical desire finds its origins in right divine desire.
. . . Dionysius' more ancient vision means that, in contemporary terms, Freud
is turned on his head. Instead of 'God' language 'really' being about sex, sex
is really about God."[16] Put differently, Coakley's view proceeds along the following lines: Gender is a desire nestled in a complex of other desires by which
human beings operate. All human desire, however, finds its source and telos
in God, the desire for whom is chief and ultimate for all of humanity. This
means that gender is swept up into our desire for God, for God is its source
and end, and our desire for God is coiled up with our gendered desire.

Here we encounter the first point of conceptual ambiguity that I would like
to explore, for it reveals some senses in which Coakley's view is inadequate,
even if I do not think it is mistaken. What does it mean to say that *gender* is
a desire? Coakley is not clear, and at points her views seem internally inconsistent. In some places, she seems to say that it is specifically *sexual* desires
that constitute gender, such that my desire for persons of a particular sex

this point, see Coakley's early work, especially Sarah Coakley, *Powers and Submissions: Spirituality, Philosophy and Gender*, Challenges in Contemporary Theology (Malden, MA: Blackwell,
2002), 68: "'Absolute dependence' is indeed at the heart of true human creatureliness and the
contemplative quest. But such *right* dependence is an elusive goal: the entanglements with
themes of power, hierarchy, sexuality and death are probably inevitable but also best brought
to consciousness; they are an appropriate reminder that our prayer is enfleshed."

13. See Coakley, *God, Sexuality, and the Self*, 316: "Why should Christianity and Platonism
here *not* genuinely converge and intersect? It has indeed all along been the burden of this volume
to suggest such." In Plato's *Symposium*, Socrates argues that the basic desires that motivate
one towards giving birth to offspring are the same desires that motivate one to giving birth to
virtuous works of philosophy. See Plato, *Symposium*, trans. Robin Waterfield, Oxford World
Classics (Oxford: Oxford University Press, 1994), 53–54 (210b).

14. Coakley, *God, Sexuality, and the Self*, 52 (emphasis original).

15. Coakley, *God, Sexuality, and the Self*, 43, 15.

16. Coakley, *God, Sexuality, and the Self*, 316.

or gender, or my sexual desire for this *particular* person, is what makes up my gender. In her treatments of gay identities, for instance, sexuality, gender, and desire are nearly synonymous with one another,[17] and the quotes in the preceding paragraph show how she tends to employ "sexuality" and "gender" interchangeably, both spoken about as the desire that turns Freud on his head. Yet Freud spoke specifically about *sexual* desire, and if that is what Coakley means by gendered desire, it would exclude desires for other goods we typically associate with gender (like desires to wear certain kinds of clothes) as well as individuals who have no sexual desire at all. On this reading of her view, someone who has no or atypical sexual desire would not be gendered. At other points, Coakley takes a much broader approach, arguing very persuasively that desire cannot be contained only to sexual desire and must be seen as a mutually implicative web in which every human category rubs elbows with all the others: "'Erotic' desire has to be seen as in a tether of connected desires: for food, drink, comfort, intimacy, acknowledgment, power, pleasure, money, relaxation, rest, etc., as well as physical sex."[18] According to this broader understanding of gendered desire, when we consider what gender is, we must take into account not just sexual desire but also our desires for food, drink, clothing, and so forth. The question, then, is this: Is gender desire *the same as* sexual desire, or does it include our desire for other goods? My suspicion, and the option that will be assumed in this chapter, is that it is the latter. Gender, if it is a desire, must be a desire informed by many objects, so as not to exclude entire classes of individuals who are intuitively gendered, like asexual (or "ace") persons. Coakley, however, does not clarify and does not seem to have a definite view about which desires are relevant for informing gendered desire.

Supposing Coakley is correct that gender is a desire, then it follows that gender itself can be ordered and purified. Like all other desires, it is situated within the divine economy such that our genders can be seen as created, fallen, redeemed, and perfected, which serves to "place the performances of gender in a spectrum of existential possibilities *between* despair and hope."[19] It is not enough simply to look around and perceive the ways gendered desire

17. See Coakley, *New Asceticism*, 141.

18. Coakley, *New Asceticism*, 8. See also: "Sexual desire cannot, in this or any other context, ultimately be divorced from other forms of desire (for food, wealth, power, status, peace, and finally for God)—not, at least, when 'desire' itself is reflected upon *theologically*" (132).

19. Coakley, *God, Sexuality, and the Self*, 54.

appears in the world and to validate it, for even if some gendered trait is ubiquitously evident, it may still be a sinful expression of gender, for sin is also everywhere we look. This means we cannot be sure that what we take to be normative and necessary for gender are not in fact fallen mutations of it simply because these gendered traits are putatively universal. Because gender is moved along the narrative of redemption, "gender is not unchangeable: it too is *in via*."[20] There is a trajectory of redemption that gender undergoes, one in which sinful aspects are being transformed by the redemptive work of Father, Son, and Holy Spirit.[21] This redemptive work, moreover, operates according to a distinct symbolism, and once again Coakley's view reveals its ambiguities. Sinful gender, Coakley maintains, operates according to a "twoness" eventually redeemed by the "threeness" of the Trinity: "It must be, then, that in this fallen world, one lives, in some sense, *between* twoness and its transfiguring interruption; so one is not, as in secular gender theory, endlessly and ever subject to the debilitating falseness of fallen gender, fallen twoness."[22] This is how God's trinitarian work redeems our genders, claims Coakley. It identifies instances of "twoness"—such as views of gender that insist on a binary—and interrupts and transforms them into "threeness." "*Twoness*," she concludes, "*is divinely ambushed by threeness*."[23]

But there are some concerns to be raised that cast doubt on this particular set of claims. It is not clear why the gender binary (and not some other binary) is undone by the work of the three persons of the Trinity, much less why the number of persons in the Trinity alters the number of gender kinds in any way. Other binaries, like the Creator/creature distinction or the binary between "me" and "not me," are not eradicated by the triune work of God. Coakley sees the purification of gender by the triune God as involving the erasure of gender as a binary, but this moves rather quickly, without showing

20. Coakley, *God, Sexuality, and the Self*, 54. This corresponds very nicely with my second principle from chapter 4 and renders problematic attempts to ground gender in something like natural law.

21. See Coakley, *God, Sexuality, and the Self*, 54: "A theological view of gender thereby also has an eschatological hope, one that it sees not as pious fiction or wish-fulfillment, but as firmly grounded in the events of Christ's incarnation and resurrection."

22. Coakley, *God, Sexuality, and the Self*, 56. Trinitarian "threeness" is of immense importance to Coakley. She criticizes Moltmann for failing to ask, "What 'difference' does it make to the issue of gender that God is *three*?" Sarah Coakley, "The Trinity and Gender Reconsidered," in *God's Life in Trinity*, ed. Miroslav Volf and Michael Welker (Minneapolis: Fortress, 2006), 139.

23. Coakley, *God, Sexuality, and the Self*, 58 (emphasis original).

how the conclusion follows from the reasons provided.[24] Linn Tonstad has therefore alleged that Coakley engages in "a kind of theological numerology" without giving an account of why it is that only certain binaries (men/women) are interrupted but not others (i.e., God/creation, divinity/humanity, me/not me).[25] Nor is it altogether obvious *what kind of difference* God's threeness is supposed to make for gender or what the connection is between gender and the number of divine persons. Finally, as we saw in the work of Kathryn Tanner, in chapter 2, there are considerable problems with drawing morally normative conclusions from the number of persons in the Trinity.[26]

If we set aside these claims about the particulars of purification, we may ask further: How *are* our desires purified, according to Coakley? The answer is deceptively simple in articulation but indicative of one of the most strenuous dimensions of the Christian life—namely, through the arduous crucible of contemplative prayer.[27] It is in prayer that our chief desire for God is transformed and purged, and this is no safe task, for here we encounter the triune God, who is eager to remake us in the image of the Christ to whom and through whom we pray in the Spirit. Through a reading of Romans 8:14–17 and 26–27, Coakley maintains that prayer is always a trinitarian act:

> What is being described by Paul is *one* experience of an activity of prayer that is nonetheless ineluctably, though obscurely, triadic. It is *one* experience of God, but God as simultaneously (i) doing the praying in me, (ii) receiving that prayer, and (iii) in that exchange, consented to in me, inviting me into the Christic life of redeemed sonship. Or to put it another way: the "Father" (so-called here) is both source and ultimate object of divine longing in us; the "Spirit" is that

24. Coakley's eschatology is not irrelevant here, though I cannot explore it in depth. For Coakley, gender in the eschaton "will certainly not conform to anything we can catch and hold in gender stereotypes *in this world*," possibly because there will be no gender in the eschaton, a position she derives from Gregory of Nyssa (*God, Sexuality, and the Self*, 283). See also Sarah Coakley, "The Eschatological Body: Gender, Transformation and God," in *Powers and Submissions*, 153–67. Coakley seems to adopt Judith Butler's view that both gender and sex are performative, such that the practices we engage in (including, for Coakley, contemplative prayer) actually change our bodies. I have argued against this position in greater depth in Fellipe do Vale, "Cappadocian or Augustinian? Adjudicating Debates on Gender in the Resurrection," *International Journal of Systematic Theology* 21, no. 2 (2019): 182–98.

25. Linn Marie Tonstad, *God and Difference: The Trinity, Sexuality, and the Transformation of Finitude*, Gender, Theology and Spirituality (New York: Routledge, 2016), 107.

26. See also Karen Kilby, *God, Evil, and the Limits of Theology* (New York: Bloomsbury, 2020), chaps. 1 and 4.

27. For Coakley on prayer, see Ashley Cocksworth, "On Prayer in Anglican Systematic Theology," *International Journal of Systematic Theology* 22, no. 3 (2020): 383–411.

irreducibly, though obscurely, distinct enabler and incorporator of that longing in creation (that which *makes* the creation divine); and the "Son" is that divine and perfected creation, into whose life I, as pray-er, am caught up.[28]

Our desires are for a trinitarian God, and in our prayers we are welcomed into the trinitarian life and are thereby transformed. As our prayers are motivated by our chief desire for God, all of those other desires entangled with divine desire, including gender, are also transformed. So, in prayer, "the specific Gift of the Spirit cracks open the human heart to the breaking of that [gender] binary, making 'gender' ultimately fluid to the priority of divine desire."[29] Or again, she maintains that "rightly channeled *eros*, whether married or celibate, is impossible without deep prayer and ascetic perseverance."[30] Because of the profound embroilment that exists between gender desire and our desire for God in prayer, our prayers transform even our gendered desires, which is not saying anything different than stating that prayer transforms gender *itself*. So, if prayer is the means by which our desires for God are radically purified, and if all of our other desires supervene on that desire for God, then changes and purgations in divine desire *entail* changes and purgations in other desires, like gender. Thus, gender, desire, and prayer are all deeply intertwined on Coakley's view.

Coakley illustrates this process in three stages through which the one who prays progresses. At the first, purgative level, people who pray "need to know in precise, even legalistic, detail what will inculcate the virtuous Christian life," discovering those beliefs that inform practices, attitudes, and postures to worldly goods that mark out a distinctively Christian life.[31] Here gender is relatively stable, and one learns how to relate to gendered goods properly, illustrated by Clement of Alexandria's *De Paedagogus*. At the second tier, the person praying receives illumination, finding out ways in which Christian practices "re-modulate beliefs," as demonstrated in the Rule of St. Benedict.[32]

28. Coakley, *New Asceticism*, 90. It is this "threeness" that Coakley maintains transforms human binaries. Since prayer transforms our desires, and prayer is always trinitarian, those fallen binaries are thereby transformed. But, again, the *number* of the persons seems to support unjustified weight. It is not inconsistent to say that God transforms our desires by prayer, that prayer is trinitarian, but that our desires are moved toward justice and love. No recourse is made to the number of divine persons on this account.

29. Sarah Coakley, "Why Gift? Gift, Gender and the Trinitarian Relations in Milbank and Tanner," *Scottish Journal of Theology* 61, no. 2 (2008): 234.

30. Coakley, *New Asceticism*, 51.

31. Coakley, *New Asceticism*, 112–13.

32. Coakley, *New Asceticism*, 115.

What does this do to gendered desire, mention of which is curiously miss-ing from Benedict's rule? Coakley states, "Societal gender expectations, it seems, have been left behind, in a curiously freeing way; but there is no hint, either, of any positive *upturning* or subverting of gender binaries."[33] This upturning is found at the third stage, which she calls the "unitive" stage. Here certain practices of prayer are *necessary* for direct and unvarnished knowledge of God, exemplified by mystical theologians like Theresa of Ávila. Gender, here, undergoes certain reversals (John of the Cross experiences a feminine posture in his soul; Theresa finds a "strong voice of authority," uniquely masculine) that reveal its fluidity.[34] The idea here is that the one who prays undergoes a process that alters her practice and belief the deeper she goes. The alteration, because it involves that desire for God upon which all other desires supervene (including gendered desire), implicates all of her life. Her gender, then, is transformed as she prays. The *particular nature of that transformation*, according to Coakley, is a removal of the twoness of gender into something fluid.

To summarize Coakley's view, we might say that the main thrust of her proj-ect is an attempt "to submit all of our desires to the test of divine longing."[35] Desire is fundamental to who we are, yet we are not passively carried along by whatever desires with which we find ourselves. Rather, we have the responsi-bility to recognize the order of desire, the chief object of which is God. God is the source of our desire, and the desire upon which all of our other desires depend, so much so that purgations and transformations to our desire for God impact them too. Gender is also a desire, liable to transformation as it depends on an ever-transforming desire for God. As we delve more deeply into the maturation of prayer, our genders are brought into a redemptive trinitar-ian presence, whereby we see more clearly and become more truly the genders God intended for us to be. Everything hinges on the nature of desire—that we are fundamentally who we are because of desire, that gender is a desire, that prayer involves our desires in a purifying way and that our desires can be

---

33. Coakley, *New Asceticism*, 117.

34. See Coakley, *New Asceticism*, 121. For more on Coakley's understanding of mystical gender reversals, see her work on Gregory of Nyssa, esp. *Powers and Submissions*, 127–29; Sarah Coakley, "Introduction—Gender, Trinitarian Analogies, and the Pedagogy of the Song," in *Re-thinking Gregory of Nyssa*, ed. Sarah Coakley (London: Blackwell, 2003), 1–13; and Sarah Coakley, "Gregory of Nyssa," in *The Spiritual Senses: Perceiving God in Western Chris-tianity*, ed. Paul L. Gavrilyuk and Sarah Coakley (Cambridge: Cambridge University Press, 2011), 36–55.

35. Coakley, *New Asceticism*, 141.

transformed. While I find this vision extremely attractive, I believe its reliance on desire needs revision. Coakley is proposing a remarkably suggestive account of gender, but it asks the concept of desire to do much more work than it is able to do. Through this objection we will see that Coakley's proposal, if it replaces desire with a more robust Augustinian account of human love, can be highly successful.

5.2.2 Desire, Love, and Selfhood: A Frankfurt-Style Critique

Though I have raised two objections so far to Coakley's view—one having to do with the ambiguities regarding which desires inform gendered desire and the other with the particular way in which she thinks gender is transformed from a binary to something more fluid—the main correction I believe her view requires regards its foundational concept: desire. In short, desire is not adequate to ground all of the moves Coakley makes; something more robust is necessary. In her work, Coakley has a tendency to collapse desire and love, terms she seems to consider fungible.[36] The trouble is that desire and love are not the same thing, even if they have a deep and mutually extensive connection. Desire is not *against* love, but love is much more than desire.

In her glossary, Coakley defines "desire" as "the physical, emotional, or intellectual longing that is directed towards something or someone that is wanted."[37] This is a fairly standard account of desire; it is fundamentally a *longing*, located in either physical, emotional, or intellectual aspects of a human person.[38] Harry Frankfurt, however, argues that dependence on the language of desire fails to account adequately for the complexities of practical reason in the shaping of human persons:

> When philosophers or economists or others attempt to analyze the various structures and strategies of practical reasoning, they generally draw upon a more or less standard but nonetheless rather meager conceptual repertoire. Perhaps the most elementary as well as the most indispensable of these limited

36. See, e.g., Coakley, *God, Sexuality, and the Self*, 316: "Physical *desire* finds its origins in divine *desire*." And just beneath that: "No one can move simply from earthly, physical *love* (tainted as it so often is by sin and misdirection of desire) to divine love" (316, emphasis added). At the very least, Coakley makes no clear distinction between desire and love.

37. Coakley, *God, Sexuality, and the Self*, 346.

38. It should be noted that a significant body of literature complicates and nuances this definition of desire. See, e.g., Timothy Schroeder, *Three Faces of Desire* (New York: Oxford University Press, 2004), which introduces notions of motivation, pleasure, and reward.

resources is the notion of what people *want*—or, synonymously . . . what they *desire*. This notion is rampantly ubiquitous. It is also heavily overburdened, and a bit limp. People routinely deploy it in a number of different roles, to refer to a disparate and unruly assortment of psychic conditions and events. Moreover, its various meanings are rarely distinguished; nor is there much effort to clarify how they are related. These matters are generally left carelessly undefined in the blunt usages of common sense and ordinary speech.[39]

Though Coakley does far better than to be *careless* in her use of "desire," she nevertheless fails to undertake the careful conceptual analysis necessary to distinguish desire within the array of terms operative in moral psychology, much less to distinguish different *instances* of desire so as to specify which ones she thinks are relevant for her theological project.

It becomes easy to see this when we think about instances of desire that would not be candidates for Coakley's robust usage of the term. Consider, for example, those desires on which we do not act. There are many of these: I desire to buy lunch today, but I also desire to save some money, so I act upon my latter desire and pack a lunch. The former, though it is a genuine desire I possess, is not an *effective* desire—that is, a desire "that moves (or will or would move) a person all the way to action."[40] Thus, there is a distinction between desires that do and desires that do not guide my conduct, those that actually lead to action and those that do not. Or again, we may consider our ability to be mistaken about what we actually desire. As Frankfurt notes, "a person may be as misguided in his preferences as in his desires," as when someone desires to enter a certain profession believing it will make her happy, only to find that it does not do so at all. What she really desired was the *idea* of the profession. But an idea of something is not the same as the thing itself, as she quickly finds out on the first day of the job. Other times, desires lack the consistency in our lives to make a difference to the individual who possesses them. Frankfurt notes, "It is possible to desire something, or to think it valuable, only for a moment. Desires and beliefs have no inherent persistence;

39. Harry Frankfurt, *The Reasons of Love* (Princeton: Princeton University Press, 2004), 10. He also says that the notion of desire "is deployed routinely, and often rather carelessly, in a variety of different roles. It is important that these roles be carefully differentiated and severally understood. Otherwise, the significance of some fundamental aspects of our lives will tend to be severely blurred" (Harry Frankfurt, *Necessity, Volition, and Love* [Cambridge: Cambridge University Press, 1998], 155).

40. Harry Frankfurt, *The Importance of What We Care About* (Cambridge: Cambridge University Press, 1988), 14.

nothing in the nature of wanting or of believing requires that a desire or a belief must endure."[41] So we might have *fleeting* desires, ones about which we forget with a passing moment. In this case, we do not care about such desires; these are the things we desire in the afternoon and forget by dinner. So there are effective and ineffective desires, desires that we identify correctly and those about which we are wrong, and desires that come and go quickly and those that stick with us for quite a long time.

Frankfurt also introduces the category of people designated as "wanton": "The essential characteristic of a wanton is that he does not care about his will. His desires move him to do certain things, without its being true of him either that he wants to be moved by those desires or that he prefers to be moved by other desires."[42] There is no reflexivity in the wanton; she may be full of desires that may or may not move her to act, but she never pauses to reflect if these are in fact the desires by which she *wants* to operate. Consider two consumers of pornography. The first has an uncontrollable desire to consume the pornography, yet because she knows that such material promotes violence and distorts sexuality, wishes desperately that she was not moved by her uncontrollable desire and feels a burden of conflict within herself. The second has a similar desire to consume, yet he does not much care whether he desires it or whether such a motivation is something he wishes were effective for him. The latter is a wanton, the former is not. The wanton reveals that there is a difference between desiring and caring about something, for it is "quite common for people to want various things without actually caring about them, and to prefer satisfying one of their desires rather than another without regarding the object of either desire as being of any importance to them."[43] The second pornography consumer wants the pornography, but the question of *whether* he wants to want it is not important to him.

So, it seems that there is actually quite a wide diversity of desires experienced in any given day. One might ask Coakley whether gendered desire includes both effective *and* ineffective desires, whether gender is something on which we always act or not. Or again, must we always correctly perceive our gendered desires, or can we be mistaken about them? What impact would that have on our gender identity? Must our gendered desires be consistent? Or can they come and go, fading according to the different stages of our lives?

41. Frankfurt, *Importance of What We Care About*, 84.
42. Frankfurt, *Importance of What We Care About*, 16.
43. Frankfurt, *Necessity, Volition, and Love*, 157.

Must we *care* about all of our gendered desires? Apart from the ones that are sinful, what criteria should we adopt for how to care about certain gendered desires? All of these questions basically boil down to this: Yes, gender is a desire, but *what kind of desire is it?* Answering this, I shall argue, requires some conceptual sharpening, leading us to identify a specific kind of desire that we call love.

The first step toward this sharpening favored by Frankfurt is to ascertain those desires that identify things about which a person cares. We care about things when they make a difference to us: "If it would make no difference at all to anything whether a certain thing existed, or whether it had certain characteristics, then neither the existence of that thing nor its characteristics would be of any importance to me."[44] So, what happens to a character in a novel in which I am immersed is important to me because it makes a difference to me that this state of affairs obtains. My life is affected by this in a way that it is not by what happens to another character in another novel in which I am uninterested. This, in addition, is because I *care* about that character and not about these other characters.

Caring, furthermore, is essentially a *second-order* desire *about* the desires that motivate us, a reflexive mental act by which "we *objectify* to ourselves the ingredient items of our ongoing mental life."[45] Caring, basically, is *when we desire to have the desires we actually have*: "People want certain of their desires to move them into action, and they usually have certain other desires that they would prefer to remain motivationally ineffective. They are concerned about their desires in other ways as well. Thus they want some of their desires to persist; and they are indifferent, or even actively opposed, to the persistence of others. These alternative possibilities—commitment to one's own desires or an absence of commitment to them—define the difference between caring and not caring. Whether a person cares about the object of his desire depends upon which of the alternatives prevails."[46] Caring occurs when our first-order desires are affirmed, appropriated, and internalized by our second-order desires, where a first-order desire is something a person wants, and a second-order desire is one held by a person when he or she identifies with a certain set of first-order desires. Those first-order desires

44. Frankfurt, *Importance of What We Care About*, 82. See also Frankfurt, *Reasons of Love*, 25: "Something is important to a person only in virtue of a difference that it makes."

45. Harry G. Frankfurt, *Taking Ourselves Seriously and Getting It Right*, ed. Debra Satz (Stanford: Stanford University Press, 2006), 4.

46. Frankfurt, *Reasons of Love*, 21.

she or he possesses but does not wish to be possessed are "external" to the desirer in a certain way, while the desires she or he accepts are internalized by taking stock of the desires that motivate them and taking ownership of the ones they find acceptable.[47] Cares are effectively second-order desires about the desires that move us. The pornography addict who desperately wishes she was not moved to consume pornography cares about her first-order desires.

It is because we care about things that our worlds contain things that are important *to us*. So, it is "by caring about things that we infuse the world with importance."[48] Caring is the means by which we *appropriate* importance. A life that did not contain anything important to it would be no life at all, contends Frankfurt, for it would have no meaningful relationships, no genuine ambitions or goals, and no direction. What is important to me, however, is not necessarily important to the next person, for objects of care are often unique; *my* daughter is important to me, while someone else's daughter is important to them, and these are not the same objects of care. Caring, more-over, provides our lives with "thematic unity": "The moments in the life of a person who cares about something, however, are not merely linked inher-ently by formal relations of sequentiality. The person necessarily binds them together, and in the nature of the case also construes them as being bound together, in richer ways."[49] There is a difference between events in our lives that merely follow one after the other and events that we weave together into a coherent narrative of ourselves. If I did not care about anything, I would be a passenger in my own life. This was a crucial addendum to the Augustin-ian account of love from the previous chapter provided by Eleonore Stump. To know a person, she argued, is a second-person kind of knowledge. It is to know the narrative of their lives shaped by the objects of their care. The things we care about—our plans, relationships, heartbreaks, favorites, and so on—cohere to narrate who we are, so much so that if we really wanted to know someone (rather than merely know *about* them), we would have to hear the story of their lives, especially with reference to the things they have loved. As I care about various things in my life, they connect one with another

47. On externalization, see Frankfurt, *Importance of What We Care About*, 63: "Passions are external to us just when we prefer not to have them, or when we prefer not to be moved by them; . . . they are internal when, at the time of their occurrence, we welcome or indifferently accept them."

48. Frankfurt, *Reasons of Love*, 23.

49. Frankfurt, *Importance of What We Care About*, 83.

because they are things that I have internalized and made my own. Care is the common thread that weaves together the variously important moments in our lives.

Caring, Frankfurt notes in addition, identifies what those final ends are by which we actually live. It "provides us with aims and ambitions, thereby making it possible for us to formulate courses of action that are not entirely pointless. . . . Without final ends, we would find nothing truly important as an end or as a means."[50] If our courses of action have no terminus, no point of completion, it would be hard to make sense of life and the things we seek to accomplish. The objects of importance about which we care locate those points of completion, what Frankfurt calls a final end. We then organize the other things we care about in virtue of accomplishing these ends. Without them, our courses of action would be meaningless. The final end of my writing this chapter is to complete this project on gender, and it is so because it is important to me that I complete the project. "If we had no final ends," maintains Frankfurt, "it is more than desire that would be empty and vain. It is life itself. For living without goals and purposes is living with nothing to do."[51] Caring and importance, then, detect the ends for which we organize our means, and this makes sense of all our courses of action in life.

So, care appropriates importance, provides thematic unity by means of our life narratives, and identifies the final ends for which we act. But we can be even more specific, for the most important type of care is *love*: "Love is a particular mode of caring."[52] Particular instances of caring count as love, just as particular desires are instances of care. Following the Augustinian theology of love from the last chapter, care is properly ordered love when it is produced by the Holy Spirit, made possible by the capacities with which we were created, implanting objects of love in our memories, shaping our narratives, forging social identities, and all the rest. Like Augustine, Frankfurt is clear that we are what we love. This extends from the nature of caring. If love consists in those desires that I have appropriated and with which I have identified, then those desires are *who I am*, in some sense. "The willing acceptance of attitudes, thoughts, and feelings transforms their status," Frankfurt claims. "They are no longer merely items that happen to appear in a certain psychic history. We have taken responsibility for them as authentic *expressions*

50. Frankfurt, *Reasons of Love*, 52–53.
51. Frankfurt, *Necessity, Volition, and Love*, 84.
52. Frankfurt, *Taking Ourselves Seriously*, 40.

of ourselves."[53] If loving provides the coherence to the sequence of my life, infuses my life with importance, and identifies the ends for which I act, then it is by loving that "our individual identities are most fully expressed and defined."[54] We organize our lives according to what we love, and without loving, our lives would be held captive to an insidious kind of boredom according to which "we have no interest in what is going on," an inhuman state where our lives do not really feel like our own.[55] Instead, most human beings feel a pull to be *wholehearted*, or not to feel a sense of division and dislocation in one's desires. There are many ways an individual may be divided: their second-order desires may conflict with their first-order desires, as is the case with the first pornography addict. Likewise, a person may have a conflicting set of second-order desires, such that she both does and does not want to be moved by certain desires.[56] The person who says "For I do not do the good I want [second order], but the evil I do not want is what I do [first order]" (Rom. 7:19) knows what it is to be divided. Being wholehearted, then, is a matter of unification: "The wholehearted person is fully settled as to what he wants, and what he cares about."[57]

Frankfurt has shown us that Coakley needs to be much more specific when claiming that gender is a desire. If gender is to form our identities, then it must not be *mere* desire, but *love*, for love is that specific kind of desire that takes into account our cares and what is important to us, thereby forming our identities. Our gendered desires are those that we appropriate and with which we identify. That is what makes them love. Not all desires do this, but only those that count as love. With this preparatory discussion in mind, let us turn to a full statement of the model I would like to defend: gender is love.

5.3 Gender as Love: The Model

I think that Coakley is basically correct in her claim that gender is defined by that which makes us who we are, our *identities*, something that cannot be separated from our basic orientation to God, the one in whom our identities are made whole. But "desire" is not the right word for what shapes identity,

---

53. Frankfurt, *Taking Ourselves Seriously*, 8 (emphasis original).
54. Frankfurt, *Reasons of Love*, 50.
55. Frankfurt, *Reasons of Love*, 54.
56. See Frankfurt, *Importance of What We Care About*, 164–65.
57. Frankfurt, *Reasons of Love*, 95.

or at least it must be specified quite heavily. Rather, gender is love, for love makes us who we are. Recall from the previous chapter that we are created as lovers by nature, for our weight is our love (a property with which we were created even before any creaturely relations into which we enter). We were created with the ability to love and with a proper object of ultimate love: God. Only when we are properly ordered to the love of God, brought about by the Holy Spirit, are we genuinely happy. Or, in Frankfurt's terms, only when we love God with undivided wills can we be wholehearted. But this does not preclude the love of earthly goods, for we can love God in these goods, recognizing them as gifts from the Divine Gift Giver. All of our objects of love are stamped into our memories and give coherence to a narrative that details our true selves, making us who we are. Loving rightly sanctifies us; loving wrongly makes us into dominators of the beloved. Communities and social identities are forged by those who share common objects of love, for they share similar identities. We love when our second- and first-order desires align toward an object that implants in our memories, shapes our stories, and forms our social identities. When the Holy Spirit indwells us, our second-order desires are radically recalibrated toward God, and the slow and sanctifying process of having our first-order desires come into alignment begins. Altering Coakley's theology of desire to an Augustinian theology of love, as I plan to do, is no slight modification, in the end. It carries with it implications for the order she invokes and for the kinds of transformation undergone by gender.

So then, what is the model of gender that I am presenting? Gender is ultimately about the organization of goods by which the sexed body is socially manifested, in which the lover identifies with the beloved, shaping who she is. A helpful way to think about this is with recourse to Eleonore Stump's notion of "the offices of love." To love something is inherently a relation, as Augustine maintained, something that binds lover and beloved together. But something must be said about how relationships of love differ from one another.[58] We can do so with recourse to the offices of love, which are "differing *kinds* of relationship of love." "The nature of an office," says Stump, "circumscribes the sort of union that is appropriate to the love of that office, and so it also

58. In the case of persons, this is bidirectional, where the persons love one another. In the case of love for nonpersonal objects, of course, the relation is unidirectional, where the beloved does not need to reciprocate the love (because it obviously cannot).

delimits the sort of love appropriate within that office."[59] Love relationships obtain between, for example, a mother and son, a student and her school, and a hungry person and his food. Stump refers to these as offices of love. Such offices specify just what kinds of acts of love are appropriate to obtain within the relationship as well as what kinds of goods are needed for that office to obtain. To love food like one loves a child, for example, is categorically mistaken. All of us occupy many different offices of love in our lives, all at once, even in a single day. On my model, one such office of love, in fact one very *sizable* office that takes into account many different objects of love, is our gender.

There are many things we love because we are sexed beings. The relation of love in question is the one that obtains between us *as sexed individuals* (or, at least, as *perceived* sexed individuals) and the objects of our love. Just as I love some goods in virtue of being a professor, a fan of Stephen King novels, and a Brazilian, I love some goods in virtue of possessing a sexed body. As we love these things, moreover, we acquire a social role by means of new norms that are attached to it. For instance, there are primary goods we love as sexed individuals. These include other people—in marriage, reproduction, or sexual attraction—but also things like clothing, the roles we play in jobs or in the household, the food we choose to consume, or the music to which we listen. Gender cannot be reduced to sexual love, and it must involve the rich array of cultural goods we encounter in ordinary experience. There are also secondary goods we love in order to facilitate the primary goods we love as sexed beings. Someone might love an activity they had previously disliked, for example, to facilitate the love they have for a particular partner, maybe to impress them. When we take into account the complex web of goods that are loved in order to facilitate primary goods, we see just how large this office of love can be. A variety of secondary objects of love have ties to the primary relation of love. Imagine a brand-new father who feels like everything about his life connects back to the primary love relationship he has with his baby, whether it is the activities with which he is involved day to day, or those from which he feels he must refrain, or the way he spends his money. The father, in virtue of his sexed body, loves a particular primary good—namely, his child—and loves many secondary goods that are informed by the primary good.[60] A separate

59. Eleonore Stump, *Wandering in Darkness: Narrative and the Problem of Suffering* (New York: Oxford University Press, 2010), 98.
60. This is my attempt to retain Charlotte Witt's insight, from the third chapter, that gender is our largest social function, organizing all of our other roles. See Charlotte Witt, *The Metaphysics of Gender* (New York: Oxford University Press, 2011), 25.

question, applicable more broadly, has to do with *whether* the things we love in virtue of our sexed bodies are appropriately loved, for it remains true that very many things are loved in virtue of sexed bodies. The basic point is this: our gender is an office of love when we love various things in virtue of our sexed bodies.

Are there inherently gendered goods that serve as appropriate objects of love for sexed human beings, or can any good be loved in this office? It seems to me that, most of the time, it is the latter, though I do not wish to close the door on the existence of intrinsically gendered goods (goods whose definitions necessarily include gender). There are particular jobs that have historically been intrinsically gendered, like the occupation of a wet nurse. It is part of the *definition* of a wet nurse to include some kind of sex or gender index. But, by and large, goods are gendered when we give to them a social meaning by loving them as sexed beings. There is nothing, for instance, *intrinsically* gendered about wearing dresses, but doing so is gendered insofar as it has been an object of love with which a particular sex identifies. This, I should say, is where social constructionist views are exactly right—many, if not most, of the goods we love in virtue of our sex are not intrinsically gendered but acquire a social meaning that is gendered.

So, we love a variety of primary and secondary goods as sexed beings, creating offices of love, which are our genders. Through our love of these goods as sexed beings, our sexes acquire a social meaning. But what is this social meaning? Recall Charlotte Witt's distinction between feeding and dining.[61] Feeding is a biological function, one that requires only biological features like mouths, digestive systems, and the like. Dining, by contrast, is what happens when feeding acquires new social roles and norms to which it is responsive and under which it is evaluable. To feed, all one needs are biological organs; dining is feeding when it takes place in a particular context, with additional norms and processes, and for a different purpose. Dining occurs in appropriate rooms (e.g., a dining room), is governed by norms of propriety (e.g., politeness), and accomplishes a different purpose (e.g., gathering friends for a time of fellowship). It would be incorrect to say that dining is entirely different from feeding. Rather, feeding is "elaborated" into dining; it is what results when feeding is socially manifested.

So it is with gender as an office of love. Sexed bodies are objective entities, something we possess apart from any creaturely social relations, but they

---

61. See chapter 3, above, and Witt, *Metaphysics of Gender*, 37.

acquire social meaning by relating to social goods that provide for them new norms, contexts, and purposes. When a male loves a social good like a particular style of dress, he acquires a new social role as a man and is evaluable under such a role by virtue of the way he appropriates that good to himself by that love. It would be misguided to say that here the gender is *constructed*, for it cannot occur apart from the sex from which it is elaborated, nor is the process by which it occurs strictly social. The love that guides us to appropriate goods according to our sexed bodies is a part of our human nature in a way that particular social goods are not, and a full explanation of the process by which gender arises could not occur merely by recourse to social explanations. In chapter 2 I distinguished between subjective social construction (where the process by which a social entity comes into being is social) and objective social construction (where the entity itself is social). On neither level is gender merely social. This is a view of gender in which social considerations are key, but just because something has a social *meaning* does not mean that it is socially *constructed*. On my view, an account of gender restricted only to social explanations would be incomplete. Claims about nonsocial human features, like the capacity to love and the sexed body, must be included, both in the process and in the result.

All the same, gender is not *just* a matter of occupying roles and being evaluable according to norms, without knowing where or when these things exist or how they are identity forming. Such a construal would appear somewhat lifeless. As the intransigence and vehemence of cultural debate indicates, gender is about *who we are*. It is about our *identities*, those aspects of who we are about which we care most deeply. This is why it is important to talk about it in terms of our loves. As Augustine and Frankfurt tell us, if we want to know someone's identity, we must inquire about what they love. If we want to inquire about someone's *gender* identity, therefore, we must see what gendered goods they love and how loving those goods gives coherence to their gendered selves. These goods, loved *qua* sexed body, are brought into the individual's very self and implanted in their memory, forming the individual's personal narratives. As we care about these goods they are incorporated into the stories we tell about ourselves that provide our lives with their thematic coherence. The variety of objects of gendered loves interweave to guide our action in the world and persist in our lives to mold our stories. We find ourselves desiring certain goods in virtue of our sexed bodies, and we affirm those desires within ourselves, incorporating them and allowing them to persist as who we are.[62] Interestingly, on this view, we might think of gender dysphoria as a particular kind of division within the system of first- and second-order gendered desires a person finds themselves having. Perhaps a person with gender dysphoria might desire a particular kind of gendered good but wish they could have other desires for different gendered goods. Such a conflict disintegrates the self, highlighting just why dysphoria is so difficult for individuals.

I must reiterate that this is not a view attempting to specify gender apart from contextual location, even if contexts do not *confine* gender. We do not have to *try* to be gendered, nor do we have to wonder which are those social goods that make up our genders. We walk out of our doors in the morning and encounter them directly, often with force. The goods are right there to be loved, and this is why I am not taking any time to specify *which* gendered goods constitute masculinity and femininity. Such a task would be impossible, for those goods will differ contextually. Rather than imagining the theological task as one in which we draw up gender from the ground up, theologies of gender instead have a two-fold task: first, they must be *descriptively* accountable, making sense of the gendered lives we already live. What are the gendered goods encountered by the individuals in these contexts? For Paul and the church in Corinth, they were veils. What are they for us? What has just been elaborated, I posit, accomplishes the descriptive task. Second, they must be *normatively* accountable, telling us not just what gender *is* but what it *ought* to be, or how to engage these goods *rightly*, as we encounter them simply by living our lives. It was the case that head veils were a gendered good, but the manner in which they were appropriated into the lives of Corinthian Christians needed reordering. The normative task is not completed by providing definitions of gender that are not descriptive.[63] Rather, the normative task must take into account the descriptions already provided and work *within those* to love rightly. So, turning to the normative task, we must ask, As we are encountered by these goods, how *should* we love them?

Christian theologians, therefore, must say more, for they are committed to the fact that there is no aspect of being human, no matter how complex

---

62. I should be clear that such affirmation need not be intentional or conscious; we might have deep desires to be certain kinds of people and come to such knowledge only through introspection, or a tragic event, or therapy, or some other moment of conscious discovery.

63. This, in the end, is the fatal flaw of "complementarian" and "egalitarian" debates, upon which so much evangelical theology has been fixated. They are, at best, only *partial* theologies of gender, forgoing the descriptive task altogether.

or culturally fraught, that is not fit for redemption by the gospel, and this must be central to our evaluation of gendered goods. This gospel provides the moral guidance necessary for the right evaluation of goods loved in virtue of sex, for very often these goods are loved wrongly or should not be loved at all as a gendered good. That is to say, there are some goods we take to be loved as gendered goods that we should not associate with the possession of sexed bodies. They should be loved merely as goods, not in virtue of the possession of sexed bodies, which is another way to claim that sexist exclusion is a moral wrong. As Coakley rightly claims, "Theology involves not merely the *metaphysical* task of adumbrating a vision of God, the world, and humanity, but simultaneously the *epistemological* task of cleansing, re-ordering, and redirecting the apparatuses of one's own thinking, desiring, and seeing."[64] Sometimes, certain goods are said to be designated solely to be loved by those with male bodies—such as ordination to the priesthood. Debates about the ordination of women are, in many ways, debates about *whether ordination is a gendered good*, a good to be loved and appropriated only by those with particular bodies. Is ordination a gendered good to be loved in virtue of one's sex, or should it be seen as a good to be loved independent of sex? For some, including myself, it is unjust to preclude in a categorical way all those with female bodies from loving this good and occupying the social role it creates. For others, that this is a gendered good is clear from revelation, and God would not reveal to the church something that is harmful to it. However we settle that question,[65] Christians should understand that there is an additional responsibility to seek the proper moral evaluation of gendered goods. Some goods will be morally *good*, able to be loved without risk of injustice. Other goods will be *unjust*, such that loving them will yield oppression and harm. Far more common, however, are morally neutral gendered goods, those whose evaluation will have to take into account contexts, cultures, and other contingent relations. The point is this: the world we inhabit is *already* filled with goods associated with gender, and our moral task is to approach them rightly.

At this juncture, it is important to recall Augustine's theology of love. For any object of love, the beloved is loved properly *when it is loved in God*. The world is full of beautiful things to love, on an Augustinian picture, but

64. Coakley, *God, Sexuality, and the Self*, 20.
65. For a particularly persuasive answer, see William G. Witt, *Icons of Christ: A Biblical and Systematic Theology for Women's Ordination* (Waco: Baylor University Press, 2020).

it is the *manner* in which they are loved that makes all the difference. They cannot be loved above God, who alone provides the true felicity for which human beings were designed. There is an order to love, and while this notion accords with Coakley's understanding of the order of desire, it also says a good deal more. Certain things are to be loved more, less, or equally. I can love my new car, my daughter, and my God, but if that is the order in which I love them, I have made a dreadful mistake. Additionally, all things are to be loved as gifts from God, in the manner specified by the gift giver. As Stump avers, "Any created good loved for the real goodness in it will lead eventually to an awareness of the creator of that good and to a love for God, if only the love for the good in that created thing is allowed to deepen."[66] Ordered love also respects the finitude of the beloved, not loving in the expectation of ulti-mate beatitude, or in any other vicious way, knowing that such a love would destroy the beloved. In short, love always has a morally evaluative aspect if it is Christian love, as will be seen more clearly in the concrete examples of the next two chapters.

So it will be with a Christian theology of gender. As Coakley crisply says, "It is not sex that is the problem, but worldly values."[67] On this model, it is not gender that is a problem, but which gendered goods are loved and the character of that love. There are various ways in which gendered goods are loved contrary to godly love. As noted above, perhaps a good is inappropri-ately turned into a gendered good, when in fact it is something to be enjoyed by anyone of any gender, so long as it is received rightly. Perhaps a gendered good is received wrongly; where it is meant to be accepted with gratitude, it is turned into an object of selfish consumption. Associating it with gender would enable a host of vices that deteriorate the lover. Or again, a gendered good may be the sort of thing a person should not allow to form their iden-tity. Perhaps the way they love it cultivates vices like arrogance, dominance, or greed. Or it may simply be the kind of thing that should not inform one's identity. When Paul states that "whoever is united to a prostitute becomes one body with her" (1 Cor. 6:16), he is saying that loving a prostitute is the wrong kind of thing to love because all objects of love are unifying, especially sexual ones, and it is wrong to treat an identity-forming union as a means to temporary and lascivious self-gratification, especially since other human beings are involved. The governing principle of the kinds of moral evaluation

66. Stump, *Wandering in Darkness*, 442.
67. Coakley, *New Asceticism*, 50.

involved requires both openness (seeing the world as full of goods that may also be gendered goods) and restrictiveness (scrutinizing the ways in which we love these goods). Once again, the point is not to come up with a list of what defines masculinity and femininity but to witness the particular contexts in which we *already* encounter these positions and bring Christian moral theological tools to bear on them. In this sense, our task is the same as Paul's in 1 Corinthians 11. Or, put differently, the normative task of gender is about the cultivation of virtue and renunciation of vice by means of our love *in light of the descriptive task*, which delivers to lovers a wide range of goods to be loved.

The interesting thing about a Christian theology of gender is that there is, in fact, nothing (or, at most, very few things) explicitly stated in Scripture about what women and men *must* be like in context-independent ways or what the specific goods are by which a woman or a man *must* be identified. Even when Paul, in 1 Corinthians 16:13, commands the Corinthian church to "*andrizesthe*," "act like men" (at least in some translations, like the ESV), he is addressing the church in its entirety, men *and* women, likely commending them to be courageous.[68] Where commands are given specifically to men or women, they are often injunctions about how best to live *as Christians* within the culture in which they find themselves, a culture having already provided gendered goods for them to love. In their world, *these* are gendered goods; how should a Christian think about them?[69] Ultimately, Scripture is concerned with the ways in which the gospel governs the love for gendered goods, whatever those goods might be (and the specification of which cannot be done apart from specific contextual analysis). The details of such a claim will be unpacked in the following chapters, especially as we consider the implications

---

68. See the discussion in Cynthia Long Westfall, *Paul and Gender: Reclaiming the Apostle's Vision for Men and Women in Christ* (Grand Rapids: Baker Academic, 2016), 50–51. Of course, I cannot survey every passage of Scripture that appears to say what traits men and women must have in order to be men and women. Here I defer to Westfall's masterful book, which covers the majority of these (since they are mostly in Paul).

69. Even the famous—or notorious—woman of Proverbs 31:10–31 is probably not best read as a straightforward description of biblical womanhood, whatever that might mean. The figures of "Lady Wisdom" and "Lady Folly" in the book's opening chapters serve as the complementary bookend to this final figure, indicating that these women are models to be imitated (or avoided, in the case of Folly) by women and men *alike*. For an argument in support of this reading, see Craig Bartholomew and Ryan P. O'Dowd, *Old Testament Wisdom Literature: A Theological Introduction* (Downers Grove, IL: IVP Academic, 2011), chap. 5; and Albert M. Wolters, *The Song of the Valiant Woman: Studies in the Interpretation of Proverbs 31:10–31* (Milton Keynes, UK: Paternoster, 2001).

of the doctrines of sin and redemption as they relate to gendered love, but for now, keep in mind the Augustinian analysis of rightly loved goods. Rightly loved gendered goods are those we recognize as gifts from God, to be used according to the specifications of the gift giver, which is to say for the flourishing of humanity, in the promotion of kindness, gentleness, and virtue. Wrongly loved gendered goods are those we love with the intent to dominate, for rapacious purposes, in a life contrary to that depicted by the kingdom of God. In the next chapter, sexual assault will be seen as the paradigm case of such wrongly loved gendered goods.

Finally, since gender is not only an *individual* matter but something that characterizes persons in their communities and cultures, it is important to provide a theological analysis of its broader social dimensions. Already we have seen that, on an Augustinian analysis, social identities are defined by the objects that characterize their love. What makes a number of persons a society rather than a random gathering is that they share objects of love. So it is with gender. As a contextually specific group of people agrees upon goods to be loved by those with male sexed bodies, this common agreement characterizes the gendering of the group. Just as a common agreement on the object of love defines a people, so also a common agreement on the objects of *gendered* love defines the *genders* of a people. Yet, the inhabitants of the heavenly city have God as their ultimate object of love, and this overarching love should qualify and reshape all other loves. Thus, in whatever culture or society a Christian finds herself, as a member of the heavenly city she must constantly adjudicate the objects of gendered love found in her society in accordance with their consistency with her love for God. The city of God does not have immutable, eternal, or context-independent gender categories, but it does constrain or widen, affirm or deny, challenge or approve the genders found in any human society in which its members find themselves. Likewise, the earthly city is characterized by a love of self and of domination, and this love warps and curves the love of gendered goods toward that end. Loving someone, especially with a supreme love, will summon the lover to love other goods *in a similar way* as their supreme object of love. Because I love my kids, I will make the effort to love what they love, to appreciate what they appreciate. The city of God will similarly love all of creation like God loves it.

Gender is about the appropriation of social goods as a means of manifesting the social body, as the previous chapter maintained, and we are now in a position to see how each of the four theses is filled in with greater detail. The most obvious is the fourth thesis: the *means* by which we appropriate these social goods is through loving them. Relevant to the first thesis, we can also see that this is a modest and attenuated form of gender essentialism, avoiding both gender skepticism and biological essentialism. On my model, the kind essence "man" requires nothing other than a male body and the identity-forming love of particular social goods, and the kind essence "woman" requires nothing other than a female body doing the same.[70] Crucially, this essentialism is useful for virtually nothing other than the prevention of gender skepticism; it does not say which social goods are properly masculine or feminine. *That* question is not answered by the essentialism; it is answered by the criteria for moral evaluation outlined above. It also takes into account the apparent arbitrariness of gendered goods pointed out by social constructionists. It also does not maintain that biology plus some theory of human action is sufficient for gender; social manifestation is part of the definition. In many ways, my model attempts to take a discussion normally held in the realm of ontology and transpose it to the world of ethics, the world where concrete individuals actually live.

The third thesis, that a viable ontology of gender must be consistent with and supportive of the cultivation of gendered justice, is also met with regard to the need to evaluate and order our loves. We must constantly ask ourselves whether our relationship to gendered goods is just and characteristic of the kingdom of God and of the kind of community shaped by Christ's gift. But this will always be a complicated business, at least until we are raised again in the new heaven and earth. A proper recognition of the noetic effects of sin is crucial, for our assurance that we are relating well to the goods that make us men and women must always be provisional. Whereas before the complexity had to do with gender's essence, now it has to do with the incomplete healing of our moral agency and ability to relate rightly to social goods. Christians must be a people willing to give up the gendered goods they enjoy the moment they have been shown to be problematic; this means that Christians must

---

70. It is worth noting that this is not necessarily a trans*-exclusive ontology of gender, for it can be developed in either direction. My account does not settle the matter either way. As many theorists have pointed out, the only modification that would need to be made to this view in order to accommodate trans* identities is that goods would need to be organized around the *perception* of a male body, and *mutatis mutandis* for female bodies. The actual possession of a female body is not needed to be perceived as having one. This is a move available to someone who finds this model of gender attractive and wishes to accommodate for certain understandings of trans* ontologies.

be ready to recognize, admit to, and correct the sexism in which virtually all societies are implicated. If it is the case—and it very often is—that men enjoy the attachment to a gendered good that is harmful to women, then they must surrender attachment to that good. It should be obvious that a good that causes and promotes harm to women cannot be a good loved in God.

So the model satisfies the theses required for an ontology of gender. We can also see that it is a suitable *theology* of gender. In the next chapters I shall trace the ways in which the biblical economy frames gender at its different stages, but for now consider one particularly powerful biblical vision of human love and gender—namely, that of the Song of Songs. Coakley's work has been remarkably important in highlighting the salience of this book for understanding gender, and she argues that it is a prime example of the intertwining of gendered desire and desire for God for which she advocates.[71] A growing number within contemporary biblical scholarship agree with this approach to the text, arguing that the Song presents a vision of humanity in which sexual love and love for God are delicately interdependent. This is a fact about how we were both created to love God supremely and called to express our sexed embodiment in appropriately social ways. The typical approaches to the Song have, however, been truncated in detrimental ways. Medieval interpreters tended to favor a strictly allegorical interpretation unrelated to sex or gender, whereas most contemporary commentators insist upon an expression of strictly human romantic love. Resisting this division requires seeing a deep connection between sexual love and the love for God, all while acknowledging that human beings do not usually compartmentalize their loves.

Here the work of Ellen Davis stands tall.[72] If the Song is merely about human love, she contends, then "nowhere within the covers of the Bible is there a truly happy story about God and Israel (or God and the church) in

---

71. Coakley especially endorses the reading of Gregory of Nyssa, whose *Homilies on the Song of Songs* illustrates the gender reversals that she maintains typify the purification of gender desire. See Coakley, *New Asceticism*, chap. 1; Coakley, "Gregory of Nyssa"; and Coakley, "Introduction—Gender, Trinitarian Analogies, and the Pedagogy of the Song." Interestingly, she does not make use of a key insight of Gregory's analysis of the Song—namely, that "human nature . . . is shaped in accordance with that which it looks upon," an insight remarkably harmonious with Augustine's and highly suggestive for a theology of gender (Gregory of Nyssa, *Gregory of Nyssa: Homilies on the Song of Songs*, trans. Richard A. Norris, Writings from the Greco-Roman World 13 [Atlanta: Society of Biblical Literature, 2012], 163).

72. A more recent example of a very similar conclusion can be found in Chloe T. Sun, *Conspicuous in His Absence: Studies in the Song of Songs and Esther* (Downers Grove, IL: IVP Academic, 2021).

love," for even in the richest expressions of love in Scripture there is a tinge of sorrow (Christ's death on the cross being a clear example).[73] Alternatively, if the Song is merely an allegory for divine love, then "the Bible lacks any strong statement about love between man and woman enjoyed in the full mutuality and equality of status."[74] Yet, there are textual reasons to hold both together, for while romantic love is readily seen in the Song, the fact that it is filled with quotations from various portions of the Hebrew Bible, specifically passages directed to God, reveals a distinct divine orientation.[75] Davis proposes that we hold on to both, allowing the Song to show "that the sexual and the religious understandings of the Song are mutually informative, and that each is incomplete without the other. For a holistic understanding of our own humanity suggests that our religious capacity is linked with an awareness of our sexuality. . . . Genuine intimacy brings us into contact with the sacred."[76] In the Song, it seems, we find love expressed toward a gendered good (in this case, the romantic partner) that also finds its culmination and perfection in the love for God.

The word consistently employed for the relationship between the two speakers of the Song is usually "love" or "beloved." That the woman addresses her lover as "you whom my soul loves" (Song 1:7, among others) is meant to trigger an allusion to the chief command of the Hebrew Bible to love the Lord with all one's heart (as in Deut. 6:5). But in 7:10, we do find the woman saying, "I am my beloved's, and his *desire* is for me." *Teshuqah*, the term translated as "desire," is found only here and in Genesis 3:16 and 4:7 (both in negative, sinful, and dominating senses), lending significant warrant to the notion that this is a deliberate echo. But the reversal is key: here the man's desire is for the woman, not the other way around, as in the cursed state of Genesis 3:16. What we find is a restoration of the original intent of creation, a reparation of the relationship characterized by sinful desire and

73. Ellen F. Davis, "'The One Whom My Soul Loves': The Song of Songs," in *Getting Involved with God: Rediscovering the Old Testament* (Lanham, MD: Rowman & Littlefield, 2001), 67.

74. Davis, "'One Whom My Soul Loves,'" 68.

75. See esp. Song 4:8–15, calling to mind the restoration of the temple's glory by reference to Lebanon (see Isa. 60:13), along with several echoes of 1 Kings 6–7. It is worth bearing in mind that quotations then did not operate in the verbatim manner of contemporary practice.

76. Ellen F. Davis, "The Song of Songs," in *Proverbs, Ecclesiastes, and the Song of Songs*, Westminster Bible Companion (Louisville: Westminster John Knox, 2000), 233, 235. For a similar approach, though much more reliant on a particular defense of the place of the Song in the canon and the nature of allegory, see Robert W. Jenson, *Song of Songs*, Interpretation: A Bible Commentary for Teaching and Preaching (Louisville: Westminster John Knox, 2005).

rule after the fall. The result is a replacement of unjust and unequal desire with harmonious and mutually beneficial love, where it is said "I am my beloved's and my beloved is mine" (Song 6:3).[77] The right kind of relation to gendered goods, so it seems, is not one of mere desire (which in the Hebrew Bible is a term designated toward sin) but specifically of love.

There are further indications that what the Song seeks to restore is the love with and for which we were created. There are frequent allusions to a "garden," and commentators do not hesitate to associate them with the Garden of Eden. Song of Songs 4:11–5:1 describes the setting in which the lovers meet, and it is a garden that flows with milk and honey, a scene at once recalling the state of creation and God's covenantal promises of land. Davis claims that such a scene "represents the reversal of that primordial exile from Eden. . . . At the theological level of interpretation, the Song as a whole represents a return to the Garden of God, the place where humanity once enjoys full intimacy with God."[78] Yet such restoration does not involve the undoing of the sexed body or any removal of the twoness according to which we were created, for "it is precisely our embracing sexually differentiated bodies whose union is sanctified by its likeness to God's own love. The heart is indeed the seat of love, but it is those hands and their placement—and the lips, and the paired organs of pleasure and procreation, and the tongues and . . . —which are the heart's actuality, at least for the Song."[79] The hope and restoration promised by the Song are in continuity with the categories of creation, including our sexed bodies.

Be that as it may, the Song does not portray the recovery of creation in uncomplicated terms, nor is it a simple return to the start. This can be seen in two places. First, in a moment of desperate seeking after her lover, the woman is stripped and assaulted by the "sentinels" of the city (Song 5:7). Here we are reminded that even as we yearn after God in this world, such yearning is constrained by enduring conditions of sin, and the particular gendered sin in question is that of sexual violence.[80] Though our love of gendered goods is purified as we seek after God, the antithesis is always lurking—namely, the desire to dominate, control, and harm the beloved. Second, and relatedly, the

77. Likely an echo of the covenantal formula, "They shall be my people, and I will be their God" (Jer. 32:38).

78. Davis, "Song of Songs," 232, 267.

79. Jenson, *Song of Songs*, 33.

80. See Davis, "Song of Songs," 278–79.

Song reminds us that our loves in this world remain fragmentary. Though it is a love poem, the Song does not seem to culminate in the permanent and blessed union of the lovers. There are moments of elated love, to be sure, but there are also moments of desperate seeking in the darkness. The Song "is not, upon close reading, a poem of love fulfilled. If the lovers do live 'happily ever after,' we never hear about it."[81] The love is proleptic, constantly seeking the beloved until that eschatological moment when it will be truly fulfilled. Thus, the Song describes a dark night of the soul: "Upon my bed at night, I sought him whom my soul loves; I sought him, but found him not; I called him, but he gave no answer" (3:1; see also 5:6–8 and 8:14). Just as God is hidden and our love for God must at times wrestle with periods of absence and dissatisfaction, so also must our love for gendered goods show the appropriate epistemic restraint, always evaluating whether they are appropriately loved. Creation's love will be restored and brought to its genuine perfection, but this is what the Song *promises*, not what it *depicts*. We know the direction in which it will head, but we do not as yet experience it fully.

These all-too-brief soundings in the Song of Songs, I submit, illustrate the central components of my model of gender. The Song interweaves the loves that make us women and men with the love we have for God, showing us that they can be mutually informative. The love we have for gendered goods is transformed by the love we have for God, just as it grants a glimpse into the kind of relationship God has with God's covenant people. Here the categories of creation are not eliminated but restored and perfected, meaning that our gendered redemption is not an elimination of masculinity and femininity but their purification from sin. So we can retain a basic gender essentialism, but we must also take into account the Song's constant seeking, reminding us that the redemption of our bodies and genders is yet incomplete. We await a resurrection in which we will see God in beatitude, and only then will our seeking end. But love will not end (1 Cor. 13:8), for the enjoyment of God knows no end. This is the standard against which one can measure the unjust practices of gender. I propose, along with Coakley, Jenson, and Davis, that we find in the Song of Songs "the chief biblical resource for a believing understanding of . . . the *lived meaning* of 'Male and female he created them.'"[82]

81. Davis, "'One Whom My Soul Loves,'" 79.
82. Jenson, *Song of Songs*, 14.

5.4 Conclusion

This chapter contains the bulk of my constructive account of gender, so let us take stock of the model of gender just proposed. Gender is the appropriation of social goods pertaining to the sexed body. We are created as sexed, with an ability to love and an impulse toward forming social bonds. These things come together in the ways we love as sexed beings, specifically in the relationship established between humans as sexed beings and the objects of their love. This relationship can be seen as a particular office of love with norms and roles specific to it, norms that elaborate it into a social plane, granting to it a social meaning. They then become *gendered* goods, the loving of which shapes our identity. They imprint themselves into our memories and weave themselves into our stories, providing our lives with thematic coherence and making us who we are as gendered beings. We care about these goods, and they shape our attitudes, establish the everyday goals of our lives, and appropriate the meaning provided by these goods. There are further theological considerations, and they come primarily in the form of the moral evaluation of these goods, in the order according to which they are loved, and so forth. Gendered goods must be loved in God, in the order intended for proper use, and according to the specifications of the gift giver. They must be loved justly, but the pursuit of such just love is necessarily incomplete this side of the eschaton. Our genders are healed in the same way that all things are healed by God—namely, by being restored to the original purposes provided in creation, yet without losing the eschatological surplus. This is an essentialist view of gender, for on it a man is a male who appropriates social goods by his love, but this view does not say *which* goods are to be loved in any one time or place. Much more relevant are the constraints placed on *how* these goods are loved. This allows gender to have sufficient cultural diversity (the beloved goods will always differ from one time and place to another) while retaining the stability of gendered categories, insofar as they are produced by the relevant properties of human nature—namely, sex, love, and sociability.

One final point must be made, a pastoral note. While what I have said is intended to be of academic and theological use, I believe it is also practical to learn to see how gender is involved with love. For so many who experience gender as burdensome and painful, a distinct sense of *longing* is involved in the pain—longing for a body that is different than their body, longing for desires that are accepted by those they love, and longing for recognition in their communities of belonging. For so many, the call to love one's enemy does not require traveling very far, for their nearest enemy looks back at them in the mirror. Augustinian love accommodates this capaciously. It is about "the unsatisfied longing of the homesick heart," as we saw.[83] It does not ignore, reject, or commodify these longings. But it does *normalize* them, claiming that this longing is expected in a world in which redemption remains incomplete. The solution is not to satisfy longing but to welcome it, to build communities in which longing is safely articulated and compassionately listened to, where it is enfolded in a patient embrace. Augustinian love expects nothing less of the church, especially of those for whom gender is a comparatively simple experience.

What remains to be seen is how gender is filtered through the different moments of the divine economy. Recall from the first chapter that human nature is narratively indexed, having the properties it has in virtue of the position it occupies within the story of creation, fall, redemption, and consummation. Identifying how this narrative implicates gender will also bring into relief the practical ramifications of my model, specifically its ability to account for intersex/DSD conditions and sexual assault.

---

83. John Burnaby, *Amor Dei: A Study of the Religion of St. Augustine* (1938; repr., Eugene, OR: Wipf & Stock, 2007), 96.

* * * * * * *

Gender in the
Story of God

* * * * * * *

SIX

Gender in Creation

In this final section, I contextualize the theological model of gender from the previous chapter by situating it within the divine economy— that is, the history of God's redemptive action spanning from creation to consummation. This is, in part, an effort to remain consistent with the theological method presented in chapter 1, where I maintained that human beings have the properties they do in virtue of the particular places they occupy in this narrative; this makes human nature "narratively indexed." This chapter engages the first moment of the divine economy, creation—a locus that has been asked to perform too much work for gender, in my opinion. As created, gender is good; it is a gift to be received, not something from which one must be redeemed. Creation is good (that is, it has proper functions), and it is the first moment of the divine economy. Here, I will apply these theological affirmations to considerations about intersex/DSD experience. Ultimately, I will contend that epistemic restraint is more important than metaphysical revision when it comes to the pursuit of justice for individuals who have experienced construals of creation as tools for oppression.

6.1 Introduction: The Narrative Indexing of Humanity

In the first chapter of this study, I made the claim that giving a theological account of gender requires observation of a central principle regarding human nature: human beings have the properties that they have in virtue of the place they occupy within the divine economy, or what John Webster calls the "historical form of God's presence to and action upon creatures."[1] So, as the trinitarian persons enter into space and time to create, redeem, and perfect all things, those divine acts acquire a specific pattern or shape, and the sum of these acts is the "divine economy" (following texts like Eph. 1:10), though it may simply be called "the gospel." At different stages within this economy, humans have particular sets of traits they do not have in others. Thus, at creation, human beings are good, but they are not perfect, for they await their confirmation and perfection. After the fall, human beings are universally sinful (with the exception of the humanity of Jesus, who is also the Son of God), but they are not *naturally* sinful, for it is not part of the definition of humanity to be that way, as creation attests. At their redemption, human beings begin to be realigned to their redeemer, getting glimpses of what they will experience fully at the perfection of their natures in the resurrection. This perspective on humanity lends credibility to the important distinction made by feminist authors like François Poulain de la Barre between universal traits and natural traits; putatively universal gender traits cannot automatically be assumed to be natural. Only when the entirety of the divine economy is in view can we make confident pronouncements about what is natural to humanity, for it is too easy to mistake a trait specific to a moment of the economy for a trait that spans its entirety.

The previous chapter had recourse to human nature without the requisite sensitivity to its narrative indexing. I maintained that gender is the social position we acquire when we appropriate certain goods to ourselves in virtue of our sexed bodies. Our sexed bodies are elaborated thereby into acquiring a social meaning. But what or whom we love, to the extent that they sediment themselves upon our memories and form the narratival coherence of our lives, tells us who we *are*, in a second-personal, nonpropositional sort of way. This makes sense of the claim that we possess a "gender identity," though not necessarily in the commonplace way this phrase is used. If one's identity, according to an Augustinian theological picture, is formed by one's loves, then one's *gender* identity must be formed by one's *gendered* loves. So, when these goods are loved, they form who we are as gendered people.

I maintain that all of this is natural to human beings, so in a sense, we are naturally gendered, though by this I do not mean biological essentialism,

---

1. John Webster, "Biblical Reasoning," in *The Domain of the Word: Scripture and Theological Reason* (London: Bloomsbury, 2012), 117.

nor does this preclude the social dimensions of gender. But since human natures are not the kinds of things that exist without temporal considerations, how does the model summarized above adapt itself to the various moments of the divine economy? What is gender like at its creation, when subject to sin, when redeemed by Christ, and at its perfection? I will attempt to answer these questions in this chapter and the next. Under the headings of *creation, fall, redemption*, and *consummation*, I will draw forth the implications the characterizing features of these stages in the divine economy have for gender.

In this chapter, the focus will be exclusively on creation. Creation merits special attention because it is often asked to bear far too much weight in theological explanations of gender. Though creation must be seen as importantly normative for reflections on gender for reasons related to matters such as Christ's own understanding of it in texts like Matthew 19:4–6, the kind of normativity in question is often far too restrictive, understanding gender to be "derivations" from creation, to the detriment of the rest of the divine economy. At times (especially with natural law approaches to gender and claims that Adam's creation temporally prior to Eve must mean that masculinity is identical to authority[2]), one could be excused for thinking that all we need to make sense of gender's complexity is a proper doctrine of creation. There are many issues with this, the chief of which is that it repeats the usual confusion in which ostensibly universal traits are assumed to be the same as natural (or in this case, created) traits. In this chapter, however, I will focus specifically on the way the divine economy is disjointed on such understandings. Creation is invoked without recognition of the ways it has been distorted by sin and without seeing eschatology as a surplus to it. In response to this theological frontloading, critics have challenged the over-reliance on the doctrine of creation for gender,[3] yet they often overcorrect to the neglect of this crucial moment in the economy. The shortcoming of both approaches, of course, is an inability to keep the entirety of the economy in view. As Oliver O'Donovan has stated about topics in theology of moral concern, "Each area has to be given, as it were, a salvation-history of its

---

2. See, e.g., Patrick Schreiner, "Man and Woman: Toward an Ontology," *Eikon* 2, no. 2 (Fall 2020): 68–87; and Wayne Grudem, *Evangelical Feminism and Biblical Truth: An Analysis of More Than 100 Disputed Questions* (2004; repr., Wheaton: Crossway, 2012).

3. For a creative theological challenge to this tendency in conversation with Judith Butler, see Daniel R. Patterson, *Reforming a Theology of Gender: Constructive Reflections on Judith Butler and Queer Theory* (Eugene, OR: Cascade, 2022).

own."[4] Between this chapter and the next, the hope is to provide exactly that for a theology of gender.

6.2 What Makes Creation Good?

A Christian doctrine of creation requires at least two central tenets. First, the creation of the world by God must be seen as the initial episode out of which the broader economy unfolds. And second, we need a positive account of what makes creation "good" (Gen. 1:4, 10, 12, 18, 21, 25).

To say that God's creation of the world is the initial episode of an unfolding economy is to recognize that inherent in the created world is an intent for growth and perfection, an unfolding toward a telos not yet realized in the first moment. Of course, creation is "good," but it cannot yet be called "perfect," for perfection entails achieving an intended completion, a culminating end. In order to obtain that end, a process of maturation along the divine economy must occur. Creation, then, must be the first moment of a coherent economy of growth.

This idea was central to the thought of Saint Irenaeus, the second-century theologian whose major work, *Adversus Haereses*, is devoted to combatting a particularly ersatz vision of creation called Gnosticism.[5] Gnosticism provides a vision of the economy according to which its constitutive moments are *disjointed*, at odds with one another. Creation and redemption are not woven into a seamless narrative, but the latter supersedes the former. That means significant elements of creation, including the body, are eliminated upon the introduction of redemption. Peter Brown summarizes: "Parts of the universe, the human body among them, would eventually be cast off as abortive and

4. Oliver O'Donovan, *Resurrection and Moral Order: An Outline for Evangelical Ethics*, 2nd ed. (Grand Rapids: Eerdmans, 1994), xvii.

5. Recently, certain scholars have begun to question whether there is any such thing as "Gnosticism." See Michael Allen Williams, *Rethinking "Gnosticism": An Argument for Dismantling a Dubious Category* (Princeton: Princeton University Press, 1996); and Karen King, *What Is Gnosticism?* (Cambridge, MA: Belknap, 2003). For these historians, the category "Gnostic" was prefabricated by an earlier wave of scholarship, which then went on to guide their readings of the primary materials. In other words, one only finds a stable and identifiable category assignable as "Gnostic" if one forces one's readings of the Nag Hammadi library into an already extant definition. For a useful introduction to this approach to the diversity of Gnosticism, see Nicola Denzey Lewis, *Introduction to "Gnosticism": Ancient Voices, Christian Worlds* (New York: Oxford University Press, 2013), chap. 1. For a defense of a measured definition of Gnosticism that is still historically defensible, see David Brakke, *The Gnostics: Myth, Ritual, and Diversity in Early Christianity* (Cambridge, MA: Harvard University Press, 2012).

misconceived creation."[6] The Gnostic "Treatise on Resurrection" makes this particularly clear: just as the savior exchanged the corruptible world for the incorruptible one, we, in union with him, die, rise, and ascend. Yet, as with his resurrection and ascension, flesh is not included: "For you will not pay back the superior element when you depart. The inferior element takes a loss; but what it owes is gratitude. . . . What is the meaning of resurrection? It is the uncovering at any given time of the elements that have 'arisen.'"[7] This is a direct result of the transience of material creation: "All changes, the world is an apparition. . . . Resurrection is not of this sort, for it is real."[8] But if resurrection does not require the body, only the ascension of the soul into that which is incorruptible, resurrection is already available insofar as one does not live "according to (the dictates of) this flesh," for anyone "rushing toward this outcome (that is, *separation from the body*)" already possesses resurrection.[9]

The main thrust of Irenaeus's response maintained that the divine economy must be consistent with itself, such that creation is seen as the first moment of a coherently unfolding whole. Thus he alleges that the Gnostics "disregard the order and the connection of the Scriptures and, as much as in them lies, they disjoint the members of the Truth."[10] The Gnostics had all of the components necessary for an understanding of the economy, but the issue was with how they assembled the parts, rearranging them into something entirely unrecognizable, like repositioning the pieces of a mosaic of a king to illustrate the image of a dog or a fox. Irenaeus, therefore, saw his task as providing the

---

6. Peter Brown, *The Body and Society: Men, Women, and Sexual Renunciation in Early Christianity*, 20th anniversary ed. (New York: Columbia University Press, 2008), 109.

7. This quotation, and all others from Gnostic texts, come from Bentley Layton and David Brakke, eds., *The Gnostic Scriptures: A New Translation with Annotations and Introductions*, trans. Bentley Layton, 2nd ed., Anchor Yale Bible Reference Library (New Haven: Yale University Press, 2021). Citations will provide the title of the particular Gnostic text followed by the pagination in Layton's translation, in this case, "Treatise on the Resurrection (Epistle to Rheginus)," 455–56. Contextually, the inferior element is the body, while the superior is the soul.

8. "Treatise on the Resurrection (Epistle to Rheginus)," 456.

9. "Treatise on the Resurrection (Epistle to Rheginus)," 457 (emphasis added).

10. Irenaeus, *Adversus Haereses* 1.8.1 (hereafter cited as *AH*). Translations of *AH* books 1 through 3 are from Irenaeus, *Against the Heresies*, trans. Dominic J. Unger, vol. 1, Ancient Christian Writers 55 (New York: Newman, 1992); Irenaeus, *Against the Heresies*, trans. Dominic J. Unger, vol. 2, Ancient Christian Writers 65 (New York: Newman, 2012); and Irenaeus, *Against the Heresies*, trans. Dominic J. Unger, vol. 3, Ancient Christian Writers 64 (New York: Newman, 2012), respectively. Translations of *AH* books 4 and 5 are from Irenaeus, *Against Heresies*, in *Ante-Nicene Fathers: The Apostolic Fathers, Justin Martyr, Irenaeus*, ed. Alexander Roberts and James Donaldson, vol. 1 (Christian Classics Ethereal Library), https://www.ccel.org/ccel/schaff/anf01.i.html.

necessary guidelines for a suitable construal of the divine economy, one that best represents the Scriptures and the God who brought all things into being.

Irenaeus begins with a *pleroma*, or fullness (a play on a central component of Gnostic thought), but he understands the fullness in question as referring to God's inner triune life. Among the Father, Son, and Spirit there exists perfect love and goodness, and the motivation for creation is an external outworking of a blessedness that already obtains immanently. Contrary to Gnostic accounts of creation, God creates not out of arrogance or overextension but from a desire to share the abundance found in God's immanent life: "In the beginning, therefore, did God form Adam, not as if He stood in need of humanity, but that He might have [someone] upon whom to confer His benefits. For not alone antecedently to Adam, but also before all creation, the Word glorified His Father, remaining in Him; and was Himself glorified by the Father, as He did Himself declare, 'Father, glorify Thou Me with the glory which I had with Thee before the world was.'"[11] This difference in motivation makes all the difference in the resulting product, for instead of instability and wretchedness, matter is an opportunity for sharing in God's goodness. As Matthew Steenberg elaborates, "God creates, that creation might participate in his glory, his goodness, which is that shared eternally by Father, Son and Spirit and exemplified by the Son's incarnate relationship to the Father through the Spirit in the economy of salvation."[12] This is best illustrated by Irenaeus's image of God creating by means of the Father's "two hands," the Son and the Spirit, who replace the lesser Gnostic deities as mediators of divine action.[13] This means that what we observe in material creation is the loving product of a craftsperson, for intra-trinitarian love and goodness take the form of external trinitarian acts of love and goodness.[14]

---

11. *AH* 4.14.1. This translation has been altered for gender inclusivity. Already detectable here is a deep resonance with the theology of John Webster from chapter 1, according to which all theological inquiry requires prior grounding in the triune God's fullness and gratuitous self-communication.

12. M. C. Steenberg, *Irenaeus on Creation: The Cosmic Christ and the Saga of Redemption*, Supplements to Vigiliae Christianae (Leiden: Brill, 2008), 36.

13. See, e.g., *AH* 4.20.1: "It was not angels, therefore, who made us, nor who formed us, neither had angels power to make an image of God, nor any one else, except the Word of the Lord, nor any Power remotely distant from the Father of all things. For God did not stand in need of these [beings], in order to the accomplishing of what He had Himself determined with Himself beforehand should be done, as if He did not possess His own hands. For with Him were always present the Word and Wisdom, the Son and the Spirit, by whom and in whom, freely and spontaneously, He made all things."

14. John Behr states Irenaeus's view as follows: "Each Person of the Trinity has a particular role: the Father plans and orders, the Son executes these orders and performs the work of

Just as God's "two hands" shaped and characterized the original creation, so too was there an equal commitment to a providential carrying out of created intent; this was no "hands off" procedure. Creation was always meant to result in ultimate participation in the divine life and included within it were intentions for creaturely maturation and growth into perfection. An aspect of the goodness of creation was a built-in teleology meant to be carried forth throughout the subsequent stages of the divine economy. With respect to the creation of humanity, Irenaeus states that Adam at creation was yet "a child; and it was necessary that he should grow, and so come to his perfection."[15] Irenaeus regularly refers to God as a "wise Architect," in reference not only to God's good fashioning of the whole world but also to God's wise design of the economy proceeding from it.[16] So, God, as Architect of creation as well as of history, is responsible for it all: "He Himself, indeed, having need of nothing, but granting communion with Himself to those who stood in need of it, sketched out, like an architect, the plan of salvation to those that pleased Him."[17] Steenberg emphasizes that for Irenaeus, creation and redemption must be seen as "two aspects of a single story," ultimately weaving into a single economy.[18] Eric Osborn captures the nature of this theological vision well: "The economy is the whole plan of God. One divine economy belongs to the one God, one plan to the wise architect. The universal economy is made up of smaller diverse economies of events which form the different saving dispositions which God has granted."[19] Motivated by love, God creates all things and sets into place a coherent economy in which all of God's acts are consistent with one another and in which all of the moments therefore share the same consistency.[20]

---

creating, and the Spirit nourishes and increases. . . . The Father is the origin of all creation, expressed by the prepositions [*ek*] and [*apo*], but he created everything through [*dia*] the Son and in [*en*] the Spirit, making the creation of man into a trinitarian activity of the one God" (John Behr, *Asceticism and Anthropology in Irenaeus and Clement* [New York: Oxford University Press, 2000], 38).

15. Irenaeus, *Epideixis* 12. English translation, with some modification for gender neutrality, from Iain M. MacKenzie, *Irenaeus's Demonstration of the Apostolic Preaching: A Theological Commentary and Translation* (Aldershot, UK: Ashgate, 2002).

16. See *AH* 2.11.1.

17. *AH* 4.14.2. See also 1.10.3, 5.17.4.

18. Steenberg, *Irenaeus on Creation*, 49. See *AH* 2.27.1, 5.30.1.

19. Eric Osborn, *Irenaeus of Lyons* (Cambridge: Cambridge University Press, 2001), 77–78.

20. A particularly interesting feature of Irenaeus's presentation of this point is his typological exegesis of the days of Genesis. For Irenaeus, the days cannot correspond to literal days; instead, they correspond to different stages of the divine economy, each lasting one thousand years, since "with the Lord one day is like a thousand years" (2 Pet. 3:8). Whatever we make

More can be said about Irenaeus's notion of creation and redemption in the economy, especially the centrality of Christ,[21] but we can conclude with the picture of eschatological redemption that results from such convictions. For Irenaeus, creatures will be retained and restored, the only difference lying in the removal of the sin within them: "For neither is the substance nor the essence of the creation annihilated (for faithful and true is He who has established it), but 'the *fashion* of the world will pass away'; that is, those things among which transgression has occurred."[22] The annihilation of creatures, for Irenaeus, is equal to an admission of wrongdoing on God's part, something the Gnostics were ready to attribute to their lesser deities. But if God is truly perfectly good and loving, thereby only making good creatures out of love, then it is the *sin* inhering in those creatures that will be removed when they are restored to their created intent, something like the purging of an infection. For human beings, this will mean the beatific vision,[23] but all things will have their place. The important thing to note, as will become important in subsequent discussions in this chapter, is that redemption does not require the replacement, annihilation, or destruction of creation, as it did for Gnostic thought, but only the removal of sin to restore all things to the design of their Architect.[24]

---

of such temporal speculation, it remains clear that if the days do in fact indicate subsequent stages of the divine economy, then *included* in creation is a subsequent sequence of events that makes up such an economy. See *AH* 5.23.2, 5.28.3–4, and 5.33.2.

21. For Irenaeus, the Divine Architect so orchestrated the flowing of events in the divine economy that they find their fulfillment in Christ, who brings all things under his rule, making sense of all time and completing the flow of redemption. This is, of course, central to Irenaeus's doctrine of recapitulation. Genesis 1 is inseparable from John 1, and so, though Irenaeus "may rightly be considered a theologian of economy, of history," this history must be "read Christocentrically—not simply taking Christ to be significant to all phases of history, but to be in his person the grounding of all history" (Steenberg, *Irenaeus on Creation*, 50).

22. *AH* 5.36.1.

23. See *AH* 4.14.1.

24. Interestingly, Irenaeus was clear that his view requires the existence of sexed bodies in the resurrection. He notes that sexed bodies must have been a feature of the created state, for otherwise the nudity of Adam and Eve would make no sense. They were naked and without shame, but nakedness without a sexed body makes no sense (an exposed ankle is rather different than exposed genitalia, for instance). So, the numerically identical sexed bodies with which humanity was created will be the ones with which they are raised. See *AH* 3.22.4 and 2.33.5 for discussions. John Behr concludes, "Not only is bipolarity as male and female man's created state, but interaction between the two, in holiness, is clearly envisaged as a dimension of their life, growth and maturation. . . . Human existence as male and female will not cease, for it is the condition and framework, as created by God, for the man's never-ending maturation and growth towards God" (*Asceticism and Anthropology in Irenaeus and Clement*, 112–13).

Creation, then, must stand as the beginning of an unfolding and internally consistent economy in the efforts to articulate a doctrine that resists the chief mistake of Gnosticism. Because it is the one God who made all things and who enjoys goodness and blessedness in the triune life, creation cannot be seen as a haphazard product of foolish semi-gods. Moreover, because it is that same God who is the redeemer of all things, creation and redemption cannot be placed in opposition to one another, as Gnostic mythology attempted to do. The created is the redeemed, for God is no feckless craftsperson. Rather, creation is good and will be perfect when it is perfectly redeemed, for the economy unified.

But what does it *mean* to say that creation is "good"? This brings us to our second tenet of creation doctrine—namely, a positive account of goodness. Often, the goodness of creation in Genesis 1 and 2 is seen *in negative terms*, as the lack or absence of sin, and surely this is true. But something *positive* must be said about this goodness, something describing the basic traits of its goodness. A proposal has been put forward by Hebrew Bible scholar John Walton, according to which the main message of Genesis 1 is that God created an orderly universe and that this order consists in the proper function of all things. Walton proposes that this is simply consistent with what would have been expected by readers and hearers in the ancient world when claims were made about bringing something into existence: "I propose that people in the ancient world believed that something existed not by virtue of its material properties, *but by virtue of its having a function in an ordered system.* . . . Unless something is integrated into a working, ordered system, it does not exist. Consequently, the actual creative act is to assign something its functioning role in the ordered system. That is what brings it into existence. Of course something must have physical properties before it can be given its function, but the critical question is, what stage is defined as 'creation'?"[25] For Walton, Genesis is silent with respect to material origins. In the historical context of which Genesis is a part (indicated through the comparison of its language with that of other creation myths), there were certain ontological principles at play, ones that prioritized the proper function of that entity (what it is supposed *to do*) more than its material properties. Thus Walton: "In the ancient world, what was most crucial and significant to their understanding of existence was the way that the parts of the cosmos functioned, not their material status."[26]

25. John H. Walton, *The Lost World of Genesis One: Ancient Cosmology and the Origins Debate* (Downers Grove, IL: IVP Academic, 2009), 24, 25 (emphasis original).
26. Walton, *Lost World of Genesis One*, 26.

The warrant for this view is not difficult to discern. He demonstrates how the Hebrew verb translated as "to create" does not necessarily require a material understanding and is often employed to emphasize the purpose the created object was meant to serve.[27] When the earth is said to be "a formless void" in Genesis 1:2 (even though it already seemed to exist materially, since there must be a referent to these descriptors), this is best understood as a description of "that which is nonfunctional, having no purpose and generally unproductive in human terms."[28] Thus, the provision of form is the endowment of function. But what is a function?

Normally, a function is understood as what an entity is *supposed* to do, not merely what it does in point of fact. The function of a heart, ostensibly, is to pump blood, and the function of a librarian is to check out books. But further qualifications are required, for not just any thing that pumps blood is a heart (machines do this too), and not everyone who checks out books is a librarian. Alvin Plantinga, who has invoked the concept of a function to advance claims in epistemology, points out that something's function carries with it specifications about a suitable *environment* for its performance.[29] A librarian with no library cannot be said to be doing the work of a librarian, for if he attempts to check out books in his local grocery store, he would not be performing his function. Likewise, if a heart is used for purposes other than to pump blood in a body (say, to pump a red dye in a laboratory setting), it cannot be said to be doing what it is supposed to.

In addition, a function requires a *design plan*. As Plantinga explains, "The notion of proper function . . . is inextricably bound with another: that of a *design plan*. Human beings and their organs are so constructed that there is a way they *should* work, a way they are *supposed* to work, a way they work when they work right; this is the way they work when there is no malfunction. . . . There is a way in which a human organ or system works when it works properly, works as it is supposed to work; and this way of working is given by its design or design plan."[30] If a function specifies what an entity ought to do in

27. See Walton, *Lost World of Genesis One*, 41–45.

28. Walton, *Lost World of Genesis One*, 48.

29. Alvin Plantinga, *Warrant and Proper Function* (New York: Oxford University Press, 1993), 7.

30. Alvin Plantinga, *Warranted Christian Belief* (New York: Oxford University Press, 2000), 154. See also Plantinga's description of a human design plan as a "set of specifications for a well-formed, properly functioning human being—an extraordinarily complicated and highly articulated set of specifications, as any first-year medical student could tell you" (Plantinga, *Warrant and Proper Function*, 14).

its proper environment, something must describe its successful performance, what it looks like when it has done what it was meant to do. For a librarian, one might reasonably find a design plan in the job description; for a heart, that might be found in the pages of an anatomy textbook. The idea, though, is that if there are such things as functions, then there are specifications for their conditions of success, for it "is the way the thing in question is 'supposed' to work, the way in which it works when it is functioning as it ought to, when there is nothing wrong with it, when it is not damaged or broken or nonfunctional."[31] It also provides the rationale for *malfunction*, or what occurs when a function does not obtain its intended purpose.

A function, then, is what something ought to do in its apposite environment and according to its design plan, and this approach can be employed to give a positive account of the claims of goodness in Genesis 1. As Walton maintains, "The repeated formula 'it was good' . . . I propose refers to 'functioning properly.'"[32] When God created the heavens and the earth, all things were good in the sense that they did precisely what they were meant to do. Each created entity functioned according to their design plan, consistent with their nature, in an order that flourished. We might expand on these details by saying that understanding goodness according to proper function requires commitment to at least three claims: first, all entities have purposes for which they were created, what they are supposed to do, or (to use an older, medieval term) their *rectitude*; second, a creation full of creatures behaving according to their proper functions forms an orderly system; third, the proper function of a being within an orderly system is its fittingness, what it ought to do in relation to a system of other beings doing what they ought to.[33]

With these two tenets in hand, what implications can be detected for gender? Let us first consider the claim that created goodness consists in proper function. Among the creatures made by God in Genesis 1 and 2 are, of course, human beings with material bodies that are sexed (1:27–28). If sexed bodies were created and called "good," then it follows that sexed bodies also have a proper function, along with all other natural human traits, like our sociability

31. Plantinga, *Warrant and Proper Function*, 21.

32. Walton, *Lost World of Genesis One*, 50.

33. I have elsewhere argued that these three claims compose St. Anselm of Canterbury's doctrine of creation, thereby lending catholic pedigree to the view I am proposing. See Fellipe do Vale, "Anselm on the *Rectus Ordus* of Creation," *Saint Anselm Journal* 14, no. 1 (Fall 2018): 93–109.

and our ability to love.[34] The claim that all aspects of the body have a proper function, moreover, seems to have canonical backing. We see it asserted in Romans 12:4, for instance: "In one body we have many members, and not all the members have the same *function* [*praxin*]." While Paul is making a claim about the church here, it is nevertheless true that he is employing certain facts about the human body to illustrate his point, and the fact to which he makes reference is that all parts of the human body have a proper function. So what might be the proper function of the sexed body?

According to a certain type of natural law theorist, the answer to the question of sexed proper function is singular: reproduction.[35] This strikes me as unnecessarily and excessively reductive. If we recall the view of Charlotte Witt from chapter 3, the role of a function was central to her gender essentialism. Witt's uniessentialism explains why there is a composite entity rather than mere parts. Why is something a house rather than wood, glass, and metal assembled in the shape of a house? These materials, for Witt, constitute a house because they are organized in such a way as to perform a function, something like the provision of shelter. Witt goes on to claim that gender is the social position acquired by the social meaning of the engendering function, and that it organizes all of the other social positions in which one finds oneself. I suggest something similar regarding the role of functions that Witt highlights. The proper function of the sexed body, in conjunction with its ability to love and its tendency toward sociability, is to organize and appropriate social goods as a means to manifest itself socially. When it does so, gender emerges. In other words, on the model presented in this project, the proper function of sex is to be gender. There are all kinds of goods, roles, relationships, and so forth that we associate with gender, and these are always differing with respect to context. What unifies these goods? Our gender identity, acting as a function. Why does wearing this kind of clothing, engaging in these types of workouts, watching these kinds of movies, reading these kinds of novels, having or lacking facial hair, drinking these kinds of beverages, or talking in this particular manner make someone a woman or a man? What brings these disparate goods together? Gender does.

34. Walton himself lists maleness and femaleness among the things with proper functions in creation (see Walton, *Lost World of Genesis One*, 67). For a discussion of the proper function of our ability to love, see Jesse Couenhoven, *Stricken by Sin, Cured by Christ: Agency, Necessity, and Culpability in Augustinian Theology* (New York: Oxford University Press, 2013), 132, 138–40.

35. This view is found, e.g., in Edward Feser, "The Role of Nature in Sexual Ethics," *National Catholic Bioethics Quarterly* 13, no. 1 (Spring 2013): 69–76.

Another implication of creation for gender is that, as created, gender must be seen as good, not as something to be overcome and done away with. The categories established at creation are, in Walton's words, *archetypal*,[36] and though there are distortions after the introduction of sin, it remains true that the categories of creation tell us what it means to be a properly functioning instance of that kind of thing, even after the introduction of sin. There is, however, some controversy around the *normativity* of the creation narrative for ongoing understandings of gender after the Garden. Does Genesis require that we understand humanity as exclusively male and female, or does it teach less than that, allowing for greater flexibility?[37] A common argument made in trans* discussions is that the binaries in the creation accounts (day/night, etc.) are not distinct but exist on a spectrum.[38] If creation stands at the head of the economy presided over by the Divine Architect, and if Genesis truly is archetypal, then it seems that its depiction of the creation of two sexes must be normative for the remainder of the economy, even if sin introduces complexities both to our perceptions of this and to the actual proper function of sexed organs.

Immediately, a further question arises. There are intersex/DSD individuals who are either born with ambiguous sexed characteristics or who have such ambiguous characteristics as a result of medical procedure. "Intersex/DSD" is in fact an umbrella term for a variety of states of affairs, one that at times has seemed inadequate for the conditions it attempts to describe. Nevertheless, a person is intersex/DSD when their "bodies do not line up clearly with the medical norms for biological maleness or femaleness (e.g.,

36. See Walton, *Lost World of Genesis One*, 69: "The fact that the ancient Near East uses the same sorts of materials to describe all of humanity indicates that the materials have archetypal significance. . . . An archetype serves as a representative for all others in the class and defines the class."

37. A rather strong thesis in this direction can be found in Deryn Guest, "Troubling the Waters: תהום, Transgender, and Reading Genesis Backwards," in *Transgender, Intersex, and Biblical Interpretation*, ed. Teresa J. Hornsby and Deryn Guest, Semeia Studies (Atlanta: SBL Press, 2016), 21–44. Guest argues that though Genesis teaches that there are two sexes, there is reason simply to reject this teaching.

38. As I have mentioned already, I do not believe my account of gender settles trans* questions conclusively, though what I say is relevant for the discussion. As with Witt's view, the only modification necessary to be friendly to trans* affirmation would be to say that what we need is a *perceived* sexed body, not a sexed body as such. All the same, because the authors I interact with in this section do not make this reading of Genesis central to their arguments, I will not consider it here. I will take it as sufficient to say that appeals to spectrums remain unconvincing to me, for ends on a spectrum are still distinguishable. Rather than "binary versus spectrum," I much prefer to speak of the world of gendered goods we encounter and the wise negotiation of those goods with which we are tasked. This is not reducible to a binary or a spectrum but is much more complex, perhaps much more like a cluster of points on a grid.

chromosomes other than XX or XY, ambiguous genitalia, internal reproductive structures of one sex with external sex features of the other sex, just to name a few possibilities)."[39] Consider the two most frequent intersex/DSD conditions as examples: Androgen Insensitivity Syndrome (AIS) and Congenital Adrenal Hyperplasia (CAH).[40] At the risk of oversimplification, someone with AIS possesses external genitalia that are either completely or partially female (with a clitoris and labia) while the internal reproductive organs are male (undescended testes, rather than ovaries, and no uterus), and though the individual is female to the eye, they are chromosomally XY and will not menstruate. In the womb, due to a variant SRY gene on the Y chromosome, the fetus's androgen receptors do not respond to the androgens produced by the gonads, which are responsible for sexual differentiation in the fetus at around the sixth week of gestation. As a result, the child is XY with external female genitals and male internal reproductive organs. Though it is difficult to say just how many infants are born with AIS, numbers range from 1 in 13,000 to 1 in 20,000 for complete AIS, while partial AIS is at about 1 in 130,000. In CAH, the body produces excesses of cortisol due to the absence of the CYP21 gene, which converts progesterone to cortisol. In an attempt to correct the low cortisol levels, the adrenal gland is overworked, making more and more testosterone. This results in an XX individual with unusually large genital development, typically a large clitoris and sometimes fused labia, which gives the appearance of small male genitalia. In general, 1 in 10,000 people have CAH, though rates differ in certain geographic locations (rates are much higher among Yupik Alaskans, for example).

Though AIS and CAH are the most common intersex/DSD conditions, included are also 5-alpha-reductase deficiencies, genetic mosaics and chimeras (a combination of XX and XY cells with varying morphological impact), having both male and female genital tissue, Klinefelter syndrome (males who have an extra copy of the X chromosome), Turner syndrome (females who are missing or partially missing one sex chromosome), hypospadias (where the urinary opening for a male is not at the tip of the penis), micropenises, and

39. Megan K. DeFranza, *Sex Difference in Christian Theology: Male, Female, and Intersex in the Image of God* (Grand Rapids: Eerdmans, 2015), xiv.
40. In the glossary to her book, Susannah Cornwall provides a helpful summary of the most well-known intersex conditions, along with their frequencies, causes, and potential health risks. See Susannah Cornwall, *Sex and Uncertainty in the Body of Christ: Intersex Conditions and Christian Theology*, Gender, Theology and Spirituality (New York: Routledge, 2010), 237–46. I draw the information in this paragraph from her glossary.

vaginal agenesis. As a rule of thumb, it is generally thought that there are about as many intersex/DSD individuals as there are people with Down syndrome.

Tragically, individuals born with intersex/DSD conditions have been subject to horrific surgical treatment. These surgeries are regularly performed while the child is quite young, often just after birth, and result in very mixed rates of enduring health, frequently requiring regular follow-up treatment well into adulthood. What is more, doctors have been noted as having a strong repulsive reaction to intersex/DSD births,[41] leading many to conclude that disgust, anxiety, and insecurity have often motivated the surgical intervention, rather than care for the health of the baby. When interviewed, individuals who have undergone these procedures report lifelong sentiments of fear and shame. They disclose feeling like a fraud in their own bodies and in the world. Follow-up treatments involved being told to lie in a prostrate position while doctors and interns probed and inspected their genitals—much less like the experience of receiving medical care and more like being the subject of a dreadful science experiment. Many intersex/DSD individuals describe such medical practices as abusive. Within the church, this sense of "freakishness" (as one person has described it) does not abate. Sally Gross, an intersex/DSD woman who initiated many conversations about this issue within the church, describes being told that, on the basis of Genesis 1:27, she is not human (since humans are either male or female) and therefore cannot have a valid baptism. To her, the church viewed her as grotesque and unfit for redemption by Christ.[42]

As Cox puts it, "Shame is above all the most significant problem."[43] Intersex/DSD individuals have suffered enormous physical and psychological trauma because of the perception that they are abject examples of humanity, cases of medical curiosity rather than image bearers reflecting the care and craft of a Creator who has made them with beauty. Regularly, the justification for their mistreatment has come from the theological position I have just defended—namely, that there are two sexes. If creation's normativity extends to the fact that humanity is female and male, does that make intersex/DSD individuals subhuman? That some have acted as if this is so is nothing short of abusive and heinous, an awful application of doctrine that any Christian

41. One urologist was quoted to have said, "Have you seen a baby with CAH? It's grotesque." See the discussion and quotations in Jennifer Anne Cox, *Intersex in Christ: Ambiguous Biology and the Gospel* (Eugene, OR: Cascade Books, 2018), 28–32. The descriptions here are drawn from her presentation.

42. Sally Gross, "Intersexuality and Scripture," *Theology and Sexuality* 11 (1999): 70n7.

43. Cox, *Intersex in Christ*, 31.

should recognize as a failure of love. But does this render the teaching of Genesis false? Does it mean that Genesis cannot be read as depicting creation in two sexes? Should we revise the number of sexes in order to better reflect the experience of intersex/DSD individuals?[44]

The theological literature has given very little attention so far to these questions, and the first two monograph-length theological attempts to answer them have argued for precisely this conclusion: because of what we now know about intersexuality/DSD, we must reject the claim that there are only two sexes, even if that claim is found in Genesis 1 and 2.[45] In the first of these treatments, Susannah Cornwall argues, "Intersex shows that human sex is *not* a simple binary; and since any exception to a dualistic model necessarily undermines the model in its entirety, this makes essentialist assumptions about what constitutes 'concrete facts' even more precarious."[46] Cornwall argues that intersex/DSD conditions *by their very existence* challenge the view that there are only two sexes, for they take what belongs to one sex and attribute it to another, questioning the very stability of the category in the first place.[47] There is, however, a deeper metaphysical commitment that makes such a conclusion possible—for, of course, some intersex/DSD individuals seek to live within a sexual binary and do so successfully. For Cornwall, intersex/DSD is a reminder of a more profound truth about reality: that claims about normativity, especially claims about what bodies are like, are strongly socially constructed. So, she maintains that the "'character' of any body, then, rests

44. This was the original proposal of Brown University biologist Anne Fausto-Sterling. See Anne Fausto-Sterling, *Sexing the Body: Gender Politics and the Construction of Sexuality*, rev. ed. (New York: Basic Books, 2000); Anne Fausto-Sterling, "The Five Sexes: Why Male and Female Are Not Enough," *Sciences* 33, no. 2 (1993): 20–24; Anne Fausto-Sterling, "The Five Sexes, Revisited," *Sciences* 40, no. 4 (2000): 18–23.

45. For a helpful overview of the theological approaches to intersex/DSD, see Elyse J. Raby, "'You Knit Me Together in My Mother's Womb': A Theology of Creation and Divine Action in Light of Intersex," *Theology and Sexuality* 24, no. 2 (2018): 98–109.

46. Cornwall, *Sex and Uncertainty*, 125. She also says, "To maintain that every human being is *exactly and ineluctably male or female* and that this entails a specific path of gendered and sexual orientation, and that any human being who cannot or will not follow this trajectory is more sinful, flawed or fallen than any other human, is unjustifiable in light of what scientific evidence tells us" (Cornwall, *Sex and Uncertainty*, 13, emphasis added). In quotes like these, Cornwall's tendency to overstate in an effort to establish her argument is clear. As far as I can tell, "exactly" introduces epistemic standards that her opponent need not take on.

47. "If something (be it tissue or something else) which 'belongs' to males, which is the sole preserve of males, is annexed by non-males . . . or if the perimeters of what constitutes access to a given category are blurred; then questions are raised about whether it is the *actuality* of the body which has socio-cosmic significance, or merely the passing appearance" (Cornwall, *Sex and Uncertainty*, 87).

both on its conscious self-projection and on its reaction from, and constitution by, others."[48] Cornwall, relying on theorists like Judith Butler,[49] is a metaphysical anti-realist about the body, claiming that its features are *constituted* by the shaping of culture. Thus, "all bodies are constituted by their wider body—political, social, religious—and constitute that body."[50] Her rejection of a sexed binary comes from her descriptions of intersexuality/DSD, but the warrant for her underlying metaphysics of gender largely relies on the work of anti-realist theorists like Butler.

If there are no objective norms for bodily traits, it is also true that there are no normative traits that inform sex. "Sex," Cornwall maintains, "is bolstered by the customs and standards of society, which are provisional human standards despite having been co-opted to back-up 'overarching' theological models."[51] It is not merely gendered properties that are socially constructed but sexed properties also, those traits that differentiate biological males from biological females from intersex/DSD individuals. Cornwall is willing to accept the metaphysical price for such a claim; she also denies the existence of human natures,[52] an insight she judges to be bolstered by disability theologies and queer theory.[53] This enables her to draw on Galatians 3:28, which will be an important text in the next chapter, to argue that redemption in Christ erases sexual differentiation: "A realized temporal world where there is no male and female—or where biological maleness and femaleness are not the only available options—has seemed too unrealistic or utopian for most theologians to take seriously. . . . The Galatians text implies that there is something about participation in Christ, about *perichoresis* between Christ and the church and between humans, which means that even such apparently self-evident concepts as sexed nature are not to be taken as read in the nascent new order."[54] Cornwall, because of the metaphysics she assumes, is able to take the "literal" reading of Galatians 3:28 and therefore maintain that, in Christ, the categories of Genesis 1 and 2 are removed. They are neither fixed nor limiting categories, and

48. Cornwall, *Sex and Uncertainty*, 100.
49. See Cornwall, *Sex and Uncertainty*, 12.
50. Cornwall, *Sex and Uncertainty*, 106.
51. Cornwall, *Sex and Uncertainty*, 232. See also 129, 135.
52. "Whether or not an action or event is 'natural' thus cannot be appealed to as the be-all and end-all of whether it is legitimate, for nature itself is a disrupted category" (Cornwall, *Sex and Uncertainty*, 215; see also 172). The implications of the incarnation for this claim are not considered by Cornwall.
53. See Cornwall, *Sex and Uncertainty*, 169 (on disability theologies), 201 (on queer theory).
54. Cornwall, *Sex and Uncertainty*, 72.

redemption will introduce new ones. Galatians 3:28 is minimally at odds with Genesis 1:26–28, and what Christ provides is an openness not yet experienced before.[55] In light of this reading, along with her metaphysical anti-realism with regard to bodies, she concludes, "For the normally-sexed male-and-female to truly take account of differently sexed bodies, it will be necessary to move to an understanding that the dichotomously-sexed world is not the 'only' or 'real' world."[56] In order to adequately "take account" (whatever that might mean) of intersexuality/DSD, one must abandon a two-sex model.

Another author, Megan DeFranza, similarly argues that intersex/DSD conditions require us to abandon commitment to the existence of only two sexes: "Christian theological anthropology can no longer assume that all humans fit into the category of either 'Adam' or 'Eve.'"[57] She points out that Christ's mention of "eunuchs who have been so from birth" in Matthew 19:12 might be a reference to intersex/DSD, elevating the status and worth of these individuals as those fit for the kingdom.[58] DeFranza draws the following conclusion from Christ's mention of eunuchs: "The eunuch provided an important supplement to the binary model of human sex and gender. The eunuch emerged as a symbol of the sexless spirit, Christian perfection, the angelic life, and life in the resurrection—when distinctions of gender would be shed and men and women would relate to one another according to a common humanity, an identity hidden in Christ."[59] Like Cornwall, DeFranza argues from intersex/DSD conditions to the conclusion that there are not only two sexes, yet she bolsters her claims with appeal to Christ's affirmation of the life of the eunuch.

DeFranza has a dedicated treatment of the creation narratives of Genesis 1 and 2, and it merits special attention. She acknowledges that Genesis depicts

---

55. For Cornwall's treatment of Genesis, see esp. *Sex and Uncertainty*, 73, 120, and 130.

56. Cornwall, *Sex and Uncertainty*, 178.

57. DeFranza, *Sex Difference in Christian Theology*, 17.

58. DeFranza, *Sex Difference in Christian Theology*, 70. For precedent in the Hebrew Bible for such an association, see John Hare, "Hermaphrodites, Eunuchs, and Intersex People: The Witness of Medical Science in Biblical Times and Today," in *Intersex, Theology, and the Bible: Troubling Bodies in Church, Text, and Society*, ed. Susannah Cornwall (New York: Palgrave Macmillan, 2015), 79–96. Hare's studies helpfully point to several categories of eunuch; the *saris khama* is said to be the one in mind in this context. It is not obvious, however, that we can easily transpose such a category to contemporary intersex/DSD individuals, for in the context of Matt. 19, Jesus is commending those who do not marry. If the eunuchs from birth really are intersex/DSD people, then it would appear as though Christ is commanding them not to marry, a conclusion no intersex/DSD advocate would adopt. If intersex/DSD people marry and are able to have stable family lives (and they are), then the association in Matt. 19 is undermined.

59. DeFranza, *Sex Difference in Christian Theology*, 106.

creation in sexually binary terms, for God creates only males and females. She rejects, however, that this depiction is normative or paradigmatic for future expressions of humanity, for Genesis serves as the fountainhead of an ever-expanding diversity of human life, including sex: "Reading the Genesis account in light of the larger biblical narrative, we are able to affirm the goodness of sex difference as the fountainhead of human difference without requiring the male-female pattern to become the paradigmatic form of the other."[60] DeFranza claims that from Adam and Eve spring forth "other ages, other languages, other cultures, and even others whose sex does not match either parent," and so the general thrust of the economy is from a simple set of categories to more and more diverse expressions of humanity.[61] Therefore, the Genesis account is "not to be understood as the final word. Rather, true humanity is found in Christ as a future toward which we are moving."[62] Like Cornwall, DeFranza takes a "literal" interpretation of Galatians 3:28, where in Christ there is literally no sex or gender.[63] Adam and Eve, therefore, "function as *progenitors* rather than *paradigms* of human difference-in-relation."[64]

Similar to Cornwall, DeFranza relies on Judith Butler[65] to argue that sex along with gender is a social construct, having the features it has in virtue of social and cultural dynamics. She is forthright about the metaphysical underpinnings of her view: "Language is now believed not only to describe the world but also to create worlds, enabling us to see some things and not others, to think some things and not others. The history of the sexes, especially the history of intersex, illustrates this very point."[66] Yet, like Cornwall, she does not offer a straightforward argument for this view; instead, the social construction of sex is taken as a "given," or we are "reminded" that sex is socially constructed, or we are "confronted with the reality of the social construction

---

60. DeFranza, *Sex Difference in Christian Theology*, 179–80. See also page 178: "Rather than identifying male and female as the paradigmatic forms of otherness, they can be interpreted as the fountainhead of others who may become more 'other' than their parents could have ever conceived."

61. DeFranza, *Sex Difference in Christian Theology*, 182.

62. DeFranza, *Sex Difference in Christian Theology*, 239.

63. DeFranza, *Sex Difference in Christian Theology*, 184. Both Cornwall and DeFranza also argue that Christ *himself* was intersex/DSD. Though he was externally male, he had no human father from whom he would have acquired a Y chromosome, suggesting that he had a severe form of CAH. This argument is found originally in Edward L. Kessel, "A Proposed Biological Interpretation of the Virgin Birth," *Journal of the American Scientific Affiliation* 35 (1983): 129–36.

64. DeFranza, *Sex Difference in Christian Theology*, 287.

65. See DeFranza, *Sex Difference in Christian Theology*, 263, for her appropriation of Butler's metaphysical anti-realism.

66. DeFranza, *Sex Difference in Christian Theology*, 137.

of sex."[67] We are not, however, given a philosophical or theological argument for this view, except for what has already been provided by Butler. Intersex/DSD individuals, nonetheless, are meant to serve as *confirmations* that this thesis is true, even if many of them do not wish to abandon a two-sex system.

DeFranza's constructive solution is intended to be flexible and open-ended. She maintains, "Statistically significant differences remain useful for medicine, politics, psychology, sociology, and theology, so long as they are not employed in oppressive ways. Intersex certainly requires an alteration of the binary model. It necessitates opening up space in between the categories of male and female. Instead of two discrete categories, intersex shows how these overlap in various ways."[68] She leaves the precise features of that space undefined, and perhaps deliberately so. Thus, she does not enumerate how many sexes there are, nor how medical practice can follow statistically significant differences. But what is clearly false, on her view, is the claim that there are only two sexes. Eunuchs illustrate this, the Genesis narrative does not confine us to it, and the social construction of sex allows for it.

There are many levels at which to engage Cornwall and DeFranza, and these scholars are to be commended for giving serious theological attention to individuals who have often been invisible. Nevertheless, there is considerable reason to question their proposals. It is not exactly clear what it is that they are proposing in the first place. At times, they seem to be moving toward a metaphysical state of affairs where there are *more* sexes, perhaps as many sexes as there are biological expressions. At other times, especially in their reliance on Galatians 3:28, they seem to indicate that there will be *no* sex. It remains unclear what kinds of metaphysical revisions to sex one is meant to make—refute the binary, expand it, or collapse its categories so that they are not exclusively expressible? Different arguments found in their books lead to different conclusions. If we follow Galatians 3:28 in conjunction with Butler's views, in the way Cornwall and DeFranza propose, then we will be inclined to think that there is no longer any sexed difference. But if we take DeFranza's suggestion that Genesis 1 gives rise to greater diversity in human expression, then we will be inclined to think that there are many sexes. But those are not the same claims, and it is unclear for which conclusion they are arguing.

Another issue with their views is their bare reliance on the metaphysical arguments of Judith Butler to show that sex is socially constructed. Since I

67. DeFranza, *Sex Difference in Christian Theology*, 29, 35, 51.
68. DeFranza, *Sex Difference in Christian Theology*, 270.

have already engaged with Butler in chapter 2, I will simply point out here that their arguments stand or fall with Butler's, and I have attempted to show that Butler's metaphysical anti-realism is indefensible. If Butler is unreliable as a theoretical foundation for the social construction of sex, one would not have warrant for advancing such a view purely on the basis of their arguments.

More relevant to the purposes of this section, it is clear that Cornwall and DeFranza reject both tenets of the doctrine of creation for which I have argued—namely, that creation must be understood as good with regard to proper function and that it must act as the beginning of an integrated economy. Yet, they do not give persuasive reasons for rejecting them, nor do they replace them with satisfactory alternatives. On the question of the internal coherence of the divine economy, both Cornwall and DeFranza maintain that the categories provided at creation are neither archetypal nor consistent with the categories of redemption. Put another way, Genesis 1 and 2 are at odds with Galatians 3:28, such that redemption means redemption *from* the categories of creation. DeFranza attempts to make sense of this by arguing that creation is a progenitor of future possibilities, but this still requires denying any normativity or continuation of created categories. Creation echoes through Scripture, even in a fallen world. Much like the theme of a classical piece of music, it is introduced at the outset and replayed in a minor key before crescendoing in another movement and finally blaring forth in a fortissimo at its conclusion.[69] An economy that severs the categories of Genesis from the world into which we are redeemed is Gnostic by definition, and it is incompatible with the resonance of Scripture. Cornwall and DeFranza, by disjointing the economy, offer a Gnostic remedy to a genuine problem.

Second, it is difficult to see what makes creation "good" on their view, even though they both seem to retain some kind of proper functional understanding of human bodies. It is virtually impossible to understand intersex/DSD conditions without reaching for language about the improper functioning of sexed organs. Thus, AIS refers to androgen receptors *unable* to respond to the androgen, and CAH describes the body's *inability* to convert progesterone to cortisol, thereby creating too much testosterone. Cornwall admits as much: "In fact, many people do not understand their conditions in this way [i.e., as

69. I borrow this illustration from Matthew Mason, "The Wounded It Heals: Gender Dysphoria and Resurrection of the Body," in *Beauty, Order, and Mystery: A Christian Vision of Human Sexuality*, ed. Gerald L. Hiestand and Todd A. Wilson (Downers Grove, IL: IVP Academic, 2017), 143.

sex identity issues], and prefer to figure their intersex/DSD state as a *medical* condition rather than one which inevitably affects sex-gender identity."[70] The rationale for this, as intersex/DSD advocates like Bo Laurent and Ellen Feder have pointed out, is to ensure that intersex/DSD individuals actually receive adequate medical care. One intersex/DSD person, for instance, died of vaginal cancer, partly because doctors did not understand the particulars of this individual's condition.[71] Thus, it is important to retain the language of proper function when it comes to sexed bodies, something that can protect the well-being of intersex/DSD individuals themselves, especially to ensure they receive the necessary care. But if this is so, much of the reasoning for revising the categories of male and female is undermined, for not all biological expressions of sex are the same. Some are properly functioning; others are not.

It is important to point out—and this can be a step forward in mitigating the stigma of intersex/DSD—that *everyone* has an improperly functioning sexed body to some extent or another, especially if we include things like our loves and desires. All sexed bodies—*all human beings*—function improperly, and intersexuality/DSD is not a uniquely inhuman instance of this. Those who have presumed that it is and who have thus abused intersex/DSD persons have seized a place of purity and superiority that is simply not theirs to claim. As Cox highlights, "Intersex is simply *one* distortion of sexuality."[72] John Hare, an OB-GYN doctor and intersex/DSD advocate, suggests that "we are all variants," with the result that intersexuality should not be thought of as anything uniquely aberrant.[73] It is not a subhuman trait, and it is simply shortsighted for anyone to say that intersex/DSD individuals are worse off than unambiguously sexed people. Instead, all of humanity is improperly functioning, every sexed body has gone awry, and all of creation needs repair. To say this is not to impugn intersex/DSD people but to acknowledge that it is a baseless mistake to mark out these image bearers as uniquely inhuman. If all creation groans under sin, then it is myopic to envision some individuals who experience a *particular* expression of improper function as less worthy than others and to treat these individuals as objects for medical curiosity and social stigma.

This brings me to the central issue: When we talk about intersex/DSD individuals in these discussions, what are we trying to do? It is sometimes hard

70. Cornwall, *Sex and Uncertainty*, 9.
71. See Cornwall, *Sex and Uncertainty*, 45.
72. Cox, *Intersex in Christ*, 58.
73. Hare, "Hermaphrodites, Eunuchs, and Intersex People," 93.

to avoid the feeling that we are speculating amongst the detritus of shattered lives. At worst, these speculations often carry overtly ideological motivations.[74] But is it not a mistake to think that *metaphysical inquiry*, as important as it is in its right place, is the right tool for the church and for society to use in caring for individuals who have been shamed and mistreated? Cornwall and DeFranza have helped the academy and the church by bringing attention and understanding to the experiences of intersex/DSD individuals, but they too quickly transition to claims about metaphysical revisions of sexed bodies in an effort to address the harms done. There is a clear difference, however, between discussion of properties and natures, on the one hand, and the treatment of people with those properties and natures, on the other. That is, it is one thing to consider what is proper functioning and what is not, and it is another thing altogether to take these considerations as a basis to mistreat, harm, or abuse someone. Of course, it is often the case that the former *does serve as a justification for the latter*; history attests to this abundantly. But the solution to this is not revising the metaphysics, especially with questionable and poorly argued alternatives. Suppose that DeFranza and Cornwall succeed, and we move to living in a world where there are not just two sexes. Nothing intrinsic to that success points in the direction of justice, for it could very well be that members of two sexes abuse members of a third, or of a fourth, and so on. In that case, instead of providing hope for intersex/DSD individuals who have experienced shame, such metaphysical revisions would only paint a clearer target on their backs. While metaphysical revision can redress abuses that stem from faulty assumptions about sex, there is nothing intrinsic to metaphysical revision that guarantees it will do so, especially when most people do not care about the details of the metaphysics of gender but care much more about the conditions for belonging and being loved.

As I will argue in the redemption section in the next chapter, the solution is working toward communities in which one's worth is attributable not to one's sex or gender but to one's status in Christ. Specifically, within the church, the pursuit of justice needs to include the communal pursuit of communities of grace, where grace is fundamentally understood as the reception of every person in Christ, without consideration of any worth or social capital—or

74. Cox worries that some "are using intersex people as pawns for their political ends. Intersex persons should not be required to change the social order nor do they exist as object lessons for radical agendas. Using people in this way undermines the humanity of intersex people" (Cox, *Intersex in Christ*, 36–37).

lack thereof—that a person might have in the eyes of the world. Receiving such a gift creates a community in which those who have experienced shame, grief, and sentiments of impurity are not treated according to any deficit of social capital attached to such experiences. In this community, whether one is male, female, or intersex/DSD is not of consequence when it comes to *worth*. Any treatment or consideration of intersex/DSD individuals that fails to meet this standard is an aberration of the gift of Christ, a new legalism where acceptance in Christ is on the basis not of grace but of sex.

But *can* we easily categorize intersex/DSD individuals as *either* female or male? Do such individuals *understand themselves* as either female or male? Should we simply wave away all ambiguity regarding sex? For some, it simply is not clear whether they are male or female. As has been emphasized throughout so much of this project, my preference is to be *epistemically restrained*, not *metaphysically revisionist*, in such cases. Perhaps there are intersex/DSD persons with irreducibly ambiguous phenotypical and genotypical traits, such that there is really no way to tell whether someone is female or male. The best course of action, I propose, is neither reckless surgery nor the creation of new metaphysical options. Both of these represent hasty attempts to categorize an ambiguity that the church and the world ought to live with; both are attempts at rapid solutions. Epistemic restraint, I recommend, is the best way forward. Instead of obeying the need to categorize the ambiguously sexed, perhaps we ought to question why such a need exists in the first place. It seems to me wiser to show patience and find ways to help individuals flourish, despite the ambiguity, and in the midst of a world eager to turn their bodies into burdens of shame. Christians have plenty of reason to provide such help, as we will see, and striving to be the kind of community where sex and gender norms carry different weight than in the world is precisely the kind of revision necessary.

It is consistent with everything just said that there are two sexes, female and male. We may not be able to say on a case-by-case basis which category fits each individual, nor does this approach require every individual to unambiguously demonstrate that they are members of either sex. My encouragement of epistemic restraint regarding cases of intersex/DSD does not mean that there is no fact of the matter regarding the issue. Rather, it means that sometimes we are simply not in a position to know, and our task is not to make the world an uncomfortable place for those whose ambiguity regarding sex is beyond our remit. Such ambiguity is resolved not with metaphysics but in the lives of communities, especially of churches who have fully appreciated the ramifications of the gift of grace. Perhaps the moment of grace is the one where epistemic surety is withheld and Christians accept not knowing, leaving the surgical and metaphysical tools off of the table.

6.3 Conclusion

Creation has remarkable relevance for a theology of gender. It is the beginning of the unfolding economy and echoes throughout it. This means that since we were created gendered, we cannot construe redemption so as to eliminate gender. Sex and gender, like all creaturely realities, will be redeemed, sustained, and perfected by the wise Architect. To posit a redemption that erodes creaturely traits runs the risk of falling into Gnosticism. Moreover, sex and gender are good, meaning that they too have proper functions and places within God's orderly universe. A picture of created gender emerges in which gender can be properly appreciated, for it has been created by God.

The doctrine of creation should not be asked to bear too much weight for gender. We need it to know the goodness that God has created, and we need it to serve as the beginning of the economy in which gender is situated. This, I hope, can be recognized as an intentionally parsimonious claim. Accounts that place creation and redemption in opposition claim that created traits must be undone, removed, or displaced because of the work of Christ. Such was the attempt of Gnostic authors, and the tendency continues to show itself in accounts of sex and gender that propose metaphysically revisionary construals, either to accommodate intersex/DSD persons or for other reasons.[75] These accounts also lose a positive and constructive appreciation for the goodness of creation, specifically for its proper functioning. Most seriously, I have argued that they are unable to deliver what their theories aim to bring about. Metaphysical revision of sex categories is not the route toward justice, toward the healing of hurt, or toward the removal of shame.

So then, what is? My proposal needs some constructive account of how such redemption occurs, but first a word must be spoken about what precisely has gone wrong in the world to bring about such pain. For that, we need the rest of the divine economy.

75. For a proposal that argues for the undoing of sex and gender on grounds unrelated to intersex/DSD, see Linn Marie Tonstad, *God and Difference: The Trinity, Sexuality, and the Transformation of Finitude*, Gender, Theology and Spirituality (New York: Routledge, 2016).

SEVEN

Gender in Fall, Redemption, and Consummation

Continuing the inquiry into how gender is implicated by the various stages of the divine economy, this chapter considers how gender is distorted by sin, redeemed by grace, and consummated in the new heaven and earth. The corruption of gender is analyzed under the rubric of the lust for domination characteristic of all sin, expressing itself in abuses of power, the paradigmatic instance of which is sexual assault. The experience of gendered shame, especially as we saw in the discussion of intersex/DSD individuals, highlights the need for an account of redemption that offers restoration. In addition to providing that account, this chapter offers a construal of grace that culminates in the pursuit of justice. Finally, in the context of eschatology, Galatians 3:28 is shown to reconfigure the social capital given to gender, which is also a call to the church now to reconfigure the weight placed on gendered structures.

7.1 Introduction

The doctrine of creation, especially in concerns related to ethics, must always be calibrated by the moments of the divine economy that come after it. Attempts to understand gender simply by returning to the beginning lose sight of the fact that things are not the way they are meant to be because of the many ways sin has distorted the goodness of creation. Additionally, our ability to tell just what is natural to that goodness and what is cultural preference is compromised, which often leads us toward unjust and sexist proclivities. At the same time, we lose sight of the normativity of the end, of the new heaven and earth fully consummated under the exalted Christ. To avoid this set of temptations, we need the whole story of God. This chapter completes that story.

Gender is very often a point of pain, burden, and difficulty, and for that reason, an examination of the nature of sin is necessary. Here I shall take sexual assault as the paradigmatic instance of gendered sin, and it will be understood as a characteristic manifestation of what Augustine called the *libido dominandi*, or the lust for domination, power, and destruction. This uses the same terms that survivors use to name assault, and it places the moral blame squarely on the assailants. While many survivors describe the shame that is occasioned by assault, particularly in ecclesial spaces that favor purity over justice, some word of hope is needed for healing and restoration. Turning to redemption, an account of grace is developed, following the work of John Barclay, according to which Christ is a gift given without regard to our worth, constituting an alternative system of worth that recognizes only one's union with Christ. This will be presented as a theological remedy for the shame and destruction wrought by patterns of gendered sin. Finally, the nature of resurrected genders will be considered, with particular attention given to Galatians 3:28. We have already seen the importance of this text in the work of Susannah Cornwall and Megan DeFranza, and it returns in the theological treatment of gender of Douglas Campbell, examined below. I shall argue that while sex and gender persist eschatologically, they do so with recalibrated worth, and such a recalibration implores churches to be spaces that reflect their eschatological end, spaces in which gender is not a tool for discrimination and bias because it has lost the burdensome significance it typically plays in such environments.

7.2 Fall

When considering the ramifications of sin for gender, I turn my attention to what I take to be the paradigmatic instance of sinful gender expression—namely, sexual assault.[1] There is a reason for this: sexual assault, by most

---

1. There is some dispute about the adequacy of terms like "sexual violence," "sexual violation," "rape," and "sexual assault," just as there is a great amount of opaqueness regarding the nature of such actions. For instance, Linda Martín Alcoff prefers to refer to this cluster of

metrics, is the most prevalent issue in sexual ethics facing the church today.[2] While it presents a morally complex challenge that ought to be resisted at various levels, theologians have a role to play in identifying the pastoral, moral, and theological dimensions involved therein, so as to promote Christian environments of healing and grace. Survivors of rape have argued as much. Christians need a credible answer to a survivor who asks, "What makes someone, a young man, want to have sex under *these* kinds of circumstances when he might have them otherwise? What is the nature of the desire that leads to such events? What are the beliefs necessary to generate such an action, or to think afterward that no harm was done?"[3] These are remarkably *theological* questions. Moreover, "without conceptual categories that can identify unjust, pathological or problematic behaviour, there can be little comprehension of what causes and maintains violence against women."[4] Survivors are in need

---

actions as "sexual violations" on the basis of the emphasis she wishes to give to sexual agency. See Linda Martín Alcoff, *Rape and Resistance: Understanding the Complexities of Sexual Violation* (Cambridge: Polity, 2018), 12. It is not my concern to settle that question here, and I acknowledge the complexity of causes and relations that surround sexual sin. The central point I emphasize is that these actions involve sexual acts (or acts relating to sexual expression, like kissing) where at least one individual lacks sexual agency. One typically lacks sexual agency when an expression of informed consent is absent; adjudications of sexual agency, however, should also look to identify whether a sense of safety is present, if the persons engaging in a sexual act exhibit mutual trust, if there is evidence of any form of manipulation in professional relationships, if economic factors were used as tools for securing false "consent," and the like. Sexual agency involves a positive contribution to engagement in the act consistent with their agency (again, whether that is consent or something stronger). In their book, Justin and Lindsey Holcomb rightly point out that sexual agency is lost through a variety of circumstances, such as "force, intimidation, violence, coercion, manipulation, threat, deception, or abuse of authority," a list to which more can be added (Justin S. Holcomb and Lindsey A. Holcomb, *Rid of My Disgrace: Hope and Healing for Victims of Sexual Assault* [Wheaton: Crossway, 2011], 28). If any of these cause the sexual act (either on its own or in conjunction with a wider complex of causes), assault is highly probable. For a cutting-edge account of sexual agency and consent, see Ellie Anderson, "A Phenomenological Approach to Sexual Consent," *Feminist Philosophy Quarterly* 8, no. 2 (2022): 1–24.

2. While accurate statistics for sexual assault and rape are notoriously difficult to ascertain due to the low number of actual reporting because of the unsafe conditions for doing so, a common statistic on the subject states that one in every six women in the United States has experienced attempted or completed rape (roughly 17 percent) and that 90 percent of victims are female. For helpful details on the statistics, see "Scope of the Problem: Statistics," RAINN (Rape, Abuse and Incest National Network), accessed February 23, 2021, https://www.rainn .org/statistics/scope-problem. While statistics do not designate importance or gravity of moral harm, this shows that sexual assault directly affects more people than any other ethical issue regarding sex and gender.

3. Alcoff, *Rape and Resistance*, 7.

4. Elaine Storkey, *Scars across Humanity: Understanding and Overcoming Violence against Women* (Downers Grove, IL: IVP Academic, 2018), 176.

of support from the church, but too often it is the church that exacerbates the harm rather than healing it. Instead of drawing "on the resources of [their traditions,] whether that's a particular historic emphasis, theological lens, or doctrinal viewpoint," the church often provides safe harbor for assailants to carry out their heinous deeds.[5] Ruth Everhart's work is filled with such instances. She tells the story of Melissa, who was raped in a dark hallway of her church when she was there for a Christmas Eve service and grieving the death of her partner. Later, when Melissa confided this painful experience to her Christian boyfriend, he immediately raped her—which, she later realized, revealed that he saw her as worthless due to her previous assault.[6] This assumption of worthlessness was tied to a perceived loss of purity, which had a distinctly theological definition in this man's mind. As this example and many others show, the church has too often been complicit in this "most detestable crime,"[7] and if a theological evaluation of such occurrences can serve to rectify this reality and begin to shift Christian perception on the issue, it is worth undertaking.

It might come as a surprise that Augustine, whose theology of love provided the core elements of the model of gender I provided, sought to give pastoral and theological consolation to rape survivors and their families—specifically, to those who were raped during the sack of Rome and then subsequently fled to Hippo—while also challenging the culture that facilitated such assault. As we have already seen, his *City of God* depicts the "most glorious city of God," whose members are guided by a primary enjoyment of God, and the "earthly city," which "seeks dominion" even though it "is itself under the dominion of its very lust for domination [*libido dominandi*]."[8] The heavenly city is characterized by glory, while the earthly city is characterized by a desire to dominate others through the greater achievement of power, after which it *lusts*. This corresponds to the two ways Augustine envisions love in a human person, either as good and directed to God or as wicked and directed to personal satisfaction and domination: "The foot of the soul is properly

---

5. Ruth Everhart, *The #MeToo Reckoning: Facing the Church's Complicity in Sexual Abuse and Misconduct* (Downers Grove, IL: IVP Academic, 2020), 237–38.

6. See Everhart, *#MeToo Reckoning*, 119–25.

7. From the title of a collection of philosophical essays on the topic: Keith Burgess-Jackson, ed., *A Most Detestable Crime: New Philosophical Essays on Rape* (New York: Oxford University Press, 1999).

8. Augustine, *De civitate Dei* 1.pref. (hereafter cited as *De civ.*). English translation from Augustine, *The City of God*, ed. Boniface Ramsey, trans. William Babcock, vol. I/6, *The Works of Saint Augustine: A Translation for the 21st Century* (Hyde Park, NY: New City, 2012).

understood as love. When it is misshapen it is called concupiscence or lust; when it is well formed it is called love or charity."[9] Interestingly, the first people to be called "glorious" in the *City of God* are the victims of rape who arrive in Augustine's community in Hippo after the sack of Rome, and the first people who are said to live by the *libido dominandi* or lust for domination are their rapists, who had sacked Rome.[10] At the outset of one of his most important works, then, Augustine identifies rape as a particularly vituperative example of sinful love and accords to its victims a singular dignity.

What does Augustine have to say about the rape of these Roman Christian women? His central diagnosis of the situation is that "the crime belongs only to the man who took the woman by force and not at all to the woman who was taken by force, without her consent and against her will."[11] The raped women are guilty of absolutely nothing. They have neither lost their "purity" nor done anything morally wrong, and whatever shame they feel is directly attributable to the wrongful act of another done *to* them, not to something for which they are responsible. Instead, Augustine points to the assailant as exemplifying the lust for domination. Augustine's pastoral response is to summon the community to believe the testimony of the survivors, offering consolation and support, even under cultural circumstances where there is every reason not to do so. Melanie Webb summarizes the theological project of the *City of God* as it relates to rape as follows: "Augustine sets out to address pastorally the pressing social and ecclesial concerns in the aftermath of the sack of Rome (410 CE), specifically through appeal to and revision of both Roman and Roman Christian virtue traditions. . . . He is reassuring his flock that the depredations of 410 CE, and others like them, were not a consequence of the community's promiscuity, and especially reassuring women in the community that they need not feel the burden and shame associated with rape."[12]

Before exploring this set of claims, it is important to gain an understanding of the historical context regarding attitudes toward rape victims. In the Roman milieu of the time, including among its Christian leaders, victims of rape were

---

9. Augustine, *Enarrationes in Psalmos* 9.15 (hereafter cited as *En. in Ps.*). English translation from Augustine, *Expositions of the Psalms, 1–32*, trans. Maria Boulding, vol. III/15, The Works of Saint Augustine: A Translation for the 21st Century (Hyde Park, NY: New City, 2000).

10. This is pointed out in Melanie Webb, "'Before the Eyes of Their Own God': Susanna, Rape Law, and Testimony in *City of God* 1.19," in *Reading Scripture as a Political Act: Essays on the Theopolitical Interpretation of the Bible*, ed. Matthew A. Tapie and Daniel W. McClain (Minneapolis: Fortress, 2015), 80.

11. *De civ*. 1.19.

12. Webb, "'Before the Eyes of Their Own God,'" 57–58.

expected to commit suicide. The reason for this had everything to do with the shame associated with notions of sexual impurity. If a victim of rape wished to safeguard her legacy as a chaste woman, she had to take her own life. Only then could her testimony be corroborated with a sufficient witness, for then "death is her witness."[13] Of course, this drastic measure was taken only because no alternative was available. In classical Rome, "a woman's will, or initiative, did not play any part" in defining adultery, elopement, and rape, which made the distinction between adultery and rape practically nonexistent. Therefore, "the only indubitable testimony that women did not in any way desire or consent to rape was suicide."[14] Only then, it seems, could her will be taken as significant in the evaluation of what occurred, even if it continued not to play a role in the legal definition of rape. If a woman wanted to avoid the shame associated with the loss of purity, then she needed to take her own life. These cultural principles of shame, purity, and rape were enforced by narratives of exemplars who did just this, the chief of which was Lucretia.[15] Lucretia was a dignified Roman woman who was raped by the king's son, Sextus Tarquinius. He threatened to leave the dead body of Lucretia's slave on top of her, to frame her for illicit sexual activity, if she retaliated in any way. The next day, she gathered her family around her and took her own life, just after requesting revenge. Her doing so motivated the overthrow of the Tarquin dynasty and the rise of the Roman Republic in the sixth century BCE. Lucretia's shadow loomed large over Roman responses to rape; a woman's suicide was expected.

Among Christian leaders, these trends were fortified rather than resisted. Jerome and Ambrose both prized a woman's chastity above her life and elevated Lucretia as an exemplar of virtue.[16] Much as in some segments of the church today, purity was prized as a distinctly feminine virtue (as more important even than a woman's life), which led to a culture in which the perceived loss of purity stripped a woman of worth and brought upon her unspeakable shame. As the above example from Everhart illustrates, such conceptions facilitate a rape culture[17] in which the loss of purity empowers

13. Webb, "'Before the Eyes of Their Own God,'" 73.
14. Webb, "'Before the Eyes of Their Own God,'" 58.
15. Lucretia's story is told in Livy, *Ab urbe condita* 1.58.1–11.
16. For their statements, see Melanie Webb, "'On Lucretia Who Slew Herself': Rape and Consolation in Augustine's *De ciuitate dei*," *Augustinian Studies* 44, no. 1 (2013): 37–38.
17. A rape culture is one where definitions and stereotypes of women and men make possible, facilitate, encourage, cover up, or otherwise promote rape, whether these are insufficient legal standards or commonly held notions about gender. See Storkey, *Scars across Humanity*, 130.

an assailant to think he can do anything he desires with a putatively impure body. As many survivors have testified, the world is filled with rape cultures, and wartime only intensifies sexual violence. Storkey reports that 90 percent of rape victims in modern warfare are civilian, and "of these 75 per cent are women and children."[18] She mentions the "Comfort Women" of the 1930s, young girls abducted from Korea, Taiwan, the Philippines, Malaysia, East Timor, and China and taken to Japan to provide Japanese forces with "sexual service." As many as 200,000 girls were taken and forced to have sex with up to forty soldiers a day, facing beatings if they resisted. Such torture often drove these girls to commit suicide.[19] Though this is a particularly odious example of sexual violence during wartime, the mechanics and motivations involved therein were not all that different from those of Augustine's time, with the crumbling of Roman civilization imminent.

Augustine recognizes that the victims of rape who had killed themselves, including Lucretia, did so out of a profound sense of shame: "When she killed herself because she had endured an adulterer (even though she was not herself an adulteress), it was not out of love of purity but out of the weakness brought about by shame. What made her feel shame was the debased act of another committed on her but not with her."[20] In a deranged Roman milieu where a woman's social capital and worth were deeply tied to her purity, the loss of purity inevitably resulted in shame. There are cultural analogues with our day here as well. Everhart, who was repeatedly raped for six hours at gunpoint, describes the aftermath: "I believed that being raped had damaged me beyond repair. I struggled with feelings of *shame* and *worthlessness*."[21] She mentions another victim who was abducted at fourteen and raped daily for nine months: "When she described her highly publicized ordeal, she said the *shame* of rape made her feel like used chewing gum. *Worthless. Used up*."[22] "Shame" and "worthlessness" are words commonly used by victims to describe the impact of rape and assault, and this experience must be taken into account in the theological reflection at hand. The reasons a survivor of sexual assault would feel shame are complex, but they at least involve a sense of being violated, of having had something taken away, of having bodily boundaries once thought

18. Storkey, *Scars across Humanity*, 136.
19. Storkey, *Scars across Humanity*, 140.
20. *De civ.* 1.19 (translation slightly modified).
21. Everhart, *#MeToo Reckoning*, 4 (emphasis added).
22. Everhart, *#MeToo Reckoning*, 52 (emphasis added).

stable and safe shown to be violable and penetrable. When a human being with richly complex emotions, identities, and memories is reduced to an object for lascivious consumption, such denigration understandably creates a sense of worthlessness and shame. For, so it is assumed, only someone who is worthless can be treated like this. Someone with dignity would have been treated better.[23] When such feelings are layered into a society that frequently distrusts survivors, leaves assailants unpunished, and otherwise facilitates abuse, the despair of feeling worthlessness is not difficult to imagine.

Augustine's response to rape in Rome, therefore, needed to address the issues surrounding shame and worth. In contrast to his ecclesiological contemporaries, who thought that the shame of rape was redeemed only through suicide, he offered a two-pronged response. First, he did not mince words about the rapist's motivation or blame, diagnosing it squarely in terms of sin and thereby shifting the focus of moral evaluation onto the assailant. What motivates rape, he maintains, is nothing other than human love sinfully distorted. He compares it to the torture of Regulus, who was forced to stand upright in a box with nails on all sides, confining him to death.[24] Here he anticipates the later judgment of survivor Mary DeMuth: "Let's call rape what it is: a murder that leaves its victim alive"—though, in the case of Lucretia and others, such a judgment carries with it a sense of heartbreaking irony.[25] Rape is not something for which one deserves scorn; it is more like the undergoing of heinous torture at the hands of wicked people. Webb concludes that "just as no one would want to be tortured, so also no one would want to be raped. Augustine does not understand rape primarily as a sexual encounter, but as torture and bereavement. Rape, as a result, warrants consolation—a judgment, it seems, that Augustine is the first to make."[26] Those who tortured Regulus, just like those who raped the Roman women, were driven by the *libido dominandi*, the lust for domination. It is fundamentally a dark desire for the exercise of power over another, since "there is hardly anyone who is free of the love of wielding power or does not long for human glory," and this wielding of power is so widespread that it "creeps like

23. For a persuasive account of the relationship between rape, memory, and identity, see Danielle Tumminio Hansen, "Remembering Rape in Heaven: A Constructive Proposal for Memory and the Eschatological Self," *Modern Theology* 37, no. 3 (2021): 662–78.
24. *De civ.* 1.15.
25. Mary E. DeMuth, *We Too: How the Church Can Respond Redemptively to the Sexual Abuse Crisis* (Eugene, OR: Harvest House, 2019), 138.
26. Webb, "'On Lucretia Who Slew Herself,'" 41.

a cancer."[27] Unsurprisingly, when one lives by the *libido dominandi*, one is prone to cultivate and exercise one's power to one's private ends, even to the point of crime: "Anyone who wants domination and power . . . will generally seek to obtain what he loves by even the most blatantly criminal acts."[28] So it was with the torturers and rapists—their sinful love drove them to obtain what they sought through the exercise of domination and power, even to the point of the destruction of life.[29] They are like Amnon, who claimed to "love" Tamar (2 Sam. 13:4), only for him to "hate" her with a hatred that exceeded his love after he raped her (2 Sam. 13:15). Here we see what the "love" that motivates rape really is: a spiteful longing for domination that aims only to destroy the beloved, leaving Tamar to be "a desolate woman" (2 Sam. 13:20). On Augustine's analysis, the rapists who invaded Rome were motivated by "lustful use," had an "utterly depraved desire," and set upon their victims "with violence," all features indicative of distorted love.[30]

There are stunning parallels here with contemporary assessments of rape, which are often said to have deep associations with the wrongful use of power for domination. Though the apothegm "Rape is not about sex; it is about power" is probably too simplistic to describe this complex reality, it has nonetheless resonated with survivors to the point of carrying wide acceptance. Storkey comments, "Power inequalities . . . often go along with incidences of rape. . . . When sin corrupts those who have power, the effects on the powerless can be overwhelming, leaving them dehumanized and objectified. . . . Sin eliminates love, and fuels loathing."[31] These power inequalities can manifest in a variety of ways—sometimes at the end of a weapon, sometimes through the social influence of the assailant, sometimes through spiritual authority—but the key idea is that if rape and assault involve, at the very least, some violation of sexual agency, there must be *something* that makes the violation possible. That variable must exercise sufficient power to break the will of the assailed, or to exercise sufficient pressure to bring them to the point of doing what the assailant wishes. After a fellow pastor kissed her against her will, Everhart recognized that leading up to it was "a larger pattern of domination

27. *En. in Ps.* 1.1.
28. *De civ.* 5.19.
29. Webb comments, "Rape . . . is a particularly salient facet of the damage wreaked by the *libido dominandi*, by which Augustine characterizes Roman society, and by extension the earthly city, in his preface to the *City of God*" (Melanie Webb, "Rape and Its Aftermath in Augustine's *City of God*" [PhD diss., Princeton University, 2016], 3–4).
30. *De civ.* 1.19.
31. Storkey, *Scars across Humanity*, 128, 223.

and control," making the occurrence "not only sexual abuse, but abuse of power."[32] By calling it a lust for domination and power that leads to acts of violence, Augustine is naming rape in the same way these survivors do. The blame for these acts falls, therefore, on the assailant, who is moved by a lust for crime and power, not on the survivor, which is an act of stunning resistance to a culture ready to shame women for failing to meet an impossible standard of purity.

This first prong of Augustine's response has to do with the causes for rape and the appropriate allocation of blame. The second prong then turns to the consolation of the survivor.[33] To offer hope, he presents these women with the love that is found in God as a contrast to the hateful cupidity demonstrated by their assailants. These women, he says in no uncertain terms, "have the glory of chastity within them, the witness of conscience. They have this in the eyes of their own God, and they need nothing more."[34] The worth and status of these women is derived from the God who sees all and tolerates no injustice, and in the eyes of this God, they are glorious. Recall that glory, in an Augustinian idiolect, is a characteristic of the heavenly city, inhabited by those people God has called, sustained, and perfected. The previous quotation is the first instance in which Augustine calls someone glorious, and with this specific terminology he is assuring these women that God sees, knows, and validates them. Augustine "appropriates God to these women, and in so doing insists that God is not the property of his male readership."[35] God is on their side. Though their male-dominated culture attributed to them shame and

32. Everhart, #MeToo Reckoning, 91, 96.

33. In De civ. 2.2, Augustine offers "consolation to those holy women of devout chastity whose treatment at the hands of the enemy brought the pangs of shame upon them, even though it actually left their unshaken virtue wholly intact. There is no wickedness in their life for which they could possibly need to feel ashamed, and so they should not feel ashamed of their life." Webb notes that consolatio is a well-established literary form of the time, intended primarily for those in exile or bereavement. "To introduce the term consolatio is to acknowledge that the addressee has suffered a grievous loss and quite understandably, is debilitated in the effort to live stably and resiliently. As a result, words of strength from that person's community members are in order so that the recipient might be nurtured toward the pursuit of healing." Rape victims were never the object of a consolatio, so Augustine's choice of the term was a countercultural choice that "pleads with the living to recognize these women as dignified and chaste" and calls on these women to "choose a different way forward and take their places among the living" (Webb, "'On Lucretia Who Slew Herself,'" 55, 57).

34. De civ. 1.19. I have modified the translation from "in the eyes of God" to "in the eyes of their own God" (habent autem coram oculis dei sui) to highlight the fact that Augustine is emphasizing that God is, without doubt, on the side of the victim. It is one of the few times where he construes God as the possession of a human being.

35. Webb, "'Before the Eyes of Their Own God,'" 77.

worthlessness, Augustine assured them that in the eyes of the One who governs history, they are without shame and beautiful. Though they are enmeshed in a culture that works against the purposes and intents of their God, they can be assured that what is most fundamentally true about them is that they are accepted and glorious in the eyes of God, a God whose justice will prevail.

Augustine's consolation then becomes even more specific as he looks to apply this to the concrete situation in which these survivors found themselves. While the consolation encountered in God is a powerful solace, Augustine also challenges the surrounding culture to conform their practices to God's standard. It is important to recall that this section of the *City of God* is not written *to the survivors as such*; it is written to government officials like Marcellinus, a Roman civil servant, and Volusianus, the imperial proconsul of Africa.[36] It can be said, therefore, that "Augustine seeks to forge theological resources for stability and strength as these women choose life day by day, moment by moment, until living can once again be experienced, consistently, as a pleasure. In their living, these women are well-regarded by God, *and society's leaders are to regard them similarly.*"[37] Since the standards set up by Roman culture informed so much of the shame these women experienced, Augustine calls this culture to recognize where significant correction is necessary. If God does not shame these women but upholds their worth, so must the society in which they live.

A crucial component of this transformation, as much in his day as in our own, is to believe the testimony of survivors. In Augustine's day, the testimony of women carried no weight, so if a woman claimed to have been raped, chances were that it would end poorly for her (perhaps even in her trial and death). Today, there is a similar concern about false allegations and the harm it can cause to the alleged abuser. However, it is generally acknowledged that *baseless* allegations (that is, not necessarily false but *unproven* ones) make up between 2 and 10 percent of all charges.[38] There is, then, an acute epistemic question regarding how to address allegations of rape and the credibility one affords to a survivor. Augustine's solution was to favor the testimony of the survivor, and he had distinctly theological reasons for doing so. Recall that

36. See *De civ.* 1.pref.

37. Melanie Webb, "Augustine, Rape, and the Hermeneutics of Love," in *Producing Christian Culture: Gospel Text and Its Interpretive Genres*, ed. Matthew Crawford, Giles E. M. Gasper, and Francis Watson (London: Routledge, 2017), 31 (emphasis added).

38. "False Reporting: Overview," National Sexual Violence Resource Center, 2012, https://www.nsvrc.org/sites/default/files/2012-03/Publications_NSVRC_Overview_False-Reporting.pdf.

the reigning exemplar for situations such as these was Lucretia, who, in an attempt to secure the validity of her testimony, was forced into transforming herself into "the murderess of an innocent and chaste woman" by taking her own life, one part of herself dividing against another.[39] Instead of affirming this act, Augustine calls his readers' attention to another exemplar, one not with Roman pedigree but with *scriptural* pedigree—namely, Susanna.[40] In Susanna's story, two men attempt to rape her while she is bathing, and though she eludes them, they falsely accuse her of adultery, which leads to her being sentenced to death. In the narrative, the prophet Daniel intervenes and defends Susanna's innocence, preventing the city from carrying out what Lucretia did on her own. Webb notes, "Susanna's story is, for Augustine, a challenge to see what is hidden,"[41] which is to say, Augustine calls upon the story of Susanna to commend the need to believe the testimony of women, just as Daniel did. Their "witness of conscience" is sufficient to safeguard their innocence,[42] a remarkably countercultural claim in a time when women's witness counted for nothing.[43] Because their testimony had validation in the eyes of God, it was the duty of all others to "coordinate their vision with the vision of God."[44] *In essence, Augustine is drawing upon Scripture to enjoin the powerful men of his day to believe women.* Webb concludes, "For Augustine, suspicion that women want rape or are defiled by rape is tantamount to a false testimony against those women. Augustine's insight is startling, and counter-intuitive within a culture, like our own, that assumes that a woman's report of rape is like a false testimony, or an attempt to cover up illicit sex."[45] For Augustine, the story of Susanna, along with the conjunction of commands not to kill (Exod. 20:13), not to bear false witness against one's neighbor (Exod. 20:16), and to love one's neighbor as oneself (Matt. 22:39) results in powerful theological impetus to believe women who are victims of rape, even in a culture providing every reason not to do so.[46]

---

39. *De civ.* 1.19.
40. In the Septuagint, Susanna's story is told in the thirteenth chapter of Daniel. Though Augustine does not mention Susanna explicitly in *De civ.* 1.19, there is reason to think that he deliberately echoes her story. He discusses Susanna in many other writings, including *Contra Julianum* 4.37, *De bono conjugali* 8.8, *De sancta virginitate* 20, *Enarrationes in Psalmos* 3.4, and substantially in *Sermones* 343.
41. Webb, "'Before the Eyes of Their Own God,'" 63.
42. *De civ.* 1.19.
43. See Webb, "'Before the Eyes of Their Own God,'" 75.
44. Webb, "'Before the Eyes of Their Own God,'" 79.
45. Webb, "Augustine, Rape, and the Hermeneutics of Love," 28.
46. All three commandments are mentioned in *De civ.* 1.20.

Rape and sexual assault have served as paradigmatic cases of sinful gendered love, both for our purposes and for Augustine's in the *City of God*. In cultures where women who are assaulted suffer from the burden of shame, as a result of both the crime committed against them and the environments that judge them to have lost something that establishes their worth, Augustine offers a two-pronged response. The first prong centers the discussion of guilt and blame directly on the assailant. The ones who do the raping are the ones who ought to be ashamed of their rapacious lust, and Augustine puts them forward as chief examples of love gone terribly awry (remembering, of course, that hatred is a species of love in the end). If sinful love is characterized by the *libido dominandi* in Augustinian theology, *they* are the ones to look at for case studies of sinful love in motion. In their grasping for power and domination, they heap guilt and shame upon themselves. This reveals that the model of this book, in which gender and its expressions are at the same time expressions of love, has sufficient explanatory scope to make moral sense of the most pressing issue in sexual ethics. The second prong is a consolation shown to the victims. They are called glorious, and Augustine offers them nothing less than God. Even if the world heaps shame upon them, Augustine assures them that in the eyes of God, they are pure and beloved, and this establishes a worth far surpassing that secured by cultural norms. This does not, however, let society off the hook, for its members are shown to be operating by a standard distinct from God's own—they are contravening the one who upholds all things by facilitating sexual assault. By drawing on Scripture, especially the story of Susanna, Augustine calls on leaders to believe the testimony of women and to work toward justice for these victims. Though "Augustine's readership was steeped in the values of a Roman society that put the knife in the hands of women who had been raped," Augustine calls them to the justice of God.[47] But how is that justice to be enacted? For that, we turn to the next moment of the divine economy, redemption.

7.3 Redemption

Shame has been the result of gendered sin, seemingly, wherever it is found. In this chapter and the last, we have witnessed how intersex/DSD individuals experience profound shame for living in a world ostensibly not made for them.

---

47. Webb, "'Before the Eyes of Their Own God,'" 66.

We have also seen how survivors of sexual abuse testify to tremendous shame on account of the harms done to them and the cultures that perceive them as lacking worth due to a perceived loss of purity or chastity. Gender, when it is mired in the corrosive forces of sin, seems to result in experiences of shame and general lack of worth. If that is so, then for the work of Christ to reach in and redeem even the darkest corners of human identity, it must address these very issues. What, then, is the redeeming work of Christ, and how is it a resource for understanding the redemption of gender, especially those sinful manifestations that bring about the greatest senses of shame and unworthiness?[48]

Christian theology has many pathways by which to approach the redemption wrought by the incarnate Son of God, but here I will focus on just one biblical concept and its ability to foster and encourage redeemed moral agency. That concept is *grace*, and though hardly anyone will demur that this is a rather important concept to Christian soteriology, there is considerable ambiguity about just what it means when it is invoked scripturally and theologically. Recently, the work of John Barclay has shone a light on these obscurities through an influential proposal for what it is that Scripture (specifically Paul) meant by "grace." Barclay observes that the English word "grace," translated from the Greek *charis*, was hardly theologically specific in its original usage. "Grace" simply meant "gift" or "benefaction," which reveals that Scripture is not conjuring up unique terminology. Where Paul *is* unique, maintains Barclay, is in the way he and other biblical authors choose to *perfect* the concept, or emphasize a particular dimension of it to the utmost, and in the way he identifies the gift with the work performed by Christ. Paul's emphasis with respect to the gift of Christ is on its *incongruity*, the fact that it is a gift given without regard for the worth of the recipient. The gift of Christ, moreover, creates a community characterized by the gift they have commonly received. Though this community has not received the gift of Christ on the basis of their worth, their reception results in a transformation whereby they are conformed into congruity with it. The chief attribute of this

---

48. There is an important question that was first raised by Rosemary Radford Ruether regarding whether a male savior such as Jesus is *able* to save women. Among feminist theologians who have argued that he cannot, the tendency is to point out that, in some way, Christ is masculine in his human nature, which renders him unfit to be a savior to all humankind, including women. The dénouement of their arguments is that Christ is disqualified from performing his soteriological task in virtue of his masculinity. I attempt to address this concern in Fellipe do Vale, "Can a Male Savior Save Women? The Metaphysics of Gender and Christ's Ability to Save," *Philosophia Christi* 21, no. 2 (2019): 309–24. In this section, I will assume that a masculine savior *can* save women, for my greater interest is in *how* he has done so.

community's interaction with one another is that no one is treated as having any worth other than that given to them by Christ, through the union they all share with him. Barclay summarizes:

> Paul . . . had an unusual, creative, and socially radical understanding of the grace of God, arising from *the Gift:* Christ. Whereas good gifts were (and still are) normally thought to be distributed best to fitting or worthy recipients, Paul took the Christ-gift, the ultimate gift of God to the world, to be given without regard to worth, and in the absence of worth—an unconditioned or incongruous gift that did not match the worth of its recipients but created it. . . . In fact, it was in the formation and the practices of these communities that the grace of God was evidenced. Moral and social transformation was not an optional extra in Paul's understanding of grace but its necessary expression, because the gift of God in Christ brought into question the whole value system of the ancient world and took place in relationships, not just in the heart. Grace, it turns out, is not an idea or a thing but a radical, divine dynamic.[49]

If the redemption offered by Christ is, at its fundamental level, distinguished by *grace*, and if grace in Scripture is a gift given without regard to the worth of the recipient but instead bestows true worth on the recipient, then grace is a robust resource for social transformation that addresses the central element of gendered sin—namely, the shame and worthlessness felt by many. Grace is a gift given *specifically to those lacking worth*, and it recasts what it is to be worthy. The resultant communities are called to realign their standards of worth and shame so as to conform to the one true standard: the gift of Christ. All those who in the eyes of the world are made to feel ashamed and worthless find solace in Jesus, whose gift lifts them out of their shame and establishes their worth. The gospel's *equalizing* power, then, lies in the fact that by it all human standards of worth are cast aside in favor of the *surpassing* worth given in Christ, which opens a door for victims of gendered sin to find a hope for healing.

Barclay's proposal begins with an observation that while grace was ubiquitous in the ancient world, it was highly diverse in its emphases, and his chosen language to reflect that diversity is that of the "perfections" of grace. For Barclay, to perfect a concept is "to draw out a concept to its endpoint or extreme, whether for definitional clarity or for rhetorical or ideological advantage."[50] It

---

49. John M. G. Barclay, *Paul and the Power of Grace* (Grand Rapids: Eerdmans, 2020), xvii–xviii.
50. John M. G. Barclay, *Paul and the Gift* (Grand Rapids: Eerdmans, 2015), 67.

is to highlight and maximize some aspect of a concept and consequently to treat entities displaying that aspect as ideal instances of that kind of thing. So, a "perfect storm" is one where some aspects of the storm (say, its wind speed and rain volume) are highlighted and maximized, such that if we wanted to look for an ideal storm, we would look for one with lots of wind speed and rain volume. According to an extensive anthropological survey of the way gifts functioned in antiquity,[51] Barclay concludes that there are least six ways that the concept "grace" can be perfected: (1) superabundance, or excessiveness in terms of scale, significance, or duration; (2) singularity, or "the notion that the giver's *sole and exclusive* mode of operation is benevolence or goodness"; (3) priority, or the fact that the gift always precedes the initiative of the recipient; (4) incongruity, or the feature of being "given without condition, that is, *without regard to the worth of the recipient*"; (5) efficacy, or the ability of a gift to achieve "what it was designed to do"; (6) non-circularity, or the freedom of obligation for any return.[52] Grace may be perfected in any or all of these dimensions, at the discretion of the one employing the concept. Additionally, while grace's perfections can be disaggregated into these six perfections, the presence of one perfection does not entail the presence of any other.

For Paul, Barclay argues, the chief perfection of grace is its *incongruity*.[53] "The gospel," emphasizes Barclay, "stands or falls with the incongruity of grace."[54] A gift given incongruously is one that does not take into account the worth, value, or social capital of the recipient, something that would have been radically countercultural in Paul's day, in which gifts were expected to be given discriminately. Paul disregarded conventional wisdom and perfected the incongruity of the divine gift. Barclay's summary of Paul's themes captures this emphasis well:

> Paul's theology . . . is significantly shaped by his conviction, and experience, of the Christ-gift, as the definitive act of divine beneficence, given *without regard to worth*. By its misfit with human criteria of value, including the "righteousness" defined by the Torah, the Christ-event has recalibrated all systems

51. See Barclay, *Paul and the Gift*, chap. 1.
52. All six of the definitions come from Barclay, *Paul and the Gift*, 70–74.
53. Incongruity is the "central," "trademark," "chief," and "primary" perfection of grace, not its exclusive perfection (Barclay, *Paul and the Gift*, 454, 545, 557, and 569, respectively). Barclay is clear that "other 'perfections' of grace . . . may be present, but they seem less prominent" in Paul (Barclay, *Paul and the Power of Grace*, 73).
54. Barclay, *Paul and the Power of Grace*, 47.

of worth, creating communities that operate in ways significantly at odds with both Jewish and non-Jewish traditions of value. The incongruous gift has subverted previous measurements of symbolic capital, establishing its own criteria of value and honor that are no longer beholden to the authority of the Torah. The Christ-event *as gift* is thus the foundation of Paul's Gentile mission, in which Paul resists attempts to reinstitute preconstituted hierarchies of ethnic or social worth, and forms alternative communities that take their bearings from this singular event.[55]

We shall turn to the creation of communities in a moment, but the main point to grasp at present is Paul's radical commitment to the disestablishment of *any* criteria of worth as a basis for receiving the Christ-gift. Since "the good news distinguishes divine from human norms," the incongruity of grace refers not just to worth acquired by Torah observance but to any worth at all, whether it is based on social status, ethnicity, gender, ancestry, education, or economic status.[56] So now "*every practice* is equally insignificant as a criterion for the favor of God."[57] In construing grace as perfectly incongruous, Paul is therefore discrediting any earthly means of accruing worth, whether religious or irreligious.

Barclay's preferred way of describing grace's incongruity is as a denial of social, cultural, or symbolic "capital."[58] Grant Macaskill, who adopts Barclay's proposal, describes this as follows:

> There is such a thing as symbolic or social capital, which is associated with perception of our status not just with God but also with the various communities in which we live and operate. It is not as straightforward as a credit sheet, since some of the elements cannot be easily quantified, but within a given community, it will say whether you are an insider or an outsider and where you might rank within the group. It will affect how others treat you and how you benefit from these interactions. Someone who has high levels of social capital will enjoy the favor (and perhaps the favors) of others, as these people look to benefit from that capital by association.[59]

---

55. Barclay, *Paul and the Gift*, 350.

56. Barclay, *Paul and the Gift*, 356. See also Barclay, *Paul and the Power of Grace*, 7.

57. Barclay, *Paul and the Gift*, 546. For further statements on the ubiquitous erasure of all systems of worth, see Barclay, *Paul and the Gift*, 567; and Barclay, *Paul and the Power of Grace*, 140.

58. For such language, see Barclay, *Paul and the Gift*, 357, 363, 383; and Barclay, *Paul and the Power of Grace*, 72.

59. Grant Macaskill, *Living in Union with Christ: Paul's Gospel and Christian Moral Identity* (Grand Rapids: Baker Academic, 2019), 48–49.

Many forms of social capital and deficit exerted influence in the ancient world in which Paul wrote—for example, men were seen as better than women and being educated as better than being uneducated—and this created a complex system of honor in Roman society. But the same dynamic is evident in any context with social hierarchies and power inequalities. The possession of certain traits is taken either to augment or to diminish one's worth in the eyes of one's community, distinguishing between the haves and the have-nots. Paul's radical claim, however, is that *in Christ, there is no social capital other than that found through union with him*: "By trusting in Christ, believers know themselves to live only as Christ lives in them, . . . and they find their only worth in him."[60]

These themes recur throughout Paul's letters. Romans 6:23 distinguishes salvation as a *gift* in contradistinction to a *wage*, which would take into account some qualification. First Corinthians 1:18–29 describes the choice of God to bestow the gift of Christ on the foolish, not on the wise. In the face of debilitation, Paul witnesses to an experience where God tells him that grace is sufficient, for divine power *perfects* his weakness (2 Cor. 8–9; 12:9). The clearest expression of Paul's radical commitment to the incongruity of grace, to my mind, is found in Philippians 3:4–11. Here Paul confesses he had "reason for confidence in the flesh" (v. 4), reasons specific to the symbolic capital of his community, such as ethnic identity, Jewish upbringing, Pharisaic allegiance, and even *blamelessness* with regard to the law (vv. 5–6). In terms of cultural capital, Paul has "more." Yet, though he had much capital "gain," he had come "to regard" all of them "as loss because of Christ" (v. 7). Paul was a possessor of great cultural capital, but the reception of Christ's gift renders all of his capital worthless in comparison to knowing Christ. The possession of such a gift leads him to regard *everything* that gave him social worth as lacking true value (v. 8). Above all, Paul wants to be "found in him," for the value brought through association with this gift far surpasses that given by anything else, even other religious practices.[61] Barclay comments that in Paul's "new value system, there is one thing, and one thing only, that is always of value, in every circumstance, for everyone. Whatever else may be useful or of relative value (in certain contexts and for certain purposes), it cannot be placed in the same category of worth as Christ."[62] Though Paul had surpassing and

---

60. Barclay, *Paul and the Power of Grace*, 49.

61. There are powerful resonances here with what theologians call "union with Christ," a massively important Pauline soteriological theme. See, e.g., Grant Macaskill, *Union with Christ in the New Testament* (New York: Oxford University Press, 2013).

62. Barclay, *Paul and the Power of Grace*, 120.

excessive reason to cash in on the cultural credit he had accrued through his various identities and practices, that he was given Christ without regard to any of these relativizes their value so much that he has come to regard them as "rubbish" (v. 8).

While Barclay is clear that the primary perfection of grace in Paul is *incongruity*, he is equally clear that Paul does *not* perfect grace's *noncircularity*, for Paul clearly believed that recipients of grace were called to offer a return both to God as giver and to the community created by the gift.[63] The upshot is that those who have received grace are now called to live together in a community characterized by the very peculiarities of the gift of Christ. Thus Barclay: "The Christ-gift thus enters into human relations, by the operation of the Spirit, equipping new patterns of social relationship where people are no longer treated by reference to the old hierarchies of worth (which have been bypassed by the gift of Christ), nor by competitive jostling for honor. These are communities that stand at odds with normal configurations, as they are released from the typical criteria by which worth is differentially distributed and acclaimed."[64] Those who have received the gift of Christ have received something that did not take into account how worthy they were or how much shame they bore; as a result, the communities formed by the reception of this gift must live in the same way. They are called to be a "community that marches to a different step"[65] than the surrounding world, a group of people among whom Paul expects "the grace of God in Christ to cascade through the life of communities, such that the grace received is passed forward by believers and shared among them."[66] In other words, the perfections of the gift define the core features of the communities it forms. The primary way the incongruity of grace takes root in the life of a community, for Paul, is through *love*, for "in disregarding previous criteria of distinction, the Christ-event has released a new creative energy, a quality of social commitment sourced in the Spirit and

63. For the circularity of grace, see Barclay, *Paul and the Gift*, 51 and 63.

64. Barclay, *Paul and the Power of Grace*, 70. He elaborates: "Paul is driven by the good news of Jesus Christ to found new communities, social experiments on the urban landscape, where old values are superseded and new relationships created. He is convinced that this is not just a human invention, a product of skill or cultural innovation. What he sees at work is, rather, a divine activity that creates new human agents, a phenomenon as fruitful and miraculous as the birth of Isaac [Galatians 4:28]. Because this derives from *elsewhere*, all kinds of new possibilities emerge on the human stage" (Barclay, *Paul and the Power of Grace*, 60).

65. Barclay, *Paul and the Gift*, 439.

66. Barclay, *Paul and the Power of Grace*, 125.

summarized as 'love.'"[67] Through our exploration of an Augustinian theology of love, we have already seen that love is characteristically definitive of moral agency. We can now see that this is a deeply biblical insight and that love is the name for a community shaped by grace. "Above all," Paul commends the church in Colossae, "clothe yourselves with love, which binds everything together in perfect harmony" (Col. 3:14). "Love," after all, "does no wrong to a neighbor" (Rom. 13:10).

Barclay is clear that there are normative implications derived from these considerations, especially for a contemporary age with contemporary issues. "Paul's theology of grace," he contends, "is, in fact, a rich resource for Christians in challenging racism, gender prejudice, and all forms of negative stereotype."[68] Because "grace is not given differentially with regard to gender, or with regard to age, wealth, status, or race," so that "we may regard everyone as accorded the same worth in that single act of unconditioned grace," it follows that "any discrimination, any inequality in treatment, any attribution of secondary status is an affront to the good news of the grace of God in Christ."[69] Remember that Paul calls for an end to esteem given on any basis other than union with Christ. Those experiencing shame are to be lifted up in the love of the community, for in this orbit shame does not correspond to worth or its lack, for all are in possession of the same worth.[70]

This also means that worth is not affected by whether one has been raped or is ambiguously sexed (or by any other form of worth attaching itself to sex and gender). Recall that one of the most pressing challenges for those who have experienced sexual trauma of one kind or another is the burden of shame, especially shame felt by a failure to meet a culture's standards of worthiness or by a capital deficit associated with their experienced trauma. Our theologies of redemption must speak to these particular expressions of

67. Barclay, *Paul and the Power of Grace*, 63. See also Barclay, *Paul and the Gift*, 430: "The prime expression of this life is love . . . , the commitment to others that forms the foundation of community." For further elaboration on the central role of love in Pauline ethics, see Richard B. Hays, "Christology and Ethics in Galatians: The Law of Christ," *Catholic Biblical Quarterly* 49, no. 2 (1987): 268–90.

68. Barclay, *Paul and the Power of Grace*, 152.

69. Barclay, *Paul and the Power of Grace*, 153. For Barclay's more explicit treatment of Paul's theology of grace in relation to contemporary questions such as slavery and race, see John M. G. Barclay, "What Makes Paul Challenging Today?," in *The New Cambridge Companion to St. Paul*, ed. Bruce W. Longenecker (New York: Cambridge University Press, 2020), 299–318.

70. Echoing the promise of Isa. 28:16, Paul is confident that no one who has trusted Christ will be put to shame (see Rom. 9:33 and 10:11), for in God's eyes, shame attaches to those who are wise apart from grace and who boast in their own worth (1 Cor. 2:11–13).

gendered sin, and in the theology of grace outlined above, I suggest, we have found such a resource. We have received Christ without regard to our worth, and whatever shame we have felt on the basis of some worldly worthlessness was not taken into consideration. Victims of rape feel great amounts of shame and worthlessness, but here Paul says that this is no obstacle to their access to God. God *specializes* in giving gifts to those without regard in the eyes of those in power, for Christ has been given precisely to those with no prior worth to speak of. Moreover, any church that exacerbates the shame felt by victims of assault or others is "not acting consistently with the truth of the gospel," as Paul once alleged of Peter (Gal. 2:14). By reestablishing patterns of worth that have been counted as nothing in Christ, they are not only doing unspeakable damage to the survivor; they are also falling back into a form of legalism they often claim to specialize in avoiding.

The woman who was raped for the second time because she told her Christian boyfriend that she had been raped once before was treated as though she were worthless. Her boyfriend measured her against a standard of worth exterior to that of the gospel and, having found her wanting, concluded that she could be treated in any sordid way he desired. This is patently at odds with the gospel of Christ. In fact, Barclay's work has shown that the gospel stands in direct condemnation of such behavior. In a Christian community, worth can only be seen as a correlative of the gift of Christ. In the Christian community, the most worthless, despised, and rejected occupy the same plane as the wealthiest, most renowned, and most attractive. Both enjoy the same quality of union with Christ. Another scriptural author, James, grants us a clear image of how this might look:

> My brothers and sisters, do you with your acts of favoritism really believe in our glorious Lord Jesus Christ? For if a person with gold rings and in fine clothes comes into your assembly, and if a poor person in dirty clothes also comes in, and if you take notice of the one wearing the fine clothes and say, "Have a seat here, please," while to the one who is poor you say, "Stand there," or, "Sit at my feet," have you not made distinctions among yourselves, and become judges with evil thoughts? Listen, my beloved brothers and sisters. Has not God chosen the poor in the world to be rich in faith and to be heirs of the kingdom that he has promised to those who love him? But you have dishonored the poor. (James 2:1–6)

One can, without much difficulty, substitute the poor person in the illustration with the person who has been raped or the person who is ambiguously sexed, or any other person who has been treated in ways incommensurate with their worth in Christ. The point is that acting on such demarcations of worth is beneath the calling of the church, of the community created by Christ's gift.[71]

There is one final question to be considered with respect to this vision of reconciliation: Does it count as justice? On one very prominent account of justice, Nicholas Wolterstorff's, the answer is yes. Wolterstorff's view is that "justice is constituted of rights: a society is just insofar as its members enjoy the goods to which they have a right."[72] Justice is constituted by rights, and rights are normative social relationships in which the right-bearer claims the obligation of others to do things that bring about goods for the right-bearer—specifically, *life-goods*, states of affairs that contribute to the right-bearer's living a flourishing life—and to refrain from doing things that bring the right-bearer harm. Human beings have a right to a flourishing life, and this right is grounded not in social contracts or in divine commands but in the worth bestowed upon human beings on account of their being loved by God. That humanity is loved by God grounds its worth, and being so loved identifies those life-goods to which one has a right. When human persons enjoy this flourishing life by enjoying their rights, ultimately, they enjoy justice.[73]

There is an intimate connection in Wolterstorff's theory of justice between *rights* and *obligations*. In fact, he argues that they are co-implicative, such that if one obtains, so does the other. He calls this the "Principle of Correlatives": "If Y belongs to the sort of entity that can have rights, then X has an obligation toward Y to do or refrain from doing A if and only if Y has a right against X to X's doing or refraining from doing A."[74] This is a rather complex way of claiming that rights *just are* the obligations others have to do something or refrain from doing something to you. From the other perspective, if others have an obligation to bring about or refrain from bringing about certain states of affairs in your life, then you have a right to them. So, if Maria has an obligation to pay Marcus back for $5 borrowed, then Marcus has a *right* to be paid back by Maria. And if Marcus has a right to $5 from

---

71. For a powerful attempt to apply this insight to the question of disabilities in the church, see Grant Macaskill, *Autism and the Church: Bible, Theology, and Community* (Waco: Baylor University Press, 2019).

72. Nicholas Wolterstorff, *Justice: Rights and Wrongs* (Princeton: Princeton University Press, 2008), xii.

73. For a fuller account of justice along these lines, see Fellipe do Vale, "Justice, Grace, and Love: A Theological Commendation," *Trinity Journal* 42 (2021): 185–200.

74. Wolterstorff, *Justice*, 8. See also 34.

Maria, then Maria has an *obligation* to pay Marcus back $5. Human beings, argues Wolterstorff, have rights primarily to "states of affairs," particularly to those states of affairs that are conducive to a flourishing life.[75]

But what grounds the obligations of others to bring about or refrain from bringing about those goods that enable one's life to flourish, those goods to which one has a right and that constitute justice? Wolterstorff rejects views that couch these obligations in terms of duties,[76] opting instead to ground these obligations to flourishing life-goods in the *worth* of the persons involved.[77] He argues that the worth of a person consists of some status, property, or relation possessed either by means of some capacity that is inherently worthy or by means of worth bestowed upon them (say, by Christ).[78] He claims that worth is bestowed upon human beings, for only then can it be said that all and only human beings possess it. In particular, the worth bestowed derives from the fact that God loves human beings and has associated closely with them.[79] Wolterstorff's account of justice, then, can be summarized as follows: Justice is constituted by rights, which are the states of affairs one must enjoy (or refrain from being subjected to) in order to flourish. If someone has a right to a life-good that brings about her flourishing, then others around her have an obligation to bring about that life-good or refrain from bringing about a situation that prevents her from having it. The grounding of this obligation is found in her worth, a bestowed trait she possesses in virtue of being loved by God. If she enjoys all of the goods proportionate to her worth to which

75. Wolterstorff, *Justice*, 137. See also 145. Wolterstorff considers, and rejects, both utilitarianism and eudaimonism as potential frameworks for states of affairs to which one has rights. See Wolterstorff, *Justice*, 176–78, 209, 212, and 217–18. He concludes that only a conception of flourishing, what he calls "eirenéism," ably identifies the life-goods to which human beings have rights (222).

76. Such views include divine command theories and social contract theories, which Wolterstorff alleges presuppose "the normative context of a standing obligation on our part to obey," but the normativity in question cannot be explained by the theory under investigation (Wolterstorff, *Justice*, 281; see also 271–76).

77. See Wolterstorff, *Justice*, 242.

78. See Wolterstorff, *Justice*, 320. He considers views of inherent worth like that of Kant (who proposes that rationality grounds worth) but rejects them on the basis of the fact that they preclude entire classes of human beings who have worth but fail to possess the capacity in question, like some elderly individuals, some disabled individuals, infants, and the comatose (see 333, 349).

79. "From these reflections I conclude that if God loves a human being with the love of attachment, that love bestows great worth on that human being; other creatures, if they knew about that love, would be envious. And I conclude that if God loves, in the mode of attachment, each and every human being equally and permanently, then natural human rights inhere in the worth bestowed on human beings by that love. Natural human rights are what respect for that worth requires" (Wolterstorff, *Justice*, 360).

she has a right, then she is inhabiting a just state of affairs. If she is failing to enjoy some good related to her flourishing, or if something in her life impedes her flourishing because she is not treated proportionately to her worth, then she is living in injustice.

I think Wolterstorff is broadly correct. Put simply, a person enjoys justice when she is treated in ways proportionate to her worth, and a person does justice when she fulfills her obligations to others in proportion to their worth. Keeping in mind Barclay's theology of grace, we can see that this question of worth is defined by the reception of the gift of Christ. Worth is not measured by any kind of social capital, but solely by the worth bestowed by having been gifted Jesus himself. This is great worth indeed, and justice is brought about when persons are treated in proportion to the worth defined by that tremendous gift. The establishment of alternative systems of worth—whether they are indexed to sexuality, ethnicity, race, gender, wealth, education, or anything else—can now be seen not just as damaging but also as unsuitable substitutes for Christ. Christians who live by grace are called to recalibrate their systems of worth to no other standard than association with Christ. When others are treated in proportion to *that* worth, and when Christians come together to help others overcome the impediments they experience to being treated according to their worth, then justice flowers in the world. This is powerful motivation to help others heal from their shame and to affirm the genuine worth they possess in virtue of Jesus. The words of Christ—"Just as you did it to one of the least of these who are members of my family, you did it to me" (Matt. 25:40)—therefore exemplify the justice of the redeemed community. The least of these—those who are perceived as having no worth—are treated as members of the family in virtue of the union they share with Christ, and feeding them is an act of justice not just to them but also *to Christ*, to whom they are united. Sexual assault victims who carry their shame with them are treated as supremely worthy, for that is what is due them. Their worth is not in their abuse; it is in their being loved by God. Justice demands no less.[80]

Does this mean, however, that categories like gender must be done away with because they do not inform worth? If only our union with Christ matters,

---

80. Space does not allow me to consider an objection frequently raised to views such as the one I am defending, an objection that goes something like this: If all worth, and the justice grounded by it, is tied up with Jesus Christ, then does this mean that only Christians are the apt recipients of justice? I do not think this follows, especially if one takes a Christologically grounded account of the image of God according to which Christ *is* the image of God and all human beings are made in his image. That alone is sufficient grounds (arguably *greater* grounds) to love even one's enemy and to perceive in them great worth.

should we hope to become nongendered beings? It is to that question that we will turn in the next section, consummation. In what does our hope lie, if our worth is no longer tied to our social identities?

7.4 Consummation

Conspicuously missing from my analysis of grace in the previous section is a verse that many have taken to be central to the theology of gender, especially as it pertains to the consummation of Christian hope. That verse is Galatians 3:28: "There is no longer Jew or Greek, there is no longer slave or free, there is no longer male and female; for all of you are one in Christ Jesus." This verse directly undergirds or indirectly lends credibility to an idea that has been gaining widespread acceptance in theology—namely, that our eschatological hopes include the removal of our sexes and genders.[81] Some theologians, such as Linn Tonstad,[82] have put forward views according to which resurrected bodies are not gendered, and the trend in the scholarship seems to be heading in that direction. Is this how Galatians 3:28 and a broader eschatology of gender is best understood?

According to a recent development in biblical studies, the answer is an emphatic yes. For the "apocalyptic school" of Pauline interpretation, Galatians 3:28 plays a central governing role in eschatological anthropology, and the particular understanding of this text put forward by some of their most prominent adherents requires that the traits with which we were created (especially gender) are actually replaced by the traits provided by Christ. Thus Beverly Gaventa: "The gospel claims all that a human is; the gospel becomes the locus of human identity; the gospel *replaces* the old cosmos."[83] On some readings of Paul's apocalyptic theology, Galatians 3:28 (and other texts) teach

81. For a much more detailed account of this movement in the theological literature, see Fellipe do Vale, "Gender Identity: To Infinity and Beyond," *Pro Ecclesia* (forthcoming).

82. See Linn Marie Tonstad, *God and Difference: The Trinity, Sexuality, and the Transformation of Finitude*, Gender, Theology and Spirituality (New York: Routledge, 2016), 246, 269–75. See also my review of this work in *Journal of Analytic Theology* 6 (2018): 710–15.

83. Beverly Roberts Gaventa, "The Singularity of the Gospel Revisited," in *Galatians and Christian Theology: Justification, the Gospel, and Ethics in Paul's Letter*, ed. Mark W. Elliott, Scott Hafemann, N. T. Wright, and John Frederick (Grand Rapids: Baker Academic, 2014), 188 (emphasis added). See also Jonathan A. Linebaugh: "Is (or are) the I as created and fallen and recreated the same? . . . According to Paul, the self does not survive salvation—the old ἄνθρωπος dies" (Jonathan A. Linebaugh, "'The Speech of the Dead': Identifying the No Longer and Now Living 'I' of Galatians 2.20," *New Testament Studies* 66, no. 1 [2020]: 104).

that we are no longer bound by created traits, for in Christ there is only new creation. The chief proponent of this view is Douglas Campbell, for whom Galatians 3:28 is central.[84]

For Campbell, the incarnate Christ (and *not* the pre-incarnate Son) is central to creation, so much so that "we must reconceptualize the very category of creation *itself* to be faithful to these truths."[85] That means that Christ *in his human nature* is the true revelation of what it means to be a creature, so that all of the traits attributable to the original creation depicted in Genesis must be relegated to a level lower than true creation. Only what is "in Christ" is truly a creature, and so it will be when we are raised again: "The structures of the new resurrected creation are in fact the indelible structures of creation, period; these are the same thing. And other things that we might previously have thought of as created are in fact temporary ordering structures and not part of God's enduring perfect creation at all."[86] Campbell, at times, claims something stronger—namely, that much of what it meant to be a creature in Genesis is put to death with Christ: "The reason for Paul's complete and universal negation seems to lie in the event he presupposes, namely, the execution of Christ. Death is a total negation. Moreover, Christ in all his humanity died, *therefore humanity as created has been executed in him.*"[87] Christ's work "displaces" all previously created categories,[88] such that redeemed, eschatological life is inconsistent with that life depicted in Eden.[89] As Joel Chopp has concluded of Campbell's work, "Paul's ethics must be unearthed: stripped

84. I cannot adequately account for the fullness of Campbell's theology here (much less for the entire apocalyptic school of Pauline interpretation). For my reading of it, I depend upon Grant Macaskill, "Review Article: The Deliverance of God," *Journal for the Study of the New Testament* 34, no. 2 (2011): 150–61; Grant Macaskill, "History, Providence and the Apocalyptic Paul," *Scottish Journal of Theology* 70, no. 4 (2017): 409–26; Joshua W. Jipp, "Douglas Campbell's Apocalyptic, Rhetorical Paul: A Review Article," *Horizons in Biblical Theology* 32, no. 2 (2010): 183–97; Joel Thomas Chopp, "Unearthing Paul's Ethics: Douglas Campbell on Creation, Redemption, and the Christian Moral Life," *Journal of Theological Interpretation* 11, no. 2 (2017): 259–76; Thomas McCall, "Crucified with Christ: The Ego and the *Omega*," *Journal of Analytic Theology* 8 (August 2020): 1–25. For a broader treatment of Campbell in particular, see Chris Tilling, ed., *Beyond Old and New Perspectives on Paul: Reflections on the Work of Douglas Campbell* (Eugene, OR: Cascade, 2014).

85. Douglas A. Campbell, *Pauline Dogmatics: The Triumph of God's Love* (Grand Rapids: Eerdmans, 2019), 576.

86. Campbell, *Pauline Dogmatics*, 584.

87. Douglas A. Campbell, *The Quest for Paul's Gospel: A Suggested Strategy* (New York: T&T Clark, 2005), 102 (emphasis added).

88. Campbell, *Quest for Paul's Gospel*, 100.

89. See also Campbell, *Quest for Paul's Gospel*, 118, 120–24.

of all their vestiges of the doctrine of creation so that the abolition of binary categories found in Galatians 3:28 may do its work."[90]

Campbell is clear that gender is one of those abolished categories. If categories that are not in Christ are abolished, and there is "no male and female" in Christ, then gender must be abolished in the consummation of our hopes. Thus Campbell: "Gender distinctions *must* be deemed transcended for those in Christ."[91] For Campbell, gender is indeed a created trait, if by that we mean an aspect of the narrative in Genesis that is not in Christ and is only present for the time being. When we are raised again, then we will know what it truly means to be a creature—namely, to be in Christ. And in Christ, there are no genders, strictly speaking. Maleness and femaleness, womanhood and manhood, were all created but have now been shown to be part of "an interim ordering structure" that will be done away with when God in Christ is all in all (see 1 Cor. 15:28).[92]

Is this the best way to understand Galatians 3:28, and the most salutary depiction of our eschatological hopes for gender more broadly?[93] The trouble in answering the latter question is that eschatological realities seem to sit patently outside of our epistemic capacities. Nevertheless, we have seen that Irenaeus and Augustine have provided some basic guidelines for theological reflection on the particulars of our eschatological bodies. Both are committed to the principle that God's intentions for creation were not thwarted with the introduction of sin and that what we hope for is not the erasure of created categories *but their purification from sin*. It is hard to see what life will be like when it is divulged from the poison of sin, but we can be assured that it exceeds expectation and perfects creation. There is strong continuity between life now and life as it will be, the main difference consisting in the permanent absence of all sin. As such, we can be assured that the best way to understand consummated genders is to claim that we will finally know what it means to be women and men without sin.[94]

---

90. Chopp, "Unearthing Paul's Ethics," 265.

91. Campbell, *Quest for Paul's Gospel*, 102. See also Douglas A. Campbell, "The Logic of Eschatology: The Implications of Paul's Gospel for Gender as Suggested by Galatians 3.28a in Context," in *Gospel and Gender: A Trinitarian Engagement with Being Male and Female in Christ*, ed. Douglas A. Campbell (New York: T&T Clark, 2003), 58–81.

92. Campbell, *Pauline Dogmatics*, 603.

93. There are more worries that must be raised than those raised about Campbell's treatment of Gal. 3:28. There are also substantial issues with his doctrine of creation and its antithetical relationship to Christ's redemption, a feature he has not persuaded his readers is not Gnostic. For initial indications, see Chopp, "Unearthing Paul's Ethics."

94. I have attempted to make a case for the view that we retain our genders in the resurrection in Fellipe do Vale, "Cappadocian or Augustinian? Adjudicating Debates on Gender in the

What, then, does it mean to say that in Christ there is no more male and female?[95] Paul ends the verse with a clear proclamation of believers' common union with Christ—"for all of you are one in Christ Jesus. And if you belong to Christ, then you are Abraham's offspring, heirs according to the promise" (Gal. 3:28–29)—a claim that serves as the theological grounding for what precedes it. The mention of union and the inheritance of Abraham ought to remind us of Paul's overarching theme in Galatians: the incongruity of grace. That all believers are one is a function of the common gift they have received, a gift that was given without regard to worth and creates communities of justice that do not operate with regard to worldly worth. Barclay reads the passage as saying that the "differences between these categories are not eradicated. Neither ethnic nor gender identity could be simply removed. . . . Paul and Peter remained Jews (2:15; cf. Titus, a 'Greek,' 2:3), and Paul was still identifiably masculine and free." So what changes? "What is altered . . . is the *evaluative freight* carried by these labels, the encoded distinctions of superiority and inferiority."[96] Or again, as Bruce Hansen concludes in his monograph on the subject, "Paul has demoted all cultural indices apart from those based on participation in Christ and refuses not their preservation but their use as bases of exclusion and judgment."[97]

What categorizes these communities also implicates the identities possessed by its members. Individuals receive the gift of Christ *as* women and men, and grace does not require the erasure of natural human traits with which God created them. But grace also *redeems* and *perfects* these traits, no longer allowing them to possess the importance they currently hold in classifying human beings and their worth. At the consummation of Christ's work, humanity *is* gendered, but gender no longer serves as a metric with which to measure the worth, esteem, or quality of a person. In addition, those for whom gender identity is complicated, a cause for shame or a vessel

---

Resurrection," *International Journal of Systematic Theology* 21, no. 2 (2019): 182–98. Aspects of the argument that I make here are made more fully in that article.

95. An additional question, raised by texts like Matt. 22:23–30, is whether there will be *marriage* in the resurrection. I take this to be a separate question, related though not consequential to my argument. Even if there is no marriage, it does not strike me as problematic to affirm that we retain our sexes and genders, for these extend far beyond the concerns of marriage. For more discussion, see Patricia Beattie Jung, *Sex on Earth as It Is in Heaven: A Christian Eschatology of Desire* (New York: SUNY Press, 2017).

96. Barclay, *Paul and the Gift*, 397.

97. Bruce Hansen, *"All of You Are One": The Social Vision of Gal 3.28, 1 Cor 12.13 and Col 3.11*, Library of New Testament Studies (London: T&T Clark, 2010), 105.

for memories that are painful, will know what it means to have the evils they have experienced defeated. Gender is not erased but *reclassified*. Macaskill summarizes this well. Gender is still present, he says, but "enclosed within a larger reality that constitutes a more basic identity, shared by all participants: you are all one in Christ. One can imagine Paul saying this in a room filled with a mixture of people (some of whom may be tacitly evaluating and judging others) and pointing at each person: a Jew, a Greek, a slave, a free person [a man or a woman]. The differences are not obliterated, but they are no longer considered to be the most basic elements of identity."[98] For those whose gender identity is not a matter of difficulty, this is good news insofar as they will not need to derive their worth from their femininity or masculinity. For those whose gender identity is a matter of great difficulty, this is a promise that their tears will be wiped away and that God will restore to them all that has been lost (1 Pet. 5:10; Rev. 21:4). Neither will be made to live in a world where sex and gender are of ultimate importance, for that which is truly of ultimate importance—union with Christ—will be made complete.

The affirmation that we will be raised gendered, though with genders that carry different evaluative freight, is also an aid to our pursuit of justice during the *saeculum*.[99] Augustine, when he famously maintained (against prevailing opinion) that women will be raised *as women*, was motivated by the nature of Christians' eschatological hope for justice. He maintains that "both sexes will rise again," for "all faults will be removed from those bodies, but their nature will be preserved." Since the "female sex is not a fault but rather a matter of nature," there is every reason to believe that God will not remove femininity from humanity when God restores creation to its intended glory. For God "both created what was not and freed what he created from corruption." Those who maintain that women will not be raised as women fail to understand that "the woman . . . is just as much God's creation as is the man."[100] It is no sin or deficit to be a woman, and it is the business of the resurrection to perfect what is good and to remove what is evil. Our genders, on Augustine's understanding, belong in the first category.

But he does recognize that until we reach that state, the world will be filled with misery and injustice, and to combat these things we need moral action

98. Macaskill, *Living in Union with Christ*, 56.

99. For a more detailed elaboration of this argument, see do Vale, "Cappadocian or Augustinian?," 192–98.

100. *De civ*. 22.17.

fueled by eschatological imagination. Margaret Miles states this well: Augustine "imagined resurrection by citing at length—and then subtracting—the painful and negative features of present bodily life, retaining its goodness and beauty."[101] For this reason, she maintains, "it is only when we understand his vision of the completion and perfection of human life that we grasp accurately his pervasive sense of the wrongness of present life."[102] Glimpsing perfect justice allows one to adjudicate the injustices of the world, just as knowing what is truly beautiful enables one rightly to perceive what is ugly about the world. Through this strategy of contrasts, Augustine was able to address what he called "the miseries of the world."

In the three places in the *City of God* where Augustine mentions the "miseries of the world" and the injustices that accompany them, he points to a future hope where all that is lost will be restored. First, he confesses that though "in this life" Christians are "schooled for eternity" as they endure evils, they are consoled by a hope not based on "anything falterable or unreliable," the promise of God's very presence.[103] Or again, when he inquires about "all the grinding evils with which human society abounds here in this mortal condition," he reminds his readers that the happiness of this life "is found to be sheer misery when compared to the happiness we call ultimate."[104] Finally, though he confesses that "this life is so wretched that it is like a sort of hell" and that "nothing delivers us from it but the grace of Christ the savior, our God and our Lord," we can be assured that upon our resurrection, we will enter into the blessed rest of God where no evil remains: "How marvelous that felicity will be, where there will be no evil, where no good will be hidden from sight, where all our time will be given to praising God, who will be all in all!"[105] This is no appeal to escapism, where the faithful are removed from the earth in an effort to make a clean getaway; Augustine is committed to the view that it is only *sin* and its consequences that are removed from creation. Instead, he points to the earth and calls those who are actively suffering to see how it can be better, how the things they see and experience are not the

101. Margaret R. Miles, "Sex and the City (of God): Is Sex Forfeited or Fulfilled in Augustine's Resurrection of the Body?," *Journal of the American Academy of Religion* 73, no. 2 (June 2005): 316.

102. Margaret R. Miles, "From Rape to Resurrection: Sin, Sexual Difference, and Politics," in *Augustine's "City of God": A Critical Guide*, ed. James Wetzel (Cambridge: Cambridge University Press, 2012), 86.

103. *De civ.* 1.29.

104. *De civ.* 19.5.

105. *De civ.* 22.22.

way they are supposed to be.[106] Eschatology is meant to provide a normative counterbalance to the sordidness of worldly sorrow, claims Augustine, calling us to imagine how the things we see with our eyes are but tawdry representations of what they will be in the fullness of glory.

So it is with the consummation of gender. To maintain that gender must be eliminated for the injustices and sins embroiling it to be made right is a Pyrrhic victory, a consolation achieved at too great a cost to be of value to the consoled. Augustine invites us to imagine what these good but broken things like our genders will be like when they are filled with the light of Christ. Having caught a glimpse of this, we are called to embody it now. Because "love cannot exist without hope nor hope without love, nor can either exist without faith," our hope shapes our moral action now.[107] Eschatology, by informing us of the ways the world has gone awry, allows and empowers us to live in ways consistent with the way it was meant to be.

This, then, is how eschatology shapes gender. It does not abolish gender in an effort to remedy the influences of sin. Because "all of [us] are one in Christ Jesus" (Gal. 3:28), we await a world in which we will be gendered in ways that do not define our worth. In the new heaven and earth, mysterious as they remain, we will be women and men who know perfect justice in accordance with our worth. No longer will gender be a burden, nor will gender make us targets for violence. Instead, we will know the glory and felicity of Christ through our sexes and genders. As we imagine a just world, we conform our lives now in anticipation. "And all of us, with unveiled faces," claims Paul, "are being transformed into the same image from one degree of glory to another" (2 Cor. 3:18). So it is with our genders; as we perceive what glorified genders will be like, we are transformed accordingly.

7.5 Conclusion

Through this disquisition into gender's place within the divine economy over the last two chapters, much has been covered. Because human beings are narratively indexed, having the properties they do in virtue of the place they

---

106. To borrow the title of Cornelius Plantinga's famous work, *Not the Way It's Supposed to Be: A Breviary of Sin* (Grand Rapids: Eerdmans, 1995).

107. Augustine, *Enchiridion* 1.8. English translation from Augustine, *The Augustine Catechism: The Enchiridion on Faith, Hope and Charity*, ed. Boniface Ramsey, trans. Bruce Harbert, vol. 1, The Augustine Series (Hyde Park, NY: New City, 1999).

occupy within the divine economy, it was important to see how gender is created, fallen, redeemed, and perfected in God's engagement with the world. In creation, two features of God's act of creating the world were highlighted. First, all things have a proper function, defining what it means for them to be "very good." Second, the state of creation was always intended to be the first stage of an internally consistent economy (so as to avoid Gnosticism). Gender, therefore, is tied to sexed bodies that themselves have proper functions, a fact that helped us to understand intersexuality/DSD. Gender, moreover, is also fallen, and the paradigmatic instance of that fallenness is sexual assault. Just as fallen love takes the form of the *libido dominandi*, we saw that gendered sin also looks to dominate others from a place of twisted power. Yet, grace is sufficient even here. Though survivors of sexual assault experience great amounts of shame and a sense of worthlessness due to twisted criteria of worth, the gospel proclaims that it is precisely those with no worth to speak of in the eyes of others that Jesus has come to redeem. The gift of God is not given on the basis of perceived worth but is given precisely to sinners who lack any worth "according to the flesh" (Rom. 8:12). The Father pours forth the Spirit, who forges the love of God in the hearts of the faithful, thereby beginning a process of reciprocity whereby they live lives offered up to God that are characterized by the gift. The communities who have been created by grace are communities in which sinful standards of worth are not observed but in which each person is treated according to the worth bestowed upon them by grace in Christ. This, ultimately, is a just society. As these pilgrims venture forth toward the consummation of their hopes, they realize that God is not taking the world away from them but taking sin away from the world. This world will one day be set right, purged from all that twists and warps it. On that day, our gender identities will no longer serve as grounds for discrimination, violence, or abuse; rather, we will see the glory of what it truly means to be men and women.

CONCLUSION

The question "What is gender?" is deceptively simple to ask and, as the foregoing discussion has shown, remarkably complex to answer. What kinds of considerations ought to be in play? Should one prize the hard facts of biology or the equally ubiquitous forces of society? How does one bridge the physical traits of human bodies and the social patterns of human gendered behavior that each of us has to navigate every day? I have attempted to provide a theological model of gender that answers such questions while also avoiding the pitfalls often ensnaring theologians who have attempted this task.

Two bifurcations dominate the field as it stands. First, one is faced with two apparently exclusive options about gender's ontology: either gender is a social construct (the view that purports to take seriously the social dimensions involved) or it is a biological essence (the view that purports to be true to the bodies with which we are created). Second, there is a division of approach regarding which tools are best suited for accomplishing the task of accounting for gender. Either theologians take gender as a serious object of investigation but set aside the recognizable tools and virtues of theology as irrelevant to the task or they uphold a commitment to the tools and virtues of theology but exclude gender and other human complexities from genuine theological investigation. On either of these approaches, theology is ill-suited for conducting an inquiry into gender. Much of the burden of the present project has been to assert and demonstrate these bifurcations as false dichotomies.

I do not think that gender is a social construct, despite the wide popularity of this view in virtually all discussions of gender. This is because it cannot allow for cross-cultural commonalities among gender kinds, for all theories

237

of social construction agree that constructs are always context specific. This means that a major commitment of feminist theory and theology (namely, that gender kinds are stable categories, so that we can speak of women and men without fission into incommensurate cultures and times) is undercut. It also means that gender is morally unevaluable, for the norms that govern good and bad instances of women and men are themselves context specific. Even though I reject the social construction of gender, I do not accept its perceived antithesis: biological essentialism. Instead, I proposed four theses for a workable ontology of gender, theses that take into account the central tenets of essentialism (like the stability of gender kinds) and the main motivations of the social constructionist position (the restraint of epistemic access to gender kinds and the importance of social identities). These theses are theologically motivated, insofar as they are warranted through theological exegesis, and they address directly some of the main controversies surrounding gender's basic properties.

My main claim is that we can understand gender as love. Or, in less arcane terms, gender is about the appropriation of social goods, an appropriation that occurs when certain goods are loved in virtue of the possession of a sexed body. Through loving, we bring the beloved into ourselves and incorporate them into our stories. Those gendered goods that we love, then, form our gender identities. But this is not just any love, for the particular account of love favored throughout has been the one put forward by Saint Augustine. For Augustine, love has its source and end in God, who is love. The social goods we are called to love are to be loved as gifts from the Creator, according to the specifications set forth by the Giver, and in a right order. Therefore, gender is a matter of moral evaluation; or better yet, it is a matter of Christian discipleship. The forces that shape us into godliness are the same forces that tell us who we are as gendered selves. There is a descriptive task (What are the gendered goods that we encounter every day?) and a normative task (What is the best way to love these goods and weave them into our stories?), and a detailed theology of human love weaves them into one. We are relieved of the burden of making up context-free gender roles, but we are given the greater task of ordering our loves.

Because gender is a matter of Christian discipleship, it must be seen within the divine economy, that grand narrative of divine action according to which God is creating, redeeming, sustaining, and perfecting creatures. Our gendered loves are always indexed to this narrative, and I attempted to illustrate how this is so by offering salient examples, such as sexual assault. God has not left humanity on its own when it comes to gender, for the One "who began a good work among you will bring it to completion by the day of Jesus Christ" (Phil. 1:6). So, the church need not feel abandoned, lost, or in panic when it is faced with what often seems like the ever-changing landscape that gender inhabits. Instead, the same promises made by God apply. Because God "will transform the body of our humiliation that it may be conformed to the body of his glory," we may rest in knowing that our genders do not fall outside of that scope (Phil. 3:21). Instead, the One who reigns over all creation and has promised to redeem it by purging it of all sin is the One who will redeem gender.

The task we now face is not new. It is the task of loving rightly. The church that is well-trained in robust love is the church that is well-equipped to face the challenges of this century and the next. Yet this is far from easy, and we will always be dependent on the Holy Spirit. So, prayer and transformation are nonnegotiable, for we are called to be women and men *in Christ*. The words of the collect for the third Sunday in Lent, therefore, are as apposite for thinking about gender as they are for any other part of our discipleship: "Heavenly Father, you have made us for yourself, and our hearts are restless until they rest in you: Look with compassion upon the heartfelt desires of your servants, and purify our disordered affections, that we may behold your eternal glory in the face of Christ Jesus; who lives and reigns with you and the Holy Spirit, one God, for ever and ever. Amen."[1]

These are the words of gendered pilgrims voyaging to their homeland, yearning for a day when the redemption of the body will be complete. Those on pilgrimage endure hardship with praise, grief with comfort, and shame with divine honor, and as they do so, they are assured of a coming day when all tears will be wiped away. Gender has caused many tears. But God will one day show the church what it means to be, finally, women and men in glory.

---

1. The Anglican Church in North America, *The Book of Common Prayer (2019)* (Huntington Beach, CA: Anglican Liturgy Press, 2019), 606. This text is available online at https://bcp2019.anglicanchurch.net/wp-content/uploads/2022/10/BCP-2019-MASTER-5th-PRINTING-05022022-3.pdf.

BIBLIOGRAPHY

Abraham, William J. *Crossing the Threshold of Divine Revelation*. Grand Rapids: Eerdmans, 2006.

Alcoff, Linda Martín. "Cultural Feminism Versus Post-Structuralism: The Identity Crisis in Feminist Theory." *Signs: Journal of Women in Culture and Society* 13, no. 3 (1988): 405–36.

———. *Rape and Resistance: Understanding the Complexities of Sexual Violation*. Cambridge: Polity, 2018.

———. *Visible Identities: Race, Gender, and the Self*. New York: Oxford University Press, 2006.

Anderson, Ellie. "A Phenomenological Approach to Sexual Consent." *Feminist Philosophy Quarterly* 8, no. 2 (2022): 1–24.

Appiah, Anthony. "'But Would That Still Be Me?' Notes on Gender, 'Race,' Ethnicity, as Sources of 'Identity.'" *Journal of Philosophy* 87, no. 10 (October 1990): 493–99.

Armstrong, D. M. *A Theory of Universals: Universals and Scientific Realism*. Vol. 2. Cambridge: Cambridge University Press, 1978.

Ásta. *Categories We Live By: The Construction of Sex, Gender, Race, and Other Social Categories*. New York: Oxford University Press, 2018.

Augustine. *The Augustine Catechism: The Enchiridion on Faith, Hope and Charity*. Edited by Boniface Ramsey. Translated by Bruce Harbert. Vol. 1. The Augustine Series. Hyde Park, NY: New City, 1999.

———. "The Catholic Way of Life and the Manichean Way of Life." In *The Manichean Debate*, translated by Roland Teske, I/19:17–106. The Works of Saint Augustine: A Translation for the 21st Century. Hyde Park, NY: New City, 2006.

———. *The City of God*. Edited by Boniface Ramsey. Translated by William Babcock. Vol. I/6. The Works of Saint Augustine: A Translation for the 21st Century. Hyde Park, NY: New City, 2012.

———. *The City of God*. Edited by Boniface Ramsey. Translated by William Babcock. Vol. I/7. The Works of Saint Augustine: A Translation for the 21st Century. Hyde Park, NY: New City, 2012.

———. *Confessions*. Translated by Carolyn Hammond. Vol. 1. Loeb Classical Library. Cambridge, MA: Harvard University Press, 2014.

———. *Confessions*. Translated by Carolyn Hammond. Vol. 2. Loeb Classical Library. Cambridge, MA: Harvard University Press, 2016.

———. "The Excellence of Marriage." In *Marriage and Virginity*, translated by Ray Kearney, I/9:29–64. The Works of Saint Augustine: A Translation for the 21st Century. Hyde Park, NY: New City, 1999.

———. *Expositions of the Psalms, 1–32*. Translated by Maria Boulding. Vol. III/15. The Works of Saint Augustine: A Translation for the 21st Century. Hyde Park, NY: New City, 2000.

———. *Expositions of the Psalms, 33–50*. Translated by Maria Boulding. Vol. III/16. The Works of Saint Augustine: A Translation for the 21st Century. Hyde Park, NY: New City, 2000.

———. *Expositions of the Psalms, 51–72*. Translated by Maria Boulding. Vol. III/17. The Works of Saint Augustine: A Translation for the 21st Century. Hyde Park, NY: New City, 2001.

———. *Expositions of the Psalms, 99–120*. Translated by Maria Boulding. Vol. III/19. The Works of Saint Augustine: A Translation for the 21st Century. Hyde Park, NY: New City, 2003.

———. *Expositions of the Psalms, 121–150*. Translated by Maria Boulding. Vol. III/20. The Works of Saint Augustine: A Translation for the 21st Century. Hyde Park, NY: New City, 2004.

———. *Homilies on the First Epistle of John*. Translated by Boniface Ramsey. Vol. III/14. The Works of Saint Augustine: A Translation for the 21st Century. Hyde Park, NY: New City, 2008.

———. *Homilies on the Gospel of John 1–40*. Translated by Edmund Hill. Vol. III/12. The Works of Saint Augustine: A Translation for the 21st Century. Hyde Park, NY: New City, 2009.

———. *On Genesis*. Translated by Edmund Hill. Vol. I/13. The Works of Saint Augustine: A Translation for the 21st Century. Hyde Park, NY: New City, 2002.

———. *Sermons 20–50*. Translated by Edmund Hill. Vol. III/2. The Works of Saint Augustine: A Translation for the 21st Century. Hyde Park, NY: New City, 1991.

———. *Sermons 94A–150*. Translated by Edmund Hill. Vol. III/4. The Works of Saint Augustine: A Translation for the 21st Century. Hyde Park, NY: New City, 1992.

———. *Sermons 151–183*. Translated by Edmund Hill. Vol. III/5. The Works of Saint Augustine: A Translation for the 21st Century. Hyde Park, NY: New City, 1992.

———. *Teaching Christianity*. Edited by John E. Rotelle. Translated by Edmund Hill. Vol. I/11. The Works of Saint Augustine: A Translation for the 21st Century. Hyde Park, NY: New City, 1996.

———. *The Trinity*. Translated by Stephen McKenna. Vol. 45. The Fathers of the Church. Washington, DC: Catholic University of America Press, 1963.

Bach, Theodore. "Gender Is a Natural Kind with a Historical Essence." *Ethics* 122, no. 2 (January 2012): 231–72.

Barclay, John M. G. *Paul and the Gift*. Grand Rapids: Eerdmans, 2015.

———. *Paul and the Power of Grace*. Grand Rapids: Eerdmans, 2020.

———. "What Makes Paul Challenging Today?" In *The New Cambridge Companion to St. Paul*, edited by Bruce W. Longenecker, 299–318. New York: Cambridge University Press.

Beauvoir, Simone de. *The Ethics of Ambiguity*. Translated by Bernard Frechtman. New York: Citadel, 1976.

———. *The Second Sex*. Translated by Constance Borde and Sheila Malovany-Chevallier. New York: Vintage, 2011.

Bennett, Jana Marguerite. "Telling the Old Story in Gendered Keys: The Theological Revivals of Katherine Sonderegger, Kathryn Tanner, and Sarah Coakley." *Anglican Theological Review* 101, no. 2 (2019): 277–88.

Bogardus, Tomás. "Evaluating Arguments for the Sex/Gender Distinction." *Philosophia* 48, no. 3 (2020): 873–92.

———. "Some Internal Problems with Revisionary Gender Concepts." *Philosophia* 48, no. 4 (2020): 45–75.

Bordo, Susan. *Unbearable Weight: Feminism, Western Culture, and the Body*. Berkeley: University of California Press, 2003.

Bornstein, Kate. *Gender Outlaw*. New York: Routledge, 1994.

Brown, Peter. *The Body and Society: Men, Women, and Sexual Renunciation in Early Christianity*. 20th anniversary ed. New York: Columbia University Press, 2008.

———. "Saint Augustine." In *Trends in Medieval Political Thought*, edited by Beryl Smalley, 1–21. Oxford: Basil Blackwell, 1965.

Burnaby, John. *Amor Dei: A Study of the Religion of St. Augustine*. 1938. Reprint, Eugene, OR: Wipf & Stock, 2007.

Burnell, Peter. *The Augustinian Person*. Washington, DC: Catholic University of America Press, 2005.

Butler, Judith. *Bodies That Matter*. New York: Routledge, 1993.

———. "Contingent Foundations: Feminism and the Question of 'Postmodernism.'" In *Feminists Theorize the Political*, edited by Judith Butler and Joan W. Scott, 1–21. New York: Routledge, 1992.

———. *Gender Trouble*. New York: Routledge, 1990.

Byrne, Alex. "Are Women Adult Human Females?" *Philosophical Studies* 177, no. 12 (2020): 3783–3803.

Campbell, Douglas A. "Apocalyptic Epistemology: The Sine Qua Non of Valid Pauline Interpretation." In *Paul and the Apocalyptic Imagination*, edited by Ben C. Blackwell, John K. Goodrich, and Jason Maston, 65–86. Minneapolis: Fortress, 2016.

———, ed. *Gospel and Gender: A Trinitarian Engagement with Being Male and Female in Christ*. London: T&T Clark, 2004.

———. *Pauline Dogmatics: The Triumph of God's Love*. Grand Rapids: Eerdmans, 2019.

———. *The Quest for Paul's Gospel: A Suggested Strategy*. New York: T&T Clark, 2005.

Chopp, Joel Thomas. "Unearthing Paul's Ethics: Douglas Campbell on Creation, Redemption, and the Christian Moral Life." *Journal of Theological Interpretation* 11, no. 2 (2017): 259–76.

Coakley, Sarah. "The Eschatological Body: Gender, Transformation and God." In *Powers and Submissions: Spirituality, Philosophy and Gender*, 153–67. Challenges in Contemporary Theology. Malden, MA: Blackwell, 2002.

———. *God, Sexuality, and the Self: An Essay "On the Trinity."* Cambridge: Cambridge University Press, 2013.

———. "Gregory of Nyssa." In *The Spiritual Senses: Perceiving God in Western Christianity*, edited by Paul L. Gavrilyuk and Sarah Coakley, 36–55. Cambridge: Cambridge University Press, 2011.

———. "In Defense of Sacrifice: Gender, Selfhood, and the Binding of Isaac." In *Feminism, Sexuality, and the Return of Religion*, edited by Linda Alcoff and John D. Caputo, 17–38. Bloomington: Indiana University Press, 2011.

———. "Introduction—Gender, Trinitarian Analogies, and the Pedagogy of the Song." In *Re-thinking Gregory of Nyssa*, edited by Sarah Coakley, 1–13. London: Blackwell, 2003.

———. *The New Asceticism: Sexuality, Gender and the Quest for God*. London: Bloomsbury Continuum, 2015.

———. "Pleasure Principles." *Harvard Divinity Bulletin* 33, no. 2 (Autumn 2005). https://bulletin.hds.harvard.edu/pleasure-principles.

———. *Powers and Submissions: Spirituality, Philosophy and Gender*. Challenges in Contemporary Theology. Malden, MA: Blackwell, 2002.

———. "A Response to Oliver O'Donovan's Ethics as Theology Trilogy." *Modern Theology* 36, no. 1 (2020): 186–92.

———. "Why Gift? Gift, Gender and the Trinitarian Relations in Milbank and Tanner." *Scottish Journal of Theology* 61, no. 2 (2008): 224–35.

Cornwall, Susannah. *Sex and Uncertainty in the Body of Christ: Intersex Conditions and Christian Theology*. Gender, Theology and Spirituality. New York: Routledge, 2010.

Couenhoven, Jesse. "Augustine's Moral Psychology." *Augustinian Studies* 48, no. 1 (2017): 23–44.

———. "'Not Every Wrong Is Done with Pride': Augustine's Proto-Feminist Anti-Pelagianism." *Scottish Journal of Theology* 61, no. 1 (2008): 32–50.

————. *Stricken by Sin, Cured by Christ: Agency, Necessity, and Culpability in Augustinian Theology*. New York: Oxford University Press, 2013.

Cox, Jennifer Anne. *Intersex in Christ: Ambiguous Biology and the Gospel*. Eugene, OR: Cascade Books, 2018.

Crisp, Oliver D. *Analyzing Doctrine: Toward a Systematic Theology*. Waco: Baylor University Press, 2019.

Crisp, Oliver D., James M. Arcadi, and Jordan Wessling, eds. *Love, Divine and Human: Contemporary Essays in Systematic and Philosophical Theology*. New York: T&T Clark, 2020.

Davis, Ellen F. "'The One Whom My Soul Loves': The Song of Songs." In *Getting Involved with God: Rediscovering the Old Testament*, 65–88. Lanham, MD: Rowman & Littlefield, 2001.

————. "The Song of Songs." In *Proverbs, Ecclesiastes, and the Song of Songs*, 231–302. Westminster Bible Companion. Louisville: Westminster John Knox, 2000.

DeFranza, Megan K. *Sex Difference in Christian Theology: Male, Female, and Intersex in the Image of God*. Grand Rapids: Eerdmans, 2015.

Dembroff, Robin. "Why Be Nonbinary?" *Aeon*, October 30, 2018. https://aeon.co /essays/nonbinary-identity-is-a-radical-stance-against-gender-segregation.

Dodaro, Robert. *Christ and the Just Society in the Thought of Augustine*. Cambridge: Cambridge University Press, 2004.

do Vale, Fellipe. "Anselm on the *Rectus Ordus* of Creation." *Saint Anselm Journal* 14, no. 1 (Fall 2018): 93–109.

————. "Book Review: *The Rise and Triumph of the Modern Self*." *The London Lyceum*. April 27, 2021, https://www.thelondonlyceum.com/book-review-the-rise -and-triumph-of-the-modern-self/.

————. "Can a Male Savior Save Women? The Metaphysics of Gender and Christ's Ability to Save." *Philosophia Christi* 21, no. 2 (2019): 309–24.

————. "Cappadocian or Augustinian? Adjudicating Debates on Gender in the Resurrection." *International Journal of Systematic Theology* 21, no. 2 (2019): 182–98.

————. "Divine Action Is Constitutive of Theology: William Abraham, John Webster, and Theological Theology." *Irish Theological Quarterly* 86, no. 4 (2021): 388–403.

————. "Justice, Grace, and Love: A Theological Commendation." *Trinity Journal* 42 (2021): 185–200.

————. "On Thomas Aquinas's Rejection of an 'Incarnation Anyway.'" *TheoLogica* 3, no. 1 (2019): 144–64.

————. "Review of *God and Difference: The Trinity, Sexuality, and the Transformation of Finitude*, by Linn Marie Tonstad." *Journal of Analytic Theology* 6 (2018): 710–15.

Dunham, Scott A. *The Trinity and Creation in Augustine: An Ecological Analysis*. New York: SUNY Press, 2009.

Everhart, Ruth. *The #MeToo Reckoning: Facing the Church's Complicity in Sexual Abuse and Misconduct*. Downers Grove, IL: IVP Academic, 2020.

Fausto-Sterling, Anne. "The Five Sexes, Revisited." *Sciences* 40, no. 4 (2000): 18–23.

———. "The Five Sexes: Why Male and Female Are Not Enough." *Sciences* 33, no. 2 (1993): 20–24.

———. *Sexing the Body: Gender Politics and the Construction of Sexuality*. Rev. ed. New York: Basic Books, 2000.

Feser, Edward. "The Role of Nature in Sexual Ethics." *National Catholic Bioethics Quarterly* 13, no. 1 (Spring 2013): 69–76.

Fiorenza, Elisabeth Schüssler. *Jesus: Miriam's Child, Sophia's Prophet; Critical Issues in Feminist Christology*. 2nd ed. New York: Bloomsbury T&T Clark, 2015.

———. "Reaffirming Feminist/Womanist Biblical Scholarship." *Encounter* 67, no. 4 (2006): 361–73.

Frankfurt, Harry G. *The Importance of What We Care About*. Cambridge: Cambridge University Press, 1988.

———. *Necessity, Volition, and Love*. Cambridge: Cambridge University Press, 1998.

———. *The Reasons of Love*. Princeton: Princeton University Press, 2004.

———. *Taking Ourselves Seriously and Getting It Right*. Edited by Debra Satz. Stanford: Stanford University Press, 2006.

Gaventa, Beverly Roberts. "The Singularity of the Gospel Revisited." In *Galatians and Christian Theology: Justification, the Gospel, and Ethics in Paul's Letter*, edited by Mark W. Elliott, Scott J. Hafemann, N. T. Wright, and John Frederick, 187–99. Grand Rapids: Baker Academic, 2014.

Gioia, Luigi. *The Theological Epistemology of Augustine's "De Trinitate."* New York: Oxford University Press, 2008.

Greene-McCreight, Kathryn. *Feminist Reconstructions of Christian Doctrine: Narrative Analysis and Appraisal*. New York: Oxford University Press, 2000.

———. "Feminist Theology and a Generous Orthodoxy." *Scottish Journal of Theology* 57, no. 1 (2004): 95–108.

Gregory, Eric. *Politics and the Order of Love: An Augustinian Ethic of Democratic Citizenship*. Chicago: University of Chicago Press, 2008.

Gregory of Nyssa. *Gregory of Nyssa: Homilies on the Song of Songs*. Translated by Richard A. Norris. Vol. 13. Writings from the Greco-Roman World. Atlanta: Society of Biblical Literature, 2012.

Griffiths, Paul J. "Secularity and the Saeculum." In *Augustine's "City of God": A Critical Guide*, edited by James Wetzel, 33–54. New York: Cambridge University Press, 2012.

Gross, Sally. "Intersexuality and Scripture." *Theology and Sexuality* 11 (1999): 65–74.

Guest, Deryn. "Troubling the Waters: תהום, Transgender, and Reading Genesis Backwards." In *Transgender, Intersex, and Biblical Interpretation*, edited by Teresa J. Hornsby and Deryn Guest, 21–44. Semeia Studies. Atlanta: SBL Press, 2016.

Hansen, Bruce. *"All of You Are One": The Social Vision of Gal 3.28, 1 Cor 12.13 and Col 3.11.* Library of New Testament Studies. London: T&T Clark, 2010.

Hansen, Danielle Tumminio. "Remembering Rape in Heaven: A Constructive Proposal for Memory and the Eschatological Self." *Modern Theology* 37, no. 3 (2021): 662–78.

Hare, John. "Hermaphrodites, Eunuchs, and Intersex People: The Witness of Medical Science in Biblical Times and Today." In *Intersex, Theology, and the Bible: Troubling Bodies in Church, Text, and Society,* edited by Susannah Cornwall, 79–96. New York: Palgrave Macmillan, 2015.

Harrison, Carol. *Augustine: Christian Truth and Fractured Humanity.* Christian Theology in Context. New York: Oxford University Press, 2000.

———. "Measure, Number and Weight in Saint Augustine's Aesthetics." *Augustinianum* 28 (1998): 591–602.

Haslanger, Sally. "Feminism in Metaphysics: Negotiating the Natural." In *Resisting Reality: Social Construction and Social Critique,* 139–57. New York: Oxford University Press, 2012.

———. "Gender and Race: (What) Are They? (What) Do We Want Them to Be?" In *Resisting Reality: Social Construction and Social Critique,* 221–47. New York: Oxford University Press, 2012.

———. *Resisting Reality: Social Construction and Social Critique.* New York: Oxford University Press, 2012.

———. "The Sex/Gender Distinction and the Social Construction of Reality." In *The Routledge Companion to Feminist Philosophy,* edited by Ann Garry, Serene J. Khader, and Alison Stone, 157–67. New York: Routledge, 2017.

Hochschild, Paige E. *Memory in Augustine's Theological Anthropology.* New York: Oxford University Press, 2012.

Holcomb, Justin S., and Lindsey A. Holcomb. *Rid of My Disgrace: Hope and Healing for Victims of Sexual Assault.* Wheaton: Crossway, 2011.

hooks, bell. *All about Love: New Visions.* New York: Harper Perennial, 2001.

———. *Feminist Theory: From Margin to Center.* 2nd ed. New York: Routledge, 2015.

Hunter, David G. "Augustine on the Body." In *A Companion to Augustine,* edited by Mark Vessey, 353–64. Malden, MA: Blackwell, 2012.

Irenaeus. *Against the Heresies.* Translated by Dominic J. Unger. Vol. 1. Ancient Christian Writers 55. New York: Newman, 1992.

———. *Against the Heresies.* Translated by Dominic J. Unger. Vol. 2. Ancient Christian Writers 65. New York: Newman, 2012.

———. *Against the Heresies.* Translated by Dominic J. Unger. Vol. 3. Ancient Christian Writers 64. New York: Newman, 2012.

———. *Against Heresies.* In *Ante-Nicene Fathers: The Apostolic Fathers, Justin Martyr, Irenaeus.* Edited by Alexander Roberts and James Donaldson. Vol. 1. Christian Classics Ethereal Library, https://www.ccel.org/ccel/schaff/anf01.i.html.

Irigaray, Luce. *Je, Tu, Nous: Towards a Culture of Difference*. New York: Routledge, 2007.

———. *Speculum of the Other Woman*. Translated by Gillian Gill. Ithaca, NY: Cornell University Press, 1985.

———. *This Sex Which Is Not One*. Translated by Carolyn Burke. Ithaca, NY: Cornell University Press, 1985.

Jenson, Robert W. *Song of Songs*. Interpretation: A Bible Commentary for Teaching and Preaching. Louisville: Westminster John Knox, 2005.

Jones, Beth Felker. "Embodied from Creation through Redemption: Placing Gender and Sexuality in Theological Context." In *Beauty, Order, and Mystery: A Christian Vision of Human Sexuality*, edited by Gerald L. Hiestand and Todd A. Wilson, 21–30. Downers Grove, IL: IVP Academic, 2017.

———. *Marks of His Wounds: Gender Politics and Bodily Resurrection*. New York: Oxford University Press, 2007.

Jones, Serene. *Feminist Theory and Christian Theology: Cartographies of Grace*. Guides to Theological Inquiry. Minneapolis: Fortress, 2000.

Jung, Patricia Beattie. *Sex on Earth as It Is in Heaven: A Christian Eschatology of Desire*. New York: SUNY Press, 2017.

Kessel, Edward L. "A Proposed Biological Interpretation of the Virgin Birth." *Journal of the American Scientific Affiliation* 35 (1983): 129–36.

Khalidi, Muhammad Ali. "Three Kinds of Social Kinds." *Philosophy and Phenomenological Research* 90, no. 1 (2015): 96–112.

LaCugna, Catherine Mowry. *God for Us: The Trinity and Christian Life*. New York: HarperSanFrancisco, 1993.

Layton, Bentley, and David Brakke, eds. *The Gnostic Scriptures: A New Translation with Annotations and Introductions*. Translated by Bentley Layton. 2nd ed. Anchor Yale Bible Reference Library. New Haven: Yale University Press, 2021.

Lee, Gregory W. "Republics and Their Loves: Rereading *City of God* 19." *Modern Theology* 27, no. 4 (2011): 553–81.

Levering, Matthew. "The Holy Spirit in the Trinitarian Communion: 'Love' and 'Gift'?" *International Journal of Systematic Theology* 16, no. 2 (April 2014): 126–42.

———. "Linear and Participatory History: Augustine's *City of God*." *Journal of Theological Interpretation* 5, no. 2 (2011): 175–96.

Macaskill, Grant. *Autism and the Church: Bible, Theology, and Community*. Waco: Baylor University Press, 2019.

———. "History, Providence and the Apocalyptic Paul." *Scottish Journal of Theology* 70, no. 4 (2017): 409–26.

———. *Living in Union with Christ: Paul's Gospel and Christian Moral Identity*. Grand Rapids: Baker Academic, 2019.

———. "Review Article: The Deliverance of God." *Journal for the Study of the New Testament* 34, no. 2 (2011): 150–61.

———. *Union with Christ in the New Testament.* New York: Oxford University Press, 2013.

MacKenzie, Iain M. *Irenaeus's Demonstration of the Apostolic Preaching: A Theological Commentary and Translation.* Aldershot: Ashgate, 2002.

Marks, Kathy. *Lost Paradise.* New York: Free Press, 2009.

Mason, Matthew. "The Wounded It Heals: Gender Dysphoria and Resurrection of the Body." In *Beauty, Order, and Mystery: A Christian Vision of Human Sexuality,* edited by Gerald L. Hiestand and Todd A. Wilson, 135–47. Downers Grove, IL: IVP Academic, 2017.

Mathewes, Charles. "A Worldly Augustinianism: Augustine's Sacramental Vision of Creation." *Augustinian Studies* 41, no. 1 (2010): 333–48.

McCall, Thomas. "Crucified with Christ: The *Ego* and the *Omega*." *Journal of Analytic Theology* 8 (August 2020): 1–25.

McCarthy, Margaret H. "Gender Ideology and the Humanum." *Communio* 43, no. 2 (Summer 2016): 274–98.

McClintock-Fulkerson, Mary. "Gender—Being It or Doing It? The Church, Homosexuality, and the Politics of Identity." *Union Seminary Quarterly Review* 47, nos. 1–2 (January 1, 1993): 29–46.

McRandal, Janice. *Christian Doctrine and the Grammar of Difference: A Contribution to Feminist Systematic Theology.* Minneapolis: Fortress, 2015.

Meconi, David Vincent. "*Grata Sacris Angelis*: Gender and the *Imago Dei* in Augustine's *De Trinitate* XII." *American Catholic Philosophical Quarterly* 74, no. 1 (2000): 47–62.

Mikkola, Mari. "Elizabeth Spelman, Gender Realism, and Women." *Hypatia* 21, no. 4 (2006): 77–96.

———. "Gender Sceptics and Feminist Politics." *Res Publica* 13 (2007): 361–80.

———. *The Wrong of Injustice: Dehumanization and Its Role in Feminist Philosophy.* New York: Oxford University Press, 2016.

Miles, Margaret R. *Augustine on the Body.* 1979. Reprint, Eugene, OR: Wipf & Stock, 2009.

———. "From Rape to Resurrection: Sin, Sexual Difference, and Politics." In *Augustine's "City of God": A Critical Guide,* edited by James Wetzel, 75–92. Cambridge: Cambridge University Press, 2012.

———. "Sex and the City (of God): Is Sex Forfeited or Fulfilled in Augustine's Resurrection of the Body?" *Journal of the American Academy of Religion* 73, no. 2 (June 2005): 307–27.

Mill, John Stuart. "On Liberty." In *J. S. Mill: "On Liberty" and Other Writings,* edited by Stefan Collini, 1–116. Cambridge Texts in the History of Political Thought. New York: Cambridge University Press, 1989.

———. "The Subjection of Women." In *J. S. Mill: "On Liberty" and Other Writings,* edited by Stefan Collini, 117–218. Cambridge Texts in the History of Political Thought. New York: Cambridge University Press, 1989.

Nussbaum, Martha C. "Human Functioning and Social Justice: In Defense of Aristotelian Essentialism." *Political Theory* 20, no. 2 (May 1992): 202–46.

———. *Sex and Social Justice.* New York: Oxford University Press, 1999.

———. *Women and Human Development: The Capabilities Approach.* Cambridge: Cambridge University Press, 2001.

O'Donovan, Oliver. *Begotten or Made?* Oxford: Oxford University Press, 1984.

———. *Common Objects of Love: Moral Reflection and the Shaping of Community.* Grand Rapids: Eerdmans, 2009.

———. *The Problem of Self-Love in St. Augustine.* 1980. Reprint, Eugene, OR: Wipf & Stock, 2006.

———. *Resurrection and Moral Order: An Outline for Evangelical Ethics.* 2nd ed. Grand Rapids: Eerdmans, 1994.

Offen, Karen. "Defining Feminism: A Comparative Historical Approach." *Signs: Journal of Women in Culture and Society* 14, no. 1 (1988): 119–56.

Ortiz, Jared. *"You Made Us for Yourself": Creation in St. Augustine's "Confessions."* Minneapolis: Fortress, 2016.

Osborn, Eric. *Irenaeus of Lyons.* Cambridge: Cambridge University Press, 2001.

Patterson, Daniel R. *Reforming a Theology of Gender: Constructive Reflections on Judith Butler and Queer Theory.* Eugene, OR: Cascade, 2022.

Pinker, Steven. *How the Mind Works.* 1997. Reissue ed., New York: Norton, 2009.

Plantinga, Alvin. *Warrant and Proper Function.* New York: Oxford University Press, 1993.

———. *Warranted Christian Belief.* New York: Oxford University Press, 2000.

Poulain de la Barre, François. "A Physical and Moral Discourse concerning the Equality of Both Sexes." In *The Equality of the Sexes: Three Feminist Texts of the Seventeenth Century*, translated by Desmond M. Clarke, 119–200. New York: Oxford University Press, 2013.

Rist, John M. *Augustine: Ancient Thought Baptized.* Cambridge: Cambridge University Press, 1996.

———. *Augustine Deformed: Love, Sin, and Freedom in the Western Moral Tradition.* New York: Cambridge University Press, 2014.

Rogers, Eugene F., Jr. *Aquinas and the Supreme Court: Race, Gender, and the Failure of Natural Law in Thomas's Biblical Commentaries.* Malden, MA: Wiley-Blackwell, 2013.

———. "Doctrine and Sexuality." In *The Oxford Handbook of Theology, Sexuality, and Gender*, edited by Adrian Thatcher, 53–66. New York: Oxford University Press, 2015.

Ruether, Rosemary Radford. "Feminist Interpretation: A Method of Correlation." In *Feminist Interpretation of the Bible*, edited by Letty M. Russell, 111–24. Philadelphia: Westminster, 1985.

―――. *Sexism and God-Talk: Toward a Feminist Theology*. Boston: Beacon, 1983.

Russell, Letty M. *The Future of Partnership*. Philadelphia: Westminster, 1979.

―――. *Household of Freedom: Authority in Feminist Theology*. Philadelphia: Westminster, 1987.

Schlabach, Gerald W. *For the Joy Set before Us: Augustine and Self-Denying Love*. Notre Dame, IN: University of Notre Dame Press, 2001.

Schreiner, Patrick. "Man and Woman: Toward an Ontology." *Eikon* 2, no. 2 (Fall 2020): 68–87.

"Scope of the Problem: Statistics." RAINN (Rape, Abuse and Incest National Network). Accessed February 23, 2021. https://www.rainn.org/statistics/scope -problem.

Searle, John R. *The Construction of Social Reality*. New York: Free Press, 1995.

Sharkey, Sarah Borden. *An Aristotelian Feminism*. Switzerland: Springer, 2016.

Soskice, Janet Martin. *The Kindness of God: Metaphor, Gender, and Religious Language*. New York: Oxford University Press, 2007.

―――. *Metaphor and Religious Language*. Oxford: Clarendon, 1985.

Spelman, Elizabeth V. *Inessential Woman: Problems of Exclusion in Feminist Thought*. Boston: Beacon, 1990.

Steenberg, M. C. *Irenaeus on Creation: The Cosmic Christ and the Saga of Redemption*. Supplements to Vigiliae Christianae. Leiden: Brill, 2008.

Stewart-Kroeker, Sarah. *Pilgrimage as Moral and Aesthetic Formation in Augustine's Thought*. New York: Oxford University Press, 2017.

―――. "Resisting Idolatry and Instrumentalisation in Loving the Neighbour: The Significance of the Pilgrimage Motif for Augustine's Usus–Fruitio Distinction." *Studies in Christian Ethics* 27, no. 2 (May 1, 2014): 202–21.

Storkey, Elaine. *Origins of Difference: The Gender Debate Revisited*. Grand Rapids: Baker Academic, 2001.

―――. *Scars across Humanity: Understanding and Overcoming Violence against Women*. Downers Grove, IL: IVP Academic, 2018.

―――. *Women in a Patriarchal World: Twenty-five Empowering Stories from the Bible*. Downers Grove, IL: InterVarsity, 2020.

Stump, Eleonore. *Wandering in Darkness: Narrative and the Problem of Suffering*. New York: Oxford University Press, 2010.

Tanner, Kathryn. *Christ the Key*. Current Issues in Theology. Cambridge: Cambridge University Press, 2010.

―――. "The Difference Theological Anthropology Makes." *Theology Today* 50, no. 4 (January 1, 1994): 567–79.

―――. "Gender." In *The Oxford Handbook of Anglican Studies*, edited by Mark Chapman, Sathianathan Clarke, and Martyn Percy, 400–412. Oxford: Oxford University Press, 2015.

———. "Globalization, Women's Transnational Migration, and Religious De-traditioning." In *The Oxford Handbook of Feminist Theology*, edited by Sheila Briggs and Mary McClintock Fulkerson, 544–59. Oxford: Oxford University Press, 2011.

———. "Social Theory concerning the 'New Social Movements' and the Practice of Feminist Theology." In *Horizons in Feminist Theology: Identity, Tradition, and Norms*, edited by Rebecca S. Chopp and Sheila Greeve Davaney, 179–97. Minneapolis: Fortress, 1997.

———. *Theories of Culture: A New Agenda for Theology*. Guides to Theological Inquiry. Minneapolis: Fortress, 1997.

Thatcher, Adrian. *Gender and Christian Ethics*. New York: Cambridge University Press, 2021.

———. *God, Sex, and Gender: An Introduction*. Malden, MA: Wiley-Blackwell, 2011.

———. *Redeeming Gender*. New York: Oxford University Press, 2016.

Tonstad, Linn Marie. *God and Difference: The Trinity, Sexuality, and the Transformation of Finitude*. Gender, Theology and Spirituality. New York: Routledge, 2016.

Torchia, Joseph. "'Pondus Meum Amor Meus': The Weight-Metaphor in St. Augustine's Early Philosophy." *Augustinian Studies* 21, no. 1 (1990): 163–76.

Torrance, Alan J. "Is There a Distinctive Human Nature? Approaching the Question from a Christian Epistemic Base." *Zygon* 47, no. 4 (December 2012): 903–17.

Walton, John H. *The Lost World of Genesis One: Ancient Cosmology and the Origins Debate*. Downers Grove, IL: IVP Academic, 2009.

Warnke, Georgia. *Debating Sex and Gender*. New York: Oxford University Press, 2010.

Watson, Francis. *Agape, Eros, Gender: Towards a Pauline Sexual Ethic*. Cambridge: Cambridge University Press, 2004.

Webb, Melanie. "Augustine, Rape, and the Hermeneutics of Love." In *Producing Christian Culture: Gospel Text and Its Interpretive Genres*, edited by Matthew Crawford, Giles E. M. Gasper, and Francis Watson, 11–43. London: Routledge, 2017.

———. "'Before the Eyes of Their Own God': Susanna, Rape Law, and Testimony in *City of God* 1.19." In *Reading Scripture as a Political Act: Essays on the Theopolitical Interpretation of the Bible*, edited by Matthew A. Tapie and Daniel W. McClain, 57–81. Minneapolis: Fortress, 2015.

———. "'On Lucretia Who Slew Herself': Rape and Consolation in Augustine's *De ciuitate dei*." *Augustinian Studies* 44, no. 1 (2013): 37–58.

———. "Rape and Its Aftermath in Augustine's *City of God*." PhD dissertation, Princeton University, 2016.

Webster, John. "Biblical Reasoning." In *The Domain of the Word: Scripture and Theological Reason*, 115–32. London: Bloomsbury, 2012.

———. *The Culture of Theology*. Grand Rapids: Baker Academic, 2019.

———. "Curiosity." In *The Domain of the Word: Scripture and Theological Reason*, 193–202. London: Bloomsbury, 2012.

———. "Eschatology and Anthropology." In *Word and Church: Essays in Christian Dogmatics*, 263–86. Edinburgh: T&T Clark, 2001.

———. "Eschatology, Anthropology and Postmodernity." *International Journal of Systematic Theology* 2, no. 1 (March 2000): 13–28.

———. "God, Theology, Universities." In *Virtue and Intellect*, 157–72. Vol. 2 of *God without Measure: Working Papers in Christian Theology*. London: Bloomsbury T&T Clark, 2016.

———. *Holiness*. Grand Rapids: Eerdmans, 2003.

———. "The Holiness and Love of God." In *Confessing God: Essays in Christian Dogmatics II*, 109–30. London: Bloomsbury, 2005.

———. *Holy Scripture: A Dogmatic Sketch*. Cambridge: Cambridge University Press, 2003.

———. "Hope." In *Confessing God: Essays in Christian Dogmatics II*, 195–214. London: Bloomsbury, 2005.

———. "The Human Person." In *Cambridge Companion to Postmodern Theology*, edited by Kevin J. Vanhoozer, 219–34. Cambridge: Cambridge University Press, 2003.

———. "On the Clarity of Holy Scripture." In *Confessing God: Essays in Christian Dogmatics II*, 33–68. London: Bloomsbury, 2005.

———. "On the Theology of Providence." In *God and the Works of God*, 127–42. Vol. 1 of *God without Measure: Working Papers in Christian Theology*. New York: Bloomsbury T&T Clark, 2016.

———. "Principles of Systematic Theology." In *The Domain of the Word: Scripture and Theological Reason*, 133–49. London: Bloomsbury, 2012.

———. "Reading Theology." *Toronto Journal of Theology* 13 (1997): 53–63.

———. "Theological Theology." In *Confessing God: Essays in Christian Dogmatics II*, 11–32. London: Bloomsbury, 2005.

———. "Theologies of Retrieval." In *The Oxford Handbook of Systematic Theology*, edited by John Webster, Kathryn Tanner, and Iain Torrance, 583–99. New York: Oxford University Press, 2007.

———. "What Is the Gospel?" In *Grace and Truth in the Secular Age*, edited by Timothy Bradshaw, 109–18. Grand Rapids: Eerdmans, 1998.

———. "What Makes Theology Theological?" In *God and the Works of God*, 213–24. Vol. 1 of *God without Measure: Working Papers in Christian Theology*. New York: Bloomsbury T&T Clark, 2016.

Westfall, Cynthia Long. *Paul and Gender: Reclaiming the Apostle's Vision for Men and Women in Christ*. Grand Rapids: Baker Academic, 2016.

Wetzel, James. "A Tangle of Two Cities." *Augustinian Studies* 43, no. 1/2 (2012): 5–23.

Williams, Rowan. *On Augustine*. New York: Bloomsbury, 2016.

———. "Politics and the Soul: Reading the *City of God*." In *On Augustine*, 107–29. London: Bloomsbury Continuum, 2016.

Witt, Charlotte. "Anti-Essentialism in Feminist Theory." *Philosophical Topics* 23, no. 2 (Fall 1995): 321–44.

———, ed. *Feminist Metaphysics: Explorations in the Ontology of Sex, Gender and the Self.* New York: Springer, 2011.

———. "Gender Essentialism: Aristotle or Locke?" In *Powers and Capacities in Philosophy: The New Aristotelianism*, edited by Ruth Groff and John Greco, 308–18. New York: Routledge, 2012.

———. *The Metaphysics of Gender.* New York: Oxford University Press, 2011.

———. *Ways of Being: Potentiality and Actuality in Aristotle's Metaphysics.* Ithaca, NY: Cornell University Press, 2003.

———. "What Is Gender Essentialism?" In *Feminist Metaphysics: Explorations in the Ontology of Sex, Gender and the Self*, edited by Charlotte Witt, 11–25. New York: Springer, 2011.

Witt, William G. *Icons of Christ: A Biblical and Systematic Theology for Women's Ordination.* Waco: Baylor University Press, 2020.

Wolterstorff, Nicholas. "Does the Role of Concepts Make Experiential Access to Ready-Made Reality Impossible?" In *Practices of Belief: Selected Essays*, vol. 2, edited by Terence Cuneo, 41–61. New York: Cambridge University Press, 2010.

———. *Justice in Love.* Emory University Studies in Law and Religion. Grand Rapids: Eerdmans, 2011.

———. *Justice: Rights and Wrongs.* Princeton: Princeton University Press, 2008.

———. "Living within a Text." In *Faith and Narrative*, edited by Keith E. Yandell, 202–13. New York: Oxford University Press, 2001.

———. "To Theologians: From One Who Cares about Theology but Is Not One of You." *Theological Education* 40, no. 2 (2005): 72–92.

———. "The World Ready-Made." In *Practices of Belief: Selected Essays*, vol. 2, edited by Terence Cuneo, 12–40. New York: Cambridge University Press, 2010.

Works, Carla Swafford. *The Least of These: Paul and the Marginalized.* Grand Rapids: Eerdmans, 2020.

Yadav, Sameer. "Christian Doctrine as Ontological Commitment to a Narrative." In *The Task of Dogmatics: Explorations in Theological Method*, edited by Oliver D. Crisp and Fred Sanders, 70–86. Grand Rapids: Zondervan, 2017.

Young, Iris Marion. *Intersecting Voices.* Princeton: Princeton University Press, 1997.

———. *Justice and the Politics of Difference.* Rev. ed. Princeton: Princeton University Press, 2011.

Zahl, Simeon. *The Holy Spirit and Christian Experience.* New York: Oxford University Press, 2020.

INDEX

255